PAKISTAN
At the Helm

Tilak Devasher has taken to writing after he retired from the cabinet secretariat, Government of India, as special secretary in 2014. His first book, *Pakistan: Courting the Abyss*, was published by HarperCollins India in 2016. During his professional career with the cabinet secretariat, he specialized in security issues pertaining to India's neighbourhood. Post-retirement, he has continued to take a keen interest in India's neighbourhood with special focus on Pakistan, Afghanistan and Bangladesh. He has written articles for *The Economic Times*, *The Indian Express*, *India Today*, Vivekananda International Foundation, *Air Power*, *India's National Security Review*, *South Asia Monitor* and Catch News among others. He did his schooling from Mayo College, Ajmer, and studied history at St Stephen's College, Delhi, at the undergraduate level and at Delhi University at the postgraduate level.

AF622099

Praise for *Pakistan: Courting the Abyss*

'… easily the best book on Pakistan.'

—**Khaled Ahmed**, *consulting editor*, Newsweek Pakistan.

'This book explains how and why Pakistan often finds itself on the brink. Devasher writes with empathy and his book is full of facts that cannot be ignored by Pakistanis or the rest of the world.'

—**Husain Haqqani**, *author and former Pakistan ambassador to the US*.

'[Devasher] unpacks Pakistan with an empathy and familiarity that many Indian authors on the subject have so far failed to bring.'

—**Suhasini Haider**, *diplomatic affairs editor*, The Hindu.

'For any study of Pakistan and for anyone formulating India's policy with respect to Pakistan, this book is a must-read.'

—**Lt Gen. J.S. Bajwa**, *Indian Defence Review*.

'Devasher's book is one of the very few books written with great depth of information and analysis … a must-read for anyone who wants to understand Pakistan.'

—**Satish Kumar**, *director, Foundation for National Security Research, former professor of diplomacy, JNU*.

'… there are few books by Indian authors that have sought to interpret the prodigal neighbour in a holistic, informed and empathetic manner. Tilak Devasher is the exception to this norm'

—**C. Uday Bhaskar**, *director, Society for Policy Studies, New Delhi*.

'… one of the best analyses of Pakistan's potential "multi-organ failure". There is no hostility in Devasher's must-read book for those who objectively wish to understand both the long-term challenges of Pakistan as well as the way forward.'

—**Aparna Pande**, *director, India Initiative, Hudson Institute*.

PAKISTAN
At the Helm

TILAK DEVASHER

HarperCollins *Publishers* India

First published India by HarperCollins
HarperCollins *Publishers* in 2018
An imprint of HarperCollins Publishers
HarperCollins *Publishers* India, Cyber City, Building 10-A, Gurugram, Haryana-122002, India
www.harpercollins.co.in

2 4 6 8 10 9 7 5 3 1
Copyright © Tilak Devasher 2018

P-ISBN: 9789352779338
E-ISBN: 9789352779345

The views and opinions expressed in this book are the author's own and the facts are as reported by her which have been verified by her to the extent possible, and the publisher is not in any way liable for the same. Names and identifying details have been changed by the author to protect the privacy of individuals. The publisher disclaims any liability to any party for any loss, damage, or disruption caused by errors or omissions, whether such errors or omissions result from negligence, accident, or any other cause.

Tilak Devasher authors asserts the moral right
to be identified as the author of this work.

All rights reserved. No part of this publication may be reproduced,
stored in a retrieval system, or transmitted, in any form or by any means,
electronic, mechanical, photocopying, recording or otherwise,
without the prior permission of the publishers.

Without limiting the exclusive rights of any author, contributor or the publisher of this publication, any unauthorized use of this publication to train generative artificial intelligence (AI) technologies is expressly prohibited. HarperCollins also exercise their rights under Article 4(3) of the Digital Single Market Directive 2019/790 and expressly reserve this publication from the text and data-mining exception.

Typeset in 10.5/14.2 Berling LT Std at
Manipal Digital Systems, Manipal

Printed and bound at
Manipal Technologies Limited, Manipal

*

HarperCollins *Publishers*, Macken House, 39/40 Mayor Street Upper, Dublin 1, D01 C9W8, Ireland

For
Anjali
Dhruv, Arati, Madhavi and Will

Contents

Pakistan: A Timeline of Events

14 August 1947:	Creation of Pakistan.
22 October 1947:	'Raiders' from Pakistan invade Jammu and Kashmir (J&K).
11 September 1948:	Muhammad Ali Jinnah dies.
1 January 1949:	UNSC Ceasefire in J&K.
17 January 1951:	Ayub Khan appointed as commander-in-chief (C-in-C).
16 October 1951:	Prime Minister Liaquat Ali Khan assassinated in Rawalpindi.
23 March 1956:	Constitution is promulgated. Iskander Mirza sworn in as first president of Pakistan.
7 October 1958:	Constitution abrogated by President Iskander Mirza, martial law imposed, Gen. Ayub Khan made chief martial law administrator, political parties banned.
24 October 1958:	Ayub Khan named prime minister.
27 October 1958:	Ayub Khan deposes Iskander Mirza and assumes power.

27 October 1959:	Ayub Khan promotes himself as field marshal.
17 February 1960:	Ayub Khan becomes president.
24 January 1963:	Z.A. Bhutto becomes foreign minister.
17 September 1964:	Fatima Jinnah files papers for presidential election.
2 January 1965:	Ayub Khan re-elected president.
April 1965:	Skirmishes in Rann of Kutch between India and Pakistan.
30 June 1965:	Pakistan and India sign accord on Rann of Kutch.
24 August 1965:	Infiltration begins in Kashmir under Operation Gibraltar.
6–22 September 1965:	Indo-Pakistan war.
23 September 1965:	Ceasefire between India and Pakistan.
3 January 1966:	Tashkent summit between Indian prime minister Lal Bahadur Shastri and Ayub Khan.
10 January 1966:	Tashkent Declaration signed by India and Pakistan.
17 June 1966:	Z.A. Bhutto resigns as foreign minister.
17 September 1966:	Gen. Yahya Khan becomes C-in-C.
9 July 1967:	Fatima Jinnah dies in Karachi.
7 November 1968:	Student demonstrations all over Pakistan.
25 March 1969:	Ayub Khan steps down, hands over power to Gen. Yayha Khan. Martial law imposed.
7 December 1970:	First general elections held. Awami League and Pakistan Peoples Party (PPP) emerge as leading parties in East and West Pakistan.

25/26 March 1971:	Operation Searchlight in Dhaka, beginning of brutal nine-month crackdown in the then East Pakistan.
3 December 1971:	Pakistan launches pre-emptive air strikes on India.
16 December 1971:	Pakistan forces surrender in Dhaka, Bangladesh created.
20 December 1971:	Gen. Yahya Khan steps down and hands over power to Z.A. Bhutto who takes over as president and chief martial law administrator.
2 July 1972:	Prime Minister Indira Gandhi and Prime Minister Bhutto sign peace accord in Simla, India.
21 February 1974:	Pakistan recognizes Bangladesh.
1 March 1976:	Gen. Zia-ul-Haq becomes chief of army staff.
10 January 1977:	Nine opposition parties form Pakistan National Alliance (PNA).
7 March 1977:	General elections: PPP wins 155, PNA thirty-five seats out of 200.
4 July 1977:	Gen. Zia-ul-Haq deposes Bhutto, declares martial law.
18 March 1978:	Lahore High Court awards death sentence to Bhutto and four others in the Muhammad Kasuri murder case.
6 February 1978:	Supreme Court upholds Bhutto's conviction in murder case.
4 April 1979:	Bhutto is hanged.
25 February 1985:	Non-party elections.
23 March 1985:	Muhammad Khan Junejo sworn in as prime minister.

10 April 1986: Benazir Bhutto returns to Pakistan.

18 December 1987: Benazir Bhutto marries Asif Ali Zardari.

29 May 1988: Gen. Zia dismisses Prime Minister Junejo and dissolves the National Assembly.

17 August 1988: Zia dies in plane crash near Bahawalpur.

6 October 1988: Eight political parties form the Islami Jamhoori Ittehad (IJI).

16 November 1988: General elections: Benazir Bhutto and her Pakistan Peoples Party win ninety-two seats out of 207; Nawaz Sharif-led IJI wins fifty-five seats.

2 December 1988: Benazir sworn in as prime minister.

13 December 1988: Ghulam Ishaq Khan elected president.

5 February 1990: Kashmir Solidarity Day observed for the first time.

6 August 1990: President Ghulam Ishaq Khan sacks Benazir's government. Ghulam Mustafa Jatoi becomes caretaker prime minister.

24 October 1990: General elections: Nawaz's Pakistan Muslim League (Nawaz) (PMLN)-led IJI wins ninety-two out of 198 seats while the PPP-led People's Democratic Alliance (PDA) wins forty-five seats.

6 November 1990: Nawaz Sharif is sworn in as prime minister.

18 April 1993: President Ishaq Khan dismisses Nawaz's government. Balkh Sher Mazari becomes caretaker prime minister.

26 May 1993: The Supreme Court restores Nawaz's government, declaring his dismissal unconstitutional.

18 July 1993:	Army chief Gen. Waheed Kakar gets both President Ghulam Ishaq Khan and Nawaz Sharif to resign.
6 October 1993:	General elections: Benazir's PPP wins eighty-six seats out of 202 compared to seventy-three won by the Nawaz's PMLN.
19 October 1993:	Benazir sworn in as prime minister for the second time.
13 November 1993:	Farooq Leghari, a Bhutto nominee, elected president.
25 April 1996:	Imran Khan launches Pakistan Tehrek-e-Insaf (PTI) party.
20 September 1996:	Murtaza Bhutto, Benazir's brother, killed by police in Karachi.
5 November 1996:	President Farooq Leghari sacks Benazir, dissolves parliament and calls for elections. Malik Mairaj Khalid becomes caretaker prime minister.
3 February 1997:	General elections: Nawaz wins 137 seats out of 204, PPP wins eighteen.
17 February 1997:	Nawaz sworn in as prime minister for second time.
2 December 1997:	President Farooq Leghari resigns after a six-month legal battle to have Sharif investigated for misuse of power.
28 May 1998:	Pakistan conducts five nuclear tests.
15 April 1999:	Benazir Bhutto and Asif Zardari sentenced in absentia to a five-year jail term on charges of corruption.
21 February 1999:	Indian prime minister Vajpayee undertakes a bus journey to Lahore.

	Lahore Declaration signed by Nawaz Sharif and A.B. Vajpayee.
April–July 1999:	Kargil intrusions by Pakistan. Serious clashes between India and Pakistan.
4 July 1999:	Nawaz dashes to Washington DC seeking President Clinton's help in extricating the Pakistan army from Kargil.
12 October 1999:	Gen. Pervez Musharraf deposes Nawaz Sharif in a military coup, Nawaz placed under house arrest.
6 April 2000:	Nawaz Sharif sentenced to life imprisonment on charges of hijacking and terrorism.
10 December 2000:	Nawaz Sharif, along with family, sent into exile in Saudi Arabia.
21 June 2001:	Gen. Pervez Musharraf assumes office of president while remaining army chief.
15 July 2001:	Agra Summit between Gen. Musharraf and Prime Minister Vajpayee.
10 October 2002:	General elections.
23 November 2002:	Zafarullah Khan Jamali sworn in as prime minister.
9 March 2007:	Gen. Musharraf dismisses the chief justice of Pakistan, Iftikhar Choudhury.
20 July 2007:	Iftikhar Choudhury restored as chief justice of Pakistan.
18 October 2007:	Benazir Bhutto returns to Pakistan, after exile, survives an assassination attempt in Karachi.
3 November 2007:	Gen. Musharraf imposes emergency.

16 November 2007: After completion of five years, National Assembly dissolved. Mohammad Mian Soomro becomes caretaker prime minister.

25 November 2007: Nawaz Sharif returns to Pakistan after seven years of forced exile.

27 December 2007: Benazir assassinated in Rawalpindi after an election rally.

18 February 2008: General elections: PPP wins 124 seats, PMLN ninety-one and Pakistan Muslim League (Quaid-e-Azam Group) (PMLQ) fifty-four.

24 March 2008: Yusuf Raza Gillani of PPP elected as prime minister.

18 August 2008: Gen. Musharraf steps down as president. Mohammad Mian Soomro takes over as acting president.

6 September 2008: Asif Zardari elected president.

11 May 2013: General elections: PMLN wins 185 seats out of 342, PPP gets forty and Imran Khan's PTI thirty-five.

5 June 2013: Nawaz Sharif sworn in as prime minister for the third time.

30 July 2013: Mamnoon Hussain elected as president.

28 July 2017: Supreme Court disqualifies Nawaz Sharif as prime minister for not fulfilling requirements of a parliamentarian.

1 August 2017: Shahid Khaqan Abbasi sworn in as prime minister.

Preface

THIS BOOK IS AN ANALYTICAL collection of anecdotes, vignettes and incidents selected from Pakistan's history of the last seven decades. I came across these nuggets while researching my first book *Pakistan: Courting the Abyss*. By themselves, some brought a wry smile to one's lips, some raised eyebrows and some the thought 'I didn't think this was possible'. I started putting away such references and rereading them occasionally to relieve the pressure of writing the book. These anecdotes provided fascinating insights into the personalities of the rulers—anecdotes that brought them to life, elucidated their whims, fancies and foibles and gave a clue why most of them fell from power and in the estimation of the people.

Although individual anecdotes were complete in themselves, they, of course, did not tell the complete story of an individual or an event, let alone of Pakistan. Despite this, I began to ask myself whether collectively the anecdotes revealed anything about Pakistan and its rulers. Did they represent any pattern, any trend and did they reveal attitudes that Pakistan's leaders consistently exhibited both internally and externally?

The search for answers to these questions led to the writing of this book.

The book is, thus, neither a conventional history of Pakistan nor a biographical one. It does not go into details about the administration and policies of each of the rulers. Thus, the reader would not find much about Zulfikar Ali Bhutto's plan to build nuclear weapons or his outreach to the Islamic world or Zia-ul-Haq's Afghan policy or about the Kashmir issue under Benazir Bhutto and Nawaz Sharif or about Pervez Musharraf's 'Enlightened moderation' and 'War on terror'. Such subjects are easily available in any standard book on Pakistan. Much has been written and, no doubt, much more will be written on them.

However, what this book does provide is a riveting glimpse into the history of Pakistan through the prism of anecdotes about those who have been at the helm and about a few seminal events that have impacted Pakistan's destiny.

In writing this book I have taken the liberty of assuming that the reader has a basic knowledge of Pakistan's history and its rulers. To help the reader I have included a timeline of the major events in Pakistan since its creation.

I would like to thank my wife for her continuing patience in allowing me to spend days, weeks and months in my 'study' reading, researching and writing this book. I would also like to thank my children for their constant support. My thanks also to my editors Udayan Mitra and Antony Thomas at HarperCollins India for all their effort in bringing out this book.

Despite the help, all the shortcomings and errors in this book are mine.

Introduction

PAKISTAN WAS CREATED ON 14 August 1947 but the British did not formally leave Pakistan till February 1948. Apart from the British military officers and civil servants who stayed back to help the government till later, the last of the British troops to leave the shores of Pakistan were the 2nd Black Watch (Royal Highland Regiment). During his farewell speech to the British troops, Muhammad Ali Jinnah (henceforth Jinnah) momentarily lost his composure and said: 'I couldn't believe that I would ever be entitled to a Royal Salute from a British Regiment.' With the massed pipes and drums of the Baloch and the Punjab Regiments playing 'Will Ye No Come Back Again', the 2nd Black Watch marched up the gangway into the ship *Empire Halladale*. Thus came to an end the ninety-six years of service of the Black Watch Regiment in India.

A grateful nation bestowed upon Jinnah the title of *Quaid-i-Azam* (the great leader) for his perseverance and single-mindedness in pursuing his dream of creating a Muslim homeland in the subcontinent. His stern photograph dots every government office in Pakistan. But there was much more to Jinnah. Few, for example, know or want to know about Jinnah's softer side; about a non-Muslim woman half his age whom he loved and who loved him 'as it is given to few men to be loved'.[1] She would, however, leave him because she could not break through his aloofness and reserve. Jinnah cried at her grave before leaving for Karachi. For a person who created Pakistan, the treatment meted out to him at the fag end of his life was disgraceful. Even more disgraceful was the way his sister and faithful companion was pushed towards the 'edges of the city' after his death and died (or was killed) in solitude.

Field Marshal Ayub Khan (henceforth Ayub) who showed 'tactical timidity' in Burma,[2] came to power after edging out his benefactor Iskander Mirza, a descendant of Mir Jaffar of Plassey fame. Mirza was exiled to London where he died a lonely death. He was denied a burial in his own country and it was the Shah of Iran who lent dignity to a president of Pakistan by arranging a state funeral in Teheran. Samuel Huntington referred to Ayub as the 'Asian de Gaulle'. Not surprisingly, his ego grew to such an extent that he claimed that during the past fifty years, Muslims had not seen a leader greater than him. A suggestion was also made that he convert Pakistan into a monarchy and become its first Badshah (king)—a proposal Ayub took seriously for a while.

Ayub referred to Indians as 'a diseased people' and that 'Hindu morale would not survive a few hard blows'. Such perceptions led to his imagination getting the better of him when he bungled into the 1965 war with India. In this, he was egged on by the assumptions made by his foreign minister Zulfikar Ali Bhutto (henceforth Bhutto) that India would not attack across the international border. When India counter-attacked on 6 September 1965, Ayub and his commander-in-chief were the most surprised people. So great was the surprise that soldiers of some infantry battalions were, in fact, busy doing morning physical exercises as the Indian forces reached the outskirts of Lahore. Like in 1947, tribal fighters were mobilized this time for the Lahore front. However, not finding the flat terrain of Punjab to their liking, the tribesmen instead indulged in looting the locals, something that was treated as 'customary exuberance' of tribesmen in pursuit of their foe.

After the war, Ayub would tell his cabinet that never again would Pakistan risk 100 million people for the sake of five million Kashmiris. With the Tashkent Agreement being perceived as surrender to India, Ayub could not restore his image in the eyes of the people. Gen. Yahya Khan (henceforth Yahya) would do to his benefactor Ayub what Ayub had done to his benefactor Iskander Mirza—ease him out of power to take charge himself. As Yahya put it, 'I did not force Ayub to relinquish power in my favour … but welcomed the chance to take power away from him.'

Yahya was a hard drinker and had a weakness for unrestrained frolicking. A telling description in the *Time* magazine was that 'between dusk and dawn, Pakistan was ruled by pimps'.[3] In the Samson mould, Yahya believed he derived his strength from his brows. He had to face events that he was not equipped to handle, either by training or temperament. A straight soldier, Yahya was out of his depth when confronted with politicians like Mujibur Rahman and especially Bhutto, the latter being called 'the catalyst of separation' who wanted to manipulate the 1970 election results for his own personal ambitions. Yahya became a victim of the woefully inaccurate analysis of the intelligence agencies that elections in 1970 would lead to a hung parliament, which the army could manipulate. Resultantly, he told Henry Kissinger, President Richard Nixon's national security adviser, that he expected that a multiplicity of parties would emerge in both West and East Pakistan and because of their infighting he would remain the central figure of Pakistan's politics. After the election result, Kissinger would chide Yahya that for a dictator he ran a lousy election.[4]

The intelligence agencies were totally ignorant of the alienation of the people of East Pakistan that had been growing for a long time. The quality of the intelligence can be gauged from the fact that one morning, during the 1971 war, the director general of the Inter-Services Intelligence (DG, ISI) told Yahya, 'Sir, Jean Dixon, the astrologer of international fame, known for accuracy of her predictions, has said that you have a long life ahead of you as Head of State—perhaps ten years or more.'[5] Yahya was thrilled to hear this, little realizing he would be kicked out in less than ten days. When Kissinger asked Yahya how they hoped to tackle Indian superiority Yahya and his colleagues answered with bravado about 'the historic superiority of Moslem fighters'.

The omens were not propitious. When Yahya left the presidency to go to Air Headquarters in the afternoon of 3 December 1971, a huge vulture blocked the passage of his vehicle and stubbornly refused to budge till it was shooed away by a gardener. When Yahya was told about the Indian attack in the then East Pakistan he said, 'What can I do for East Pakistan? I can only pray.' Such was the state of affairs that Pakistan's naval chief learnt of the Pakistani air strikes of 3 December 1971 from a Pakistani radio broadcast while driving to work the next morning. On the eastern front, Lt Gen. A.A.K. Niazi learnt of the air strikes while listening to the BBC World Service. Ultimately, Yahya presided over the brutal dismemberment of the country. Like what Ayub before him had said about the Kashmiris, Yahya would say that he was not going to endanger West Pakistan 'for the sake of Bengalis'.

Bhutto claimed Indian citizenship till 1958 when he became a minister under Ayub Khan. Born of a Hindu mother, Bhutto, by all accounts, was a complex personality and his mother's humiliation by the Bhutto family may have accounted for this. When he first burst on the political firmament, he was hailed as someone 'with an exceptional mind, highly educated and charismatic'.[6] He was at ease both with the *awam* (people) and in the sophisticated international diplomatic circles. Once during a public speech, when caught consuming alcohol he retorted, 'Fine I am drinking sharab (alcohol). Unlike you sister-f....rs, I don't drink the blood of our people.' This brought the crowd to their feet and they chanted in Punjabi, 'Long may our Bhutto live, long may our Bhutto drink.'

Bhutto's approach to politics was best expressed by his statement in an interview: To succeed in politics 'one must have light and flexible fingers to insinuate them under the bird sitting on its eggs in the nest and take away the eggs. One by one. Without the bird realizing it.'[7] Bhutto potentially could have changed Pakistan. His was the first national popular political party in Pakistan with an innovative and catchy slogan—roti, kapda aur makan (food, clothing and shelter). He, however, could not realize this potential because of his complex personality and feudal mindset that could not tolerate dissent or opposition or brook any slight. His obsession with winning, and winning big, led him to rig the 1977 elections that provoked a reaction that saw him being removed in a coup and ultimately led him to the gallows. Sir James Morrice, British high commissioner to Pakistan (1962–65) and high commissioner to India (1968–71) was to write with uncanny prescience when, in an assessment he sent to London, he wrote about Bhutto: 'It seems to me that he was born to be hanged.'[8]

Gen. Zia-ul-Haq (henceforth Zia) obsequiously wriggled his way into Bhutto's confidence to become the army chief. Bhutto used to humiliate him by calling him his 'monkey general'[9] not realizing that Zia forgot no insult. Bhutto would pay dearly for his arrogance. When Benazir saw him for the first time, she thought Zia looked like an English cartoon villain. Referred to as 'a chess player in a nation of cricketers'[10] Zia showed an uncanny ability to outmanoeuvre his opponents to become the longest-serving military dictator. He did this by masking his true feelings and capabilities and allowing himself to be misjudged by friends and foes alike. Consequently, errors about him were frequent. For example, one of his contemporaries advised another colleague, 'Gen. Zia-ul-Haq is not very bright. If you have to make a point, say it slowly and never repeat less than three times.'[11]

During his career, Zia got an annual confidential report stating, 'he is not fit to be an officer in the Pakistan Army'.[12] Luckily his stars were favourable. On the intervention of Lt Gen. Gul Hassan, Yahya Khan quashed the report.

Though Zia hanged Bhutto, like Macbeth, Zia was spooked by 'Banquo's ghost'. On a visit to the UN, Zia visited the Pakistani consulate general in New York in October 1980. In the library, he casually picked up a book and a photograph of Bhutto stared Zia in the face. Impulsively, Zia threw the book down and shouted, 'Don't you have better books?' and irritably walked out of the library.[13]

Following the death of Zia in a plane crash, there was euphoria that democracy would be restored. The swearing in of Benazir Bhutto as the first woman prime minister in the Muslim world electrified many with hopes of change for the better. Bhutto had groomed Benazir from a very young age—reading her books on Napoleon, introducing her to Zhou Enlai, telling her about President Kennedy's assassination, and taking her to the Simla summit in 1972 where she met Indira Gandhi who both unnerved and intrigued her.

During both her tenures as prime minister, the hopes and expectations were belied very quickly. Benazir, called 'Alice in Blunderland' by some of her colleagues, got bogged down in tackling the establishment on the one hand and competing with Nawaz Sharif on the other. As a result, governance suffered. There was disappointment all around, especially when her husband Asif Zardari came to be known as Mr Ten Per Cent for his rampant corruption. For Zardari, Pakistan was his personal estate and as the PM's spouse he considered it his right not to make a distinction between personal and public money. Such was her isolation in her first term that right till the moment troops surrounded her secretariat, Benazir did not believe that she could be dismissed.

Though the Americans had worked out a deal between Benazir and Gen. Pervez Musharraf (henceforth Musharraf) for her return to Pakistan in 2007, there were ominous signs. When she asked him over the phone from the US if American officials had made it clear to him that her safety was his responsibility, Musharraf's cryptic response was that the Americans could call all they want but Benazir should understand that 'Your security is based on the state of our relationship'.[14] Did Benazir have a premonition about her impending fate? During a flight to Aspen, Colorado, just prior to her return to Pakistan, a flight attendant offered Benazir some freshly baked cookies. She declined on the pretext of watching her weight. However, she called the attendant back and said, 'Oh what's the difference, I'll be dead in a few months anyway.'[15]

Nawaz Sharif (henceforth Nawaz) and his brother Shahbaz are by far the longest-serving duo in Pakistani politics with Nawaz having been in and out of government since 1981. However, he has fared no better than Benazir in his three tenures as prime minister. Not very bright to begin with, Nawaz's father despaired about him till the governor of Punjab, Gen. Jilani Khan, started building a house in Lahore and sought the father's help in construction. The family hasn't looked back since then. The governor and Zia catapulted Nawaz Sharif into politics. Hamid Gul, DG, ISI, often remarked with delight that Nawaz Sharif was a product of their agency, their pride and symbol. However, this child of the 'establishment' would turn against his benefactors after becoming prime minister.

During Nawaz's prime ministership, the family's business empire grew by leaps and bounds. As noted commentator Ayaz Amir puts it, '... the first interest of this dynasty was always the building up of their business empire. Politics and power were means to that end.'[16] Nawaz considered himself above accountability and 'managed' the system, including the judiciary, so well that he could not be brought to book. It was the 'Panama Papers', however, in which his children were named and for which he has not been able to provide the money trails for acquiring property abroad that have become his nemesis. Corruption apart, what Nawaz would be remembered for most is that all his three tenures as prime minister were cut short prematurely by the president, the army chief and the judiciary respectively. The reason, at least partly, has been his 'monarchical style of governance'. He once told a journalist that he fancied himself as a Mughal king; she, however, felt that with his balding head and short stature he looked like a little Buddha.[17]

Benazir and Nawaz were autocratic. The difference was that Benazir never enjoyed the majorities in parliament that Nawaz did to push through her plans. It was Nawaz who was prone to leverage the one weakness of democracy—destroying democracy by democratic means—by using his brute majority to enact legislation that would destroy the spirit of democracy. This authoritarian streak in him has come to the fore whenever he has been prime minister, especially during his second and third terms. His big majorities have tempted him to advance his personal agenda and build a personalized political fiefdom.

The marked feature of the 1990s that has been called the 'barren years' or the 'democratic interlude' was that every civilian government since then had to look over its shoulder to see when and how the army would pull it down. This is, perhaps, best represented by this graffiti on a Karachi wall, in August 1990: 'We apologize for this temporary democratic interruption. Normal martial law will be resumed shortly.'[18] Another example was a cartoon published in a leading Pakistani newspaper: 'Ask not what Dictatorship can do for you. Ask what Democracy can do for Dictatorship.'[19] Clearly, the last word has not yet been heard on this score.

Musharraf by his own admission was 'an ill-disciplined young man – quarrelsome, irresponsible and careless'.[20] He had earned a dubious name for himself as army chief due to his Kargil misadventure. When the operation failed, both he and Nawaz pointed fingers at each other. An interesting aspect of the Kargil affair was that both Musharraf and Sharif had agreed to troop withdrawal *before* Sharif went to Washington for his meeting with President Clinton,[21] though both have studiously avoided mentioning this for their own reasons.

Musharraf should have been a footnote in Pakistan's history. He, however, came to occupy centre stage due to the fatal flaw in Nawaz Sharif's personality of seeing and treating his appointee army chief as 'his man'. As has been demonstrated repeatedly, a Pakistan army chief is no one's man except his own. As a result, Musharraf could successfully launch a 'counter-coup' against Nawaz Sharif. However, his survival was fortuitous because of the terrorist attack on the twin towers in New York on 9/11 that led to Pakistan once again becoming a front-line state against terrorism. Musharraf's misfortune was that his duplicitous game of simultaneously supporting the American war effort and the Taliban was bound to be counterproductive sooner or later. The assassination of Benazir on his watch will always be a stigma. He too had to quit under the force of political resentment.

The Indo-Pak wars of 1965 and 1971 (discussed in the chapters on Ayub and Yahya) and the Kargil intrusions (discussed in the chapter on Nawaz and Musharraf) provide a fascinating account of the Pakistani military mindset. They reflect their assumptions about India, the poor planning and worse implementation of plans, the lack of adequate decision making and, above all, a tactical mindset that either cannot or did not see the big picture. For example, after having launched the infiltrators into Kashmir in 1965, the army did not expect India to retaliate. In 1971, the crackdown in the then East Pakistan seemed to have no specific aim except that the danda—the big stick—would cow down the Bengali babu. In 1999, during Kargil, Musharraf and his three henchmen totally underestimated Indian reaction with Musharraf telling Nawaz that he did not expect India to 'carpet-bomb'.

What do these anecdotes and incidents about the rulers of Pakistan tell us? While the reader will, no doubt, draw his/her own conclusions, a few trends are highlighted here.

One political trend that has increasingly become visible is a reversion to the pre-British structures of governance. The pre-

British subcontinental empires were characterized, in broad terms, by two main principles: first, the entire empire was the personal estate of the ruler; the bureaucracy functioned at his whims and fancies. Second, instead of the rule of law there was the law of the ruler; all power and authority flowed from the ruler and he was the final authority in all matters—political, military, administrative and judicial.[22]

In the martial law periods of Ayub Khan, Yahya Khan, Zia-ul-Haq and Pervez Musharraf, the constitution itself was suspended and the word of the dictator was law. However, even under civilian governments, the noticeable feature has been increasing arbitrariness of governments. The governance model of Nawaz Sharif during his three tenures is a case in point. Behaving like a king, Nawaz ignored parliament, the real bastion of his strength, rarely consulted his cabinet and considered himself to be above accountability. Civil servants were at his beck and call as if they were his servants rather than employees of the state. Thus, capricious exercise of power has become the prevailing form of governance replacing institutions and democratic functioning; 'there is routine oppression of opponents, massive corruption and violation of the law.' Institutions have been eroded to such an extent that instead of protectors of the democratic system, they have become complicit in the erosion of the system.[23]

Innumerable politicians and commentators have testified to this state of affairs. For example, Syeda Abida Hussain, a politician from south Punjab, writes, 'Certainly, my country's history would have been quite different had our leaders been less self-serving and our institutions stronger. Almost from the outset, state power was exercised in a manner that served only to erode it.'[24] Even the UN commission that came to investigate Benazir's assassination, '... soon encountered a country deeply skeptical of authority and the justice system because of widespread corruption, abundant behind-the-scenes political deal making, and the regular impunity that had met previous unsolved political assassinations.'[25]

During Benazir's first government, she was furious at one cabinet meeting, complaining that of the 106 applications for jobs that she had received and sent to various ministries, not one had received a positive response. She accused the civil service of wilful obstruction. Cabinet Secretary Hassan Zaheer explained recruitment rules and regulations, the need to advertise and so forth. One cabinet minister cut him short to assert, 'The PM's orders surely override all rules and regulations.'[26]

A second trend is of political polarization that is increasingly becoming vicious. One reason for this was the clash of legacies earlier in the 1990s—the legacy of Zia represented by Nawaz Sharif and that of Bhutto represented by Benazir. Following her assassination, that legacy has all but disappeared under Asif Zardari. In fact, with the entry of Imran Khan as a serious player, the polarization has become multi-pronged and more bitter since the electoral prize is Punjab that has more than 50 per cent of the seats in the National Assembly. Unlike the PPP that seems to have lost its base in Punjab, Imran is building his base there, much to the annoyance of the Sharifs. This multi-pronged contest is no longer about legacy but a no-holds-barred contest for power, for the sake of power.

One symptom of polarization is the legal disabling of political opponents on account of corruption and abuse and misuse of power. Benazir, her husband Asif Zardari, and Nawaz Sharif have all been victims of it. Interestingly, such disqualifications have rarely stopped politicians from staging a comeback.

Asif Zardari's case is a fascinating study of the Pakistan political system. When Benazir became prime minister for the first time in 1988, he moved into the PM's house; when she was dismissed in 1990, he went from the PM's house to jail. When she returned to power in 1993, he went from jail to the PM's house; and in 1996 when she was dismissed for a second time he went back to jail. When the PPP won the 2008 elections after the assassination of Benazir, he moved into the President's House and all cases against him were slowly settled. As Imran Khan puts it: 'the justice system only acted against those out of power. In power, the justice system became part of the executive.'[27]

Another symptom is the effort to grab the levers of 'thana-kutchery', i.e., law and order to be used to influence the elections results. For example, the inspector general of police of Punjab, Abbas Khan, in the 1990s told the Lahore High Court that 25,000 policemen had not been recruited on merit, and amongst them were known criminals. He attributed the situation to the Punjab government under the Sharifs. The PPP and MQM (Muttahida Quami Movement) governments in Sindh were no better, filling up the police with their party cadres, even though some of them had a criminal past. Notes Imran Khan, 'the destruction of the police system was done at the cost of law and order in Pakistan and it was deliberate because the police typically play a major role in manipulating the elections and intimidating the opposition. The whole moral fabric of the country began to fall apart.'[28]

Due to such polarization, any challenge to the sitting elected government is often described as playing into the hands of the adversaries of democracy, i.e., the opposition's democratic right of criticism of the government has come to be equated with inviting martial law. Elected leaders have come to think that electoral victory gives them an insurance policy to pursue any political and personal agenda until the next general elections and they should not be criticized for it. No wonder, Nawaz Sharif equated corruption charges levelled against him by the opposition in the Panama Papers case[29] as akin to terrorism. Often, politicians indulge in massive amounts of corruption as a financial insurance against the day they will be out of power. The memory of Iskander Mirza, Pakistan's last Governor General and first president, who lived in penury in London after Ayub Khan deposed him possibly haunts all politicians. When he died, he left behind the princely sum of £859. Not surprisingly, politicians of all shades and hues have learnt the lesson well and have stashed away fortunes abroad including houses in fancy locations to be used when they are out of power.

The years 2008–13 did mark the successful completion of a democratic tenure in the country and the smooth transfer of power to another political party. However, commentators noted that in Pakistan, democracy has come to mean the holding of elections and not how far democratic norms have been internalized and how far they are practised. Due to political polarization, personal and party interest have come to be equated with the national interest. Development work is now projected as personal favours by the ruler.

The level of democracy can be gauged from a hilarious but representative example of an incident in the Punjab assembly narrated by Marvi Sirmed. On a motion presented by the then law minister, all the members blindly said 'aye'; the Speaker had to remind them they had to say 'no' to it. The poor members didn't even know the significance of a 'no' on a ministry-sponsored motion. They were never consulted perhaps. Their 'aye' and 'no' were taken as a given privilege of the party head.[30]

Three trends have marked the dictators. One is that when they arrived on the political scene they were all 'reluctant' and all of them promised to restore democracy as soon as possible because they did not hanker after power. Second, all of them have exhibited the desire for public acclaim and popularity. Whether it were the farcical 'referendums' of Zia and Musharraf or the co-opting of politicians to 'civilianize' their rule, almost all the dictators have tried to perpetuate themselves in this manner and ultimately failed. This was also borne out by the realization that a country as complex as Pakistan could not be governed without the politicians. Ayub Khan and Yahya co-opted Z.A. Bhutto, Zia used Muhammad Khan Junejo and Musharraf had to get Taj Muhammad Jamali and Shaukat Aziz. In June 2001, Musharraf declared himself president in the 'supreme national interest'. The *Dawn* summed this up brilliantly: 'Military rulers in Pakistan traverse a familiar and well-trodden route, sooner or later assuming the title and office of president. It took Gen. Ayub Khan three weeks to arrive at this stage, Gen. Yahya Khan a few days, Gen. Zia-ul-Haq about a year and it has taken Gen. Pervez Musharraf a little over eighteen months to cover the same journey.'[31]

Interestingly, while the dictators have moved from a one-man show towards their brand of democracy by civilianizing their governments, the civilian rulers have moved in the reverse direction by becoming autocrats. This was most visible under the second and third terms of Nawaz Sharif as PM.

A third feature of martial law regimes in Pakistan is that they have all come to power in bloodless coups. The people hailed the men on horseback when they assumed power, such had been the low ebb of popularity of the politicians. And all of them except Zia were forced from power without violence. Zia, of course, died in a plane accident. If anything, it was the loss of their core constituency—the military—and public unrest that made them see the writing on the wall. No wonder, it has been said that while the generals knew when to take over they were never sure when to step down. There have been no military purges. Conspiracies from among the lower ranks for a military takeover have been detected and dealt with efficiently.

Pakistan has been essentially calm immediately following the removal of any government. Starting from Iskander Mirza abrogating the constitution in 1958, to Ayub Khan's coup, to Yahya Khan's takeover, to Zia's coup, to the dismissals of the Benazir and Nawaz Sharif governments in the 1990s and of Nawaz in 2017, a cynical population has not reacted. This is probably a reflection of their realization of the inability or unwillingness of the leaders to improve their lot. A classic example is when Nawaz Sharif was deposed in a coup in October 1999; for the populace it seemed to be a day of deliverance and they distributed sweets for many days. The popular mood was clearly in favour of Musharraf who had sent Nawaz home.

What of the future? Leadership in Pakistan, whether military or civil, will continue to be autocratic. Pakistan has a long way to go before democracy can be said to have taken roots. Undoubtedly, elections will be held but other aspects of democracy like a functioning cabinet, parliament being more than a rubber stamp, acceptance of the role of an opposition, internal party democracy, strong regulatory institutions, etc., are still in the future.

1

End of the Raj: The Last Hurrah

THERE WAS LITTLE LOVE LOST between Lord Louis Mountbatten (henceforth Mountbatten), the last viceroy of India, and Jinnah as revealed by the references to Jinnah in the former's dispatches.

In his weekly Personal Report dated 17 April 1947 to the British prime minister, the Secretary of State and some other ministers, Mountbatten summed up his estimate of Jinnah by saying: 'I regard Jinnah as a psychopathic case; in fact, until I had met him I would not have thought it possible that a man with such a complete lack of administrative knowledge or sense of responsibility could achieve or hold down so powerful a position.'[1]

On 4 July 1947, in his weekly Personal Report, Mountbatten gave a detailed account of his efforts to persuade Jinnah to accept the proposal of a common Governor General: 'He [Jinnah] is suffering from megalomania in its worst form, for when I pointed out to him that if he went as a constitutional Governor-General his powers would be restricted but, as Prime Minister, he really could run Pakistan, he made no bones about the fact that his Prime Minister would do what he said. "In my position, it is I who will give the advice and other will act on it." ... I asked him, "Do you realize what this will cost you?" He said sadly, "It may cost me several crores of rupees in assets", to which I replied somewhat acidly, "It may cost you the whole of your assets and the future of Pakistan."'[2]

On 25 July 1947, a frustrated Mountbatten wrote in his report: 'He [Jinnah] was only saved from being struck by the arrival of other members of the Partition Council at this moment. However, I sent Ismay (Lord-Chief of Staff) round to beat him up as soon as possible…'[3]

To discuss the partition plan, Mountbatten had called a meeting on 2 June 1947 of one representative each from the Congress, the Muslim League and the Sikh community. Jinnah asked for more time to consider but Mountbatten told him firmly, 'Mr Jinnah, I do not intend to let you wreck all the work that has gone into this settlement. Since you will not accept it for the Muslim League, I will speak for them myself.' Mountbatten added that the next morning, he would announce to all the leaders that Jinnah had given him an assurance with which he was satisfied and on no account would he allow Jinnah to contradict him. He continued, 'After this announcement, when I look at you Mr Jinnah, you would nod, signifying that whatever I am saying is correct.'[4]

At the meeting held the next morning, on 3 June 1947, when Mountbatten looked at him, Jinnah, dutifully nodded his head.

This raises the interesting question: Did the Muslim League or Jinnah actually accept the decision of the 3 June partition plan? The proposal and counter-proposal were made on behalf of the Muslim League by Mountbatten, on the basis that he was given the authority to represent and decide on behalf of the party. Whether the Muslim League had given this authority or whether Mountbatten grabbed this initiative from them remains an untold story.

Mountbatten had to swear in Jinnah as Governor General on 14 August 1947. When on 13 August 1947 Mountbatten arrived in Karachi for the transfer of power, Jinnah did not personally welcome him and instead sent the governor of Sindh, Sir Ghulam Hussain Hidayatullah.[5]

For the ceremony, Jinnah insisted that he sit on a chair higher than that of Mountbatten since he was the Governor General of Pakistan and the president of the Constituent Assembly. This caused considerable embarrassment and the British had to turn this down diplomatically by hinting that Jinnah would assume the office of Governor General only after Mountbatten as the viceroy of India delivered the oath of office. Till that was done and all powers inherent in the office were transferred to him, Jinnah did not have an official position. Jinnah had to accept the logic of the argument with some reluctance.[6]

There was an interesting incident in the run-up to the swearing in. There was a rumour that some Sikhs had planned an assassination attempt on Jinnah by throwing a bomb at him when he went to the assembly in a ceremonial procession. When informed about this and asked what he would like to do, Mountbatten made it clear that the decision was not his to make, it was up to Jinnah and party. When he realized that Jinnah had left this decision to him, Mountbatten said that if he accompanied Jinnah, quite likely there would be no such attack because it would kill the Governor General of India together with a Governor General of Pakistan. That's why he had no objection to the procession being taken out.

The ceremonial procession went off without any incident. Later when they arrived back at the Government House safe and sound, Jinnah told Mountbatten, 'Thank God, I have got you back alive.' To this Mountbatten replied: 'Thank God, I have got *you* back alive.'[7]

The whole Karachi programme had had to be changed at the last minute because Jinnah had overlooked that it was Ramzan. Therefore, the lunch reception that he had himself suggested had to be changed to a dinner reception.[8]

Last Days

The last remnants of the Raj that left India were soldiers of the British Army. Successive generations of the army had served in

India, first guarding the possessions of the East India Company and later the 'Jewel in the crown'. It was a toss-up as to which regiment would be the last to leave and from which of the two dominions—India or Pakistan.

Ultimately, the honour went to the 1st Somerset Light Infantry in Bombay that had been in India longer (126 years) than any other regiment. The date for their departure was fixed for 28 February 1948. But, in typically British style, it was decided that the 2nd Black Watch (Royal Highland Regiment) in Karachi would be the second last to leave, two days earlier.

Trevor Royle describes the departure ceremony in his book *The Last Days of the Raj*. On 26 February, soldiers of the 2nd Battalion of the Black Watch regiment 'with colours flying, bayonets fixed and pipes and drums playing', began the march through the streets of the Empress Market into Elphinstone Street to say farewell to Jinnah. Unfortunately, there was a massive downpour totally soaking the soldiers. Despite this, the soldiers continued their march to the cheers of the enormous crowd that had collected to see them. According to the commander of the battalion, Neville Blair, even when the music stopped the crowds kept on roaring their approval and it was their enthusiasm, above anything else, that stuck in his mind as he marched at the head of his column of men. 'I was absolutely astounded by the reception. The crowds were vast and the police had to clear them away while they went on cheering ... to see amongst those crowds proud old turbaned Pathans saluting the colours was really quite something. I shall never forget it.'[9]

The battalion formed up in line outside the Governor General's house and accorded Jinnah a royal salute. During his farewell speech Jinnah momentarily lost his composure: 'I couldn't believe that I would ever be entitled to a Royal Salute from a British Regiment,' he told an embarrassed Blair.[10]

Following the civil ceremony at the Governor General's house, the battalion was given a military farewell at the Keamari docks by the massed pipes and drums of two battalions of the Baloch and the Punjab regiments. There was another large crowd to witness the last British battalion leaving the shores of Pakistan. Maj. Gen. Akbar Khan read out the farewell speech and he also gave permission to Blair to continue the parade. The battalion presented arms and with the Pakistani regiment's guard of honour playing massed pipes and drums, the colours were slow-marched up the gangway into the ship *Empire Halladale*. Thus came to an end, the ninety-six years of service of the Black Watch Regiment in India.

Trevor Royale notes that the last set to be played jointly by the massed Pakistani bands was the slow march, 'Will Ye No Come Back Again'—Lady Nairne's sentimental chorus for the lost cause of the Jacobites ringing down the years to mark the Highlanders' farewell:

Will ye no come back again,
Will ye no come back again,
Better lo'ed ye canna be,
Will ye no come back again?[11]

Iqbal Akhund noted that it was unlikely that the Baloch and Punjab regiments' bandsmen knew the words or significance of the Jacobites' farewell chorus for the vanquished Bonnie Prince Charlie—or that the cheering crowds wanted the British to come back.[12] However, the music did seem suitable. Blair's wife Isabel, who was already on board the ship with the other wives, remembered that 'the Scots were blubbing like babies'.[13]

With the colours on board, the battalion had officially left Pakistan, though in reality it sailed on 28 February due to handing over/taking over of stock to the Pakistan Army.

2

Muhammad Ali Jinnah: *Quaid-i-Azam*

Early Life

MUHAMMAD ALI JINNAH (HENCEFORTH JINNAH), nicknamed Mamad, was born on 20 October 1875. His date of birth was recorded as such by the Sindh Madressatul Islam, which he joined in 1887. Jinnah changed his date of birth to 25 December, Christmas Day, perhaps due to the influence of the Church Mission Society High School that he joined on 8 March 1892. Pakistan observes 25 December as his birthday.[1]

Jinnah's grandfather Poonja Gokuldas Meghji aka Punjalal Meghji Thakkar was born a Gujarati Hindu who converted to Islam and adopted the Ismaili faith. Jinnah converted to Athnaashri Shiism from Ismailism.[2] He also changed his name from Muhammadali Jeenabhai Poonja to Muhammad Ali Jinnah in 1894 while studying for the bar in London.

Jinnah's first marriage took place in 1892 to Emibai, daughter of Gokal Lera Khemji, when he was seventeen years old. At that time, he was still a fifth-grade student of the Sindh Madressatul

Islam in Karachi.[3] Emibai died due to a cholera outbreak when he was in London.

One amusing anecdote that Jinnah was fond of narrating was about his first night in an English boarding house, though he said it in the third person: 'When he slipped into bed and felt the hot water bottle near his feet he thought it was an animal and threw it out. As he peered at it in the dark, he could see water oozing out of it which he was quite convinced was blood. 'I have killed it', he screamed, but there was no one to hear him.'

(Sheela Reddy, *Mr and Mrs Jinnah: The Marriage that Shook India*, Gurgaon, India: Penguin Random House, 2017, p. 84.)

Ruttie Jinnah

Later, Jinnah would get married to Rutten Bai Petit (Ruttie), a Parsi, who was twenty-two years younger to him. Rutten Bai was the daughter of Sir Dinshaw Manockjee Petit[4] (1873–1933) who was a client and friend of Jinnah. Her father was opposed to the marriage. He got a high court injunction against Jinnah marrying or having any contact with his daughter who was a minor (when Jinnah sought to marry her, Ruttie was only sixteen). Jinnah fully respected the court injunction and did not meet Ruttie during this period. However, within two months of her reaching the age of eighteen on 20 February 1918, they got married on 19 April 1918. She converted to Islam and the marriage was performed according to Shiite rites.[5] There was much consternation in the Parsi community at Ruttie's conversion to Islam.[6]

Ruttie had the ability of drawing out Jinnah, using her charm and making him talk and even laugh at himself.[7] Jinnah did not even try to hide the power she had over him. To please her, he even shaved off his moustache and wore his hair longer, 'brushed sleekly backwards in the style favoured by the more fashionable young Parsis. In her inimitable, playful way, she insisted on it before accepting his proposal.[8]

Ruttie was a fascinating person and stories about her abound. For one, she was not very religious and despite embracing Islam, she rarely practised Islamic rites. What was marked about her was her frankness and spontaneity. In public, she went about without a veil unlike most upper-class Muslim women of India at that time.[9]

It was Ruttie's sartorial style that irked Lady Willingdon, the wife of the governor of Bombay. On one occasion, at a party held at Government House, Ruttie Jinnah wore a low-cut dress that offended her hostess. At the dining table, Lady Willingdon asked an ADC to bring a wrap for Mrs Jinnah, in case she felt cold. Jinnah is said to have risen and said, 'When Mrs Jinnah feels cold, she will say so, and ask for a wrap herself.' Then he led his wife from the dining room, and from that time refused to go to Government House again so long as the Willingdons occupied it.[10]

Ruttie never concealed her dislike of the ruling classes. She expressed this in a striking way during a visit to Kashmir in 1926. Asked to complete a form that required information about the purpose of her visit, she wrote, 'The purpose of visit is to spread sedition.' Years later, Maharaja Hari Singh and Jinnah would have a good laugh about the incident.[11]

Stories of Ruttie's frankness, sense of humour and disregard of the British are legion. Once when the Jinnahs were visiting Simla in 1918, they were invited to dinner at the Viceroy's Lodge. When presented to the viceroy, Lord Chelmsford, Ruttie after shaking his hand chose to greet him in the traditional Indian way by folding her hands, rather than curtseying to him. After dinner Chelmsford advised her that in order to avoid jeopardizing her husband's political career she should, when in Rome, do as the Romans do. Undeterred, Ruttie pointed out: 'That is exactly what I did Your Excellency. In India, I greeted you in the Indian way.'[12]

On another occasion Lord Reading sought to elicit Ruttie's help to persuade Jinnah to accept an offer of knighthood. He asked whether she would not like to be called Lady Jinnah? Ruttie disappointed him by retorting that should her husband accept, she would seek separation from him.[13]

On another occasion, she was seated next to Lord Reading at a dinner party. The conversation happened to be about Germany where the viceroy had spent time as a student. He was keen to return there but believed that, '… the Germans will not like us, the British, any more after the war and I cannot go there.' 'Oh!' said Ruttie Jinnah, adding: 'How is it then that you came to India?'[14]

The marriage, however, did not last long. Jinnah was too busy in politics and Ruttie could not bear the separation. Once married, Ruttie discovered that Jinnah was not the 'fierce and passionate lover of her dreams who she thought would burn "storming passions into the very fibre of her being", but someone altogether more timid and naïve.' In her youthfulness, she had not factored in Jinnah's long years of living alone and 'lack of physical demonstrativeness'. His lack of showing deep emotion frustrated her.[15] Ruttie once told Sarojini Naidu that Jinnah was unable 'to satisfy her mind and soul. He stifled her by his lack of understanding and his lack of the spirit of the joy of life.' She revealed that she had even wilfully tried to put an end to herself.[16]

In September 1922, Ruttie left Jinnah and along with their baby went to London. This was the first of many departures in their stormy relationship. She did return to Bombay eventually, 'but it was the first of many endings to their relationship. From September 1927, the couple lived apart'.[17]

However, she could not bear the break-up of the marriage. Writes Rafia Zakaria, 'Unable to wrest the only man she wanted from his political commitments, the girl who had all her life been feted and fretted over, coveted and coddled, whose wit and charm and beauty were all legendary, fell ill.'[18]

When the end was close, both her father and husband returned to her. Her father who had disowned her when she married Jinnah, forgave his daughter and supported her in her last days when she was staying at the Taj Hotel in Bombay. Jinnah wept at her bedside when he saw her life slipping away, realizing it was too late to save her. In her last letter to him she wrote:

> When one has been as near to the reality of Life (which after all is Death) as I have been dearest, one only remembers the beautiful and tender moments and all the rest become a half-veiled mist of unrealities. Try and remember me as the flower you plucked and not the flower you tread upon ... Darling I love you – I love you – and had I loved you just a little less I might have remained with you – only after one has created a very beautiful blossom one does not drag it through the mire. The higher you set your ideal the lower it falls. I have loved you my darling as it is given to a few men to be loved. I only beseech you that the tragedy which commenced in love should also end with it.[19]

Ruttie Jinnah died on 20 February 1929 on her twenty-ninth birthday. Her death certificate made no mention of the cause. Forty years later, her close friend Kanji Dwarkadas in an interview explicitly stated that Ruttie had committed suicide by taking sleeping pills that were always on her bedside. 'She chose to die on her birthday,' Kanji told the Pakistani writer, Syed Shahabuddin Dosnani on 16 February 1968.[20]

She was buried in a Muslim cemetery in Bombay. Jinnah visited her grave just before he left Bombay for Karachi for the last time. 'Here at the grave of the woman he had lost for the sake of the country he had to create, Jinnah was said to have wept.'[21] Much later Jinnah was to admit to a friend's wife: 'She was a child and I should never have married her. The fault was mine.'[22]

After her death, sometimes Jinnah, according to his driver, would peer into a trunk full of Ruttie's clothes. 'His gaunt, transparent face would become clouded. "It's all right, it's all right," he would say, then remove his monocle, wipe it and walk away.'[23]

Ruttie's death deeply impacted Jinnah. According to Kanji Dwarkadas, Jinnah became so bitter that 'he could not stand abuse, ridicule, misunderstanding and misrepresentation of his actions and never forgave those who, unwisely and unjustly indulged in them'. It was this bitterness that got transposed into his political life.[24]

Jinnah's life and times are extensively taught in schools and colleges of Pakistan. But the children seldom learn about his non-Muslim wife, about the woman he had loved and who loved him 'as it is given to a few men to be loved'.

Jinnah and the Muslim League

When Jinnah became Governor General of Pakistan, his opinion of the Muslim League was made perfectly clear to Iskander Mirza when the latter pleaded, 'We must try to be considerate to the Muslim Leaguers as, after all, they gave us Pakistan.' Jinnah retorted haughtily: 'Who told you the Muslim League gave us Pakistan? I brought Pakistan – with my stenographer.'[25]

A.K. Fazlul Haq, prime minister of united Bengal, was known as the Sher-e-Bangla (the Bengal Tiger). Even Jinnah had to acknowledge Haq's popularity, albeit in his own style. While addressing the historic Muslim League session in Lahore in 1940, where the Lahore Resolution was adopted, Jinnah found that there was spontaneous applause when Fazlul Haq entered the hall. Finding his voice drowned by the public eruption, Jinnah resumed his seat saying, 'Now that the tiger has arrived, the lamb must retire.'[26]

While Jinnah could forge the Muslim League as an instrument for the creation of Pakistan, his disparaging attitude towards it resulted in the instrument beginning to crumble even before his demise. As a well-known commentator put it, 'Even before the Quaid-i-Azam's demise ... the uninspired and uninspiring Muslim League leadership had begun to devote most of its time merely to maintaining its position. The party was soon riven into hostile factions, with intrigue and low-level manoeuvre their main weapons and the grabbing of personal power and wealth their single common aim.'[27]

This was confirmed by Ayub Khan, who wrote in his autobiography that the affairs of the Muslim League were in a mess, the party had no organizational structure. 'It seems to me, however, that this disintegration had started earlier, even in the Quaid-e-Azam's time, with people like Choudhry Khaliquzzaman challenging his authority.[28]

Jinnah's Properties

While leaving Delhi for the last time on 7 August 1947, Jinnah had remarked enigmatically, 'That's the end of that;' that this was the last time he would be seeing Delhi. Despite such assertions, his two houses—one in Bombay (Malabar Hill) and the other in Delhi (Aurangzeb Road)—kept Jinnah tied to India.

The Bombay house, which Jinnah dearly loved, was left undisturbed by the Government of India out of consideration for him. However, there was pressure on the government on this score. Ultimately, Prime Minister Nehru had to call up India's high commissioner in Karachi, Sri Prakasa, to say that the government was under pressure to requisition the house. He instructed Sri Prakasa to see Jinnah, find out his wishes and the rent he would like to have. Jinnah was taken aback with Nehru's message and told Sri Prakasa, 'Tell Jawaharlal not to break my heart. I have built it brick by brick. Who can live in a house like that? What fine verandahs! It is a small house fit only for a small European family or a refined Indian prince. You do not know how I love Bombay. I still look forward to going back there.'

'Really Mr Jinnah', Sri Prakasa said, 'You desire to go back to Bombay? I know how much Bombay owes to you and your great services to the city. May I tell the Prime Minister that you want to go back there?'

He replied: 'Yes, you may.'[29] The high commissioner informed Prime Minister Nehru accordingly and the house remained as it was.

However, after some months Nehru again spoke to the high commissioner saying that the government was being embarrassed by the adverse remarks on the house being left untouched. It would have to be requisitioned. The prime minister asked Sri Prakasa to inquire from Jinnah the rent he would like to have. Jinnah, who by then was unwell and recuperating in Quetta/Ziarat in Balochistan, said he had been offered Rs 3,000 a month and hoped his wishes regarding the nature of the tenant would be respected. The British deputy high commissioner rented the house for Rs 3,000. He had a small family and so Jinnah's wishes were fulfilled. Another condition for the lease was that should Jinnah ever want the house for himself, the tenant would have to vacate it immediately.[30]

For the Delhi house, Jinnah managed to negotiate its sale but there were complications since it had become evacuee property and so the sale could not be registered. Jinnah was very upset about this and even complained to the Indian high commissioner. As a very special case, the Government of India allowed the registration of the sale of the house a few months later. Jinnah was informed about this and according to the high commissioner, instead of getting a thank you note, he got a brusque answer saying that he was glad that the right thing was done which should really have been done long ago.[31]

Jinnah was also attached to his house in Karachi and concerned about finding a suitable tenant. On 17 March 1948, Jinnah and his sister invited the newly arrived American ambassador to Pakistan, Paul H. Alling, for tea. After inquiring whether the ambassador was making progress in the acquisition of property, Jinnah and Fatima asked whether the ambassador would be interested in their house 'Flagstaff'. A few days earlier Jinnah had told Alling that it would be available for purchase. The ambassador replied that they were already negotiating the purchase of the ambassador's residence before they became aware that 'Flagstaff' was available, and it would be impossible to withdraw from that negotiation. Jinnah then asked if 'Flagstaff' could be suitable for other personnel of the embassy. The ambassador had to regret again saying that they would not be able to justify the purchase of such a large property for any subordinate personnel. The ambassador sensed that Jinnah and his sister were disappointed that the Americans had not been able to purchase 'Flagstaff'.[32] On receiving the details of the ambassador's meeting with Jinnah, a thoughtful secretary of state cabled the American embassy in Karachi to present to Jinnah four twelve-inch oscillating fans with the compliments of the United States.[33]

> At the dinner reception that Jinnah hosted on 14 August 1947, Lt Col (later Maj. Gen.) Akbar Khan expressed his disappointment that higher posts in the armed forces continued to be held by British officers. Jinnah retorted, 'Never forget that you are the servants of the state. You do not make policy. It is we, the people's representatives, who decide how the country is to be run. Your job is only to obey the decision of your civilian masters.' Present-day civilian leaders would do well to recall this incident in their dealings with the army.
>
> (M. Asghar Khan, *We've Learnt Nothing from History: Pakistan: Politics & Military Power*, Karachi: OUP, 2005, p. 3.)

Jinnah's love for his own properties was in sharp contrast to the treatment he meted out to Shivrattan Mohatta whose Mohatta Palace in Karachi was requisitioned by Pakistan's Ministry of

Foreign Affairs in 1947. When he managed to meet Jinnah at a state function for Karachi businessmen, he interceded for his house. He received no sympathy. 'It is a matter of state,' Jinnah simply said before walking off,[34] unmindful of the fact that his properties in India too were matters of state.

> After Gandhiji was assassinated, the Pakistan Constituent Assembly made a reference to him. Prime Minister Liaquat Ali Khan and Muhammad Ayub Khuhro, the chief minister of Sindh paid fulsome compliments and repeatedly referred to him as 'Mahatma'. However, when his turn came to speak, Jinnah did not mention Gandhiji by name and neither did he call him 'Mahatma'. Instead, he referred to Gandhiji as 'he', and said that he served his community as he thought best, and that he (Jinnah) would convey to the Governor-General of India, the feelings of the House at an appropriate time.
>
> (Sri Prakasa, *Pakistan: Birth and Early Days*, Meerut: Meenakshi Prakashan, 1965, p. 109.)

Fatima Jinnah

Fatima Jinnah, described as 'the frail-looking, graceful but gritty sister of Jinnah'[35] was a qualified dental surgeon having received a degree (in dentistry) from the University of Calcutta in 1914. She opened a dental clinic in Bombay in 1923. After the death of Ruttie in 1929, Fatima closed her clinic and moved in with Jinnah at his Malabar Hill bungalow. Henceforth, she would be a political worker and a close and trusted confidante of her brother.

That Jinnah was extremely fond of his sister was well known. One of the tributes he paid to her was at a dinner in his honour at the Karachi Club soon after his arrival in Karachi. Jinnah described Fatima Jinnah in the following words: 'Miss Fatima Jinnah is a constant source of help and encouragement to me. In the days when I was expecting to be taken as a prisoner by the British Government, it was my sister who encouraged me, and said hopeful things when revolution was staring me in the face. Her constant care is about my health.'[36] On another occasion he said, 'My sister was like a bright ray of light and hope whenever I came back home and met her. Anxieties would have been much greater and my health much worse, but for the restraint imposed by her.'[37]

According to their driver, Jinnah depended on Fatima for everything. Even when he played billiards, the one sport he liked, Fatima had to watch him play. 'If the shot went through as planned, he would smile triumphantly at his sister.'[38]

After Jinnah died, Fatima Jinnah was requested to address the nation on the radio. However, the address was curtailed. The director general of Radio Pakistan was given instructions to switch off the speech as soon as she started criticizing Prime Minister Liaquat Ali.[39]

Fatima Jinnah's book *My Brother*, though written in 1955, was published only in 1987, thirty-two years later. The reason appears to be the criticism that she levelled against the early leaders of Pakistan. She made five important points in the book, as noted by Nadeem F. Paracha:

- that her brother was 'betrayed' by even some of his closest comrades who had worked with him during the Pakistan Movement;
- that the deterioration in his health was due to such betrayal;
- that she was especially resentful towards Prime Minister Liaquat Ali Khan, regarded as Jinnah's closest colleague;
- that Jinnah told her that many of his former colleagues were coming to meet him when he was recuperating in Ziarat only to determine how much life there was left in him, implying that they were most probably waiting for him to quietly perish;
- and that she was particularly pained by the treatment meted out to Jinnah at the end when the ambulance carrying him from

Mauripur airport to the Governor General's residence on 11 September 1948 broke down in the middle of the road. Jinnah expired that night after having been stuck in the ambulance in an oppressive atmosphere.[40]

For two years after Jinnah's death, Fatima Jinnah was not allowed to address any public meetings. It was only on Jinnah's third death anniversary that she was allowed to address the nation on Radio. However, when she started speaking about the ambulance breaking down, she was cut off.[41]

Following Jinnah's death in September 1948, Fatima Jinnah ebbed further and further from the political awareness of the country. No longer the Governor General's sister, she lived all alone in the twenty-four-room, red-stone Mohatta Palace (that had been requisitioned) near the sea.

The combined opposition parties pulled her out of her self-imposed political retirement in 1964 to challenge Field Marshal Ayub Khan in the presidential elections that were to be held in January 1965. Contesting against Ayub in the presidential elections was her final political foray. It was, however, ironic that she was contesting against Ayub Khan. In 1958, after Ayub had taken over power, and there were spontaneous celebrations throughout the country, she had summed up the feelings by saying: 'A new era has begun under Gen. Ayub Khan and the Armed Forces have undertaken to root out the administrative malaise and the antisocial practices, to create a sense of confidence, security and stability and eventually to bring the country back to normalcy. I hope and pray that God may give them wisdom and strength to achieve their objective.'[42]

In her election speeches Fatima Jinnah criticized Ayub and his family for corruption. She particularly zeroed in on Bhutto, then a minister in Ayub's government, for personal condemnation, calling him an 'inebriate and a philanderer' in a speech in Hyderabad. Ayub retaliated in a press conference in Lahore by accusing her of leading an 'unnatural' life (a reference to her spinsterhood) and being surrounded by 'perverts'.[43] He also accused her of being an Indian and American agent. This was also reported in an article in *Time* magazine.[44] This shocked everyone but Ayub managed to get away with it since the campaign rhetoric had sunk to a really low level with rival parties freely abusing each other.

Ayub won the 1965 elections with a narrow margin—only 49,591 of the 80,000 electors voted for him. It was in East Pakistan and Karachi that Fatima Jinnah's democracy argument had great resonance.[45]

Abida Hussain, who would later become a prominent politician from south Punjab and Pakistan's ambassador to the US, provides a graphic description of Fatima Jinnah's condition. She and her mother visited Fatima Jinnah at Mohatta Palace in late July 1965. After ringing the front bell for a long time, the door was opened by Fatima Jinnah herself. She led them into a dark and stifling sitting room. 'Open the latches of the windows, Kishwar,' she said, addressing Abida Hussain's mother by her name, 'you and your daughter are taller and stronger than I am.' Abida did as she was asked. As the windows opened and the light and air entered the room, Abida was taken aback to see how old and frail Fatima Jinnah looked.[46]

Fatima Jinnah then asked Abida Hussain to ring the bell so that her deaf old servant could bring some tea or limbo paani (lemonade). She added sorrowfully, 'Kishwar, as you can see, my sofas have loose covers on because I seldom have visitors. They all go to see my half-sister, Shireen Bai, these days, since she has an "in" with the Ayub Khan's government. Had my brother foreseen all this, would he have struggled so hard for the creation of Pakistan? Would he have wanted a country without a constitution, without justice, where skilled sycophants become powerful while people with integrity and dignity start falling behind? If this was what Pakistan was to become, then making Pakistan was a foolish mistake.'[47]

According to Rafia Zakaria, 'Every night Fatima Jinnah locked herself in the second-story bedroom of Mohatta Palace. Every morning when she awoke, she dropped the key from the balcony upstairs so that her attendant below could retrieve it and bring her morning tea.'[48]

However, on 9 July 1967, no key was dropped from the bedroom balcony but no one noticed. It was only in the evening that the domestic maid finally told a neighbour. It was near dusk by the time a locksmith opened the door. Inside her bedroom, Fatima Jinnah lay cold, having passed away hours before she was found.[49] She was seventy-one. While the government announced the cause of the death to be a heart attack, many including Jinnah's nephew Akber Pirbhai, insisted that she was murdered. He even met Ayub Khan and requested that a judicial commission be appointed to examine if she had been assassinated, a request that was turned down by Ayub. This was reported under the headlines 'New Twist to Miss Jinnah's controversy'.[50] It is believed that her followers were not allowed to see her face to confirm that she had not died unnaturally.

She was buried in Karachi. Almost half a million people took part in her funeral procession. Many in the procession raised slogans against the Ayub Khan regime. There was some rioting in which members of the Jamaat-i-Islami (JI) and left-wing groups were involved. The police first resorted to tear gas and later opened fire in which about twelve people were killed.[51]

In 1972, the Urdu daily *Jang* reported that a court in Karachi had admitted a petition which stated that the government did not allow the people to have a last look at Fatima Jinnah. The people who bathed her body said there were deep wounds on her body, signs of torture and a deep gash in her stomach. While a date for the hearing was announced, no one knows what happened to the petition.

Her book *My Brother* was banned by the Quaid-i-Azam Academy on the grounds that her ideas were against the 'Nazariae-Pakistan' since it contained unfavourable references to Liaquat Ali. When the book was published after thirty-two years of its writing, those portions were censored.

She left behind a small poodle, a goat and a duck.[52]

Jinnah and Liaquat Ali

That there was a serious rift between Jinnah and Liaquat Ali, the first prime minister of Pakistan, was made public by several, including Jinnah's secretary Syed Sharifuddin Pirzada and Fatima Jinnah. According to Pirzada, Jinnah had lost trust in Liaquat during his last days. He linked to this rift the unusual incident in Karachi when the military ambulance carrying a terminally ill Jinnah ran out of petrol and broke down on the road from Mauripur airport to the Governor General's house.[53]

Syed Hashim Raza, the then administrator of Karachi and his brother Syed Kazim Raza, inspector general of police, were required to be at the airport whenever Jinnah left or returned to Karachi. Both were completely unaware of his return to Karachi from Quetta on 11 September 1948.[54] When Liaquat was asked why the administrator and the IG were not informed of Jinnah's return, he said, 'No one except Col Knowles, Military Secretary to the Governor General, knew about the return of the Quaid. It was Col Knowles who had ordered the ambulance which unfortunately broke down on the way.'[55]

Jinnah and Choudhry Rahmat Ali

Choudhry Rahmat Ali, the man who coined the acronym PAKISTAN, worked as private secretary to Mir Dost Muhammad Khan Mazari, the Mazari chief, in order to fight a family court case between 1919 and 1928. Dost Muhammad Khan won the case in 1929 and in appreciation, rewarded Rahmat Ali handsomely for his services. Rahmat Ali used the money to finish his education at Cambridge.[56]

According to Sherbaz Mazari, Rahmat Ali was ahead of his time. When he contacted the Indian delegation during the 1930–31 Round Table Conference at London, they scoffed at his views and regarded him an idealistic dreamer.[57]

In January 1933, he, together with three other students in Cambridge, coined the acronym PAKISTAN (literally meaning land of the pure) in a four-page leaflet entitled 'Now or Never'. According to Rahmat Ali, Pakistan was an acronym composed of Punjab, Afghania (NWFP), Kashmir, Sindh and Balochistan. Rahmat Ali had met Jinnah in 1934, soon after he had authored his pamphlet. According to K.K. Aziz, Jinnah, after noticing the restless and impulsive nature of the young ideologue, told him, 'My dear boy, don't be in a hurry; let the waters flow and they will find their own level ...'[58]

In 1948, Rahmat Ali visited Pakistan, the country he had named and dreamt of for many years ago. However, the security agencies hounded him constantly, making him feel unwelcome. He became disillusioned and even accused the leaders of the Pakistan movement of a sell-out. Frustrated, he went back to England never to return. He died there in 1951.[59]

Jinnah was the lawyer for the Khan of Kalat and had even argued the case for Kalat's independence before the Cabinet Mission in 1946. The Khan of Kalat had weighed Jinnah in gold to raise money for the creation of Pakistan, which the Khan had supported, but not the accession of his state, Kalat, to it. According to the Khan's servant Syed Bahar Shah who did the weighing, 'Jinnah weighed exactly ninety pounds and he got his weight in gold. Then I weighed his sister, Fatima and His Highness presented her with a chain that was worth $1 million at that time. It was gold, with diamonds, emeralds and rubies.' Later, after the creation of Pakistan, Jinnah sent the army into Kalat and forced the Khan to accede to Pakistan.

(Mary Anne Weaver, *Pakistan: In the Shadow of Jihad and Afghanistan*, New York: Straus and Girous, 2002, Indian edition, New Delhi: Viking, Penguin Books India, 2003, p. 102.)

Jinnah's 11 August 1947 Speech

Jinnah's famous 11 August 1947 speech to the Constituent Assembly of Pakistan, where he said, 'You are free to go to your temples ... etc.' came as a bit of a shock to many in the Muslim League. The press in Karachi was instructed not to print the statement. According to Khaled Ahmed, 'In the years to come, it was not allowed to figure in official publications.'[60] 'Zia had historians commissioned to say that Jinnah was not completely in his senses when he addressed the Constituent Assembly.'[61] To maintain Jinnah in the national pantheon, the state took pains to describe him as a non-secular, non-liberal leader who had promised the sharia as a part of his political programme.[62] Ahmed further notes that Jinnah's daughter Dina Wadia, then living in New York, was secretly asked to clarify Jinnah's culinary habits, especially that he never drank alcohol or ate ham. She, however, refused to oblige. She was thereafter threatened with 'disclosures' about her private life if she ever revealed that she had been contacted in this regard. She was never officially invited to visit Pakistan.[63]

Jinnah hand-picked his colleague and friend, M.A.H. Ispahani to be the first ambassador of Pakistan to the US. Ispahani laid the foundation of Pakistan's dealings with American officials. He reported back to Jinnah in these memorable words: 'I have learnt that sweet words and first impressions count a lot with Americans. They are inclined to quickly like or dislike an individual or organization.' This would be the mantra that succeeding generations of Pakistan leaders would chant and follow.

(Dennis Kux, *The United States And Pakistan, 1947-2000: Disenchanted Allies*, London: OUP, 2001, p. 10.)

Jinnah's Health and Death[64]

Jinnah developed fatal spots on his lungs before the end of the Second World War. The one person who knew about this was Dr Jal R. Patel who had taken the X-Rays. However, he maintained a professional silence. Had the news leaked, according to Wolpert, Pakistan might never have been born, at least not in 1947.[65]

Towards the end of July 1948, without prior notice, Liaquat Ali, the prime minister, accompanied by Ch. Mohammad Ali, Secretary General, arrived in Ziarat where Jinnah was recuperating. He asked Jinnah's doctor Col Illahi Bux about his diagnosis of Quaid's health. The doctor declined to comment saying that he had been invited by Fatima Jinnah to attend to the Quaid; he could say what he thought of the patient only to her. When Liaquat asserted that as prime minister he wanted to know, the doctor answered he could not do it without the patient's permission.[66]

On 11 September 1948, Jinnah, weighing barely 70 pounds and suffering from consumption, compounded by cancer of the lungs, was carried on a stretcher aboard the Governor General's Viking for the flight from Quetta to Karachi. Despite his condition, however, he found the energy to return, from his stretcher, the salute given by the flight crew. There was no one to receive him at Mauripur airport (Karachi's military airport) barring his military secretary Col Geoffrey Knowles and an army ambulance, sans any nurse. The diplomatic corps had not been informed about his arrival, which was the norm whenever Jinnah landed in Karachi so that he was received in the approved official way. The ambulance would break down halfway to his residence and it took Col Knowles two hours to fetch another, from the local Red Cross. Meanwhile, Jinnah was stranded on the road for two hours in an 'oppressive' ambulance that completely exhausted him. No one knew that Jinnah was in the stranded ambulance. His pulse was weak and irregular. Jinnah was to die later that night.

The tragic manner of his death was compounded by his last rites. A Twelver Shia, following his conversion from the Ismaili sect, Jinnah had to have two separate funerals—one according to the Sunni rituals in the open and the other before that according to Shia norms in his home.[67]

3.1

Ayub Khan I: Unchartered Waters

Early Life and Personality

AYUB KHAN, A TAREEN PAKHTUN, was born in Rehana, a village in the Hazara district of North West Frontier Province (NWFP) (now known as Khyber Pakhtunkhwa or KPK) on 14 May 1907. His father, Mir Dad had retired as a risaldar major from the 9th Hodson Horse in the British Indian Army. Despite his small pension, Mir Dad managed to send Ayub to the Aligarh Muslim University in 1922. By a stroke a good fortune, when Ayub was preparing for graduation, the adjutant general of the British Indian Army, Gen. Andrew Skeen, spotted him. Skeen had come to Aligarh looking for suitable soldierly material and was struck by Ayub's appearance: tall, well built, of fair complexion. Ayub was accordingly chosen for training at Sandhurst as one of the earliest Indian cadets to go there. Ayub did remarkably well at Sandhurst, securing top position among Indian cadets.[1] Interestingly, apart from his military endeavours, Ayub was musically inclined and played the flute in Sandhurst's music club. In recognition of his musical accomplishments he was even awarded a silver flute.[2]

Iskander Mirza's son Humayun Mirza, who knew Ayub well since he was a frequent visitor to their house when his father was the defence secretary, had this to say about Ayub: 'He [Ayub] had a presence about him that radiated authority, enhanced by his general's uniform. Tall, with an erect military posture, he spoke in short, clipped sentences, devoid of humour.'[3]

In one of his telegrams, the then US ambassador to Pakistan, James Langley, made an assessment of President Iskander Mirza and Gen. Ayub Khan: 'Neither Mirza nor Ayub has much patience with the way the democratic processes are working in Pakistan (nor does anybody else).' Commenting on the two principals, the ambassador stated, 'Mirza has more imagination than Ayub. He probably has a greater sense of loyalty to individuals than Ayub. This sense of loyalty extends to foreign friends also. Of the two, Ayub is the more moody, and the more easily exasperated. Even in the isolation of the presidency, Mirza seems to retain closer personal friendships than Ayub manages. Ayub seems more self-centered.'[4]

On another occasion, Langley said, 'Ayub has native talents of charm and quick wit, which conceal administrative and intellectual deficiencies. When the latter are made to show through, quick and high temper results.'[5]

Army Career

Ayub was commissioned as a second lieutenant on 27 February 1928 in the 1/14 Punjab Regiment, known as the 'Sherdils' (lion-hearted) in the British Indian Army. By the time of the Second World War, Ayub was a major and was later promoted to lieutenant colonel in 1942. He was posted to Burma as second in command of the 1st Assam Regiment that saw heavy fighting.[6] He was later promoted to colonel and assumed command of the Punjab Regiment. However, his initial record as an army officer was quite dismal. He was suspended and removed from command in Burma in 1945 'for visible cowardice under fire'. Again, in 1947, he escaped a court martial ordered by Jinnah himself through the inquiry officer Major Musa Khan whom Ayub would later elevate as the commander-in-chief.[7]

After Ayub's appointment as commander-in-chief (C-in-C), Sir Gilbert Laithwaithe, the British high commissioner to Pakistan, recorded a note on Gen. Ayub stating, 'I would not put him in the highest intellectual class by any means. He was, according to our records, a failure as a Commanding Officer on active service and had to be relieved.'[8] Shaukat Hayat Khan confirmed this in his book; Gen. Reese of the British Army had told him that he 'had sent [Ayub Khan] back from Burma when he showed tactical timidity'.[9]

At the time of Partition, Ayub was the tenth-ranking officer in the Pakistan Army with service number PA-10. After being sent back from Burma, Ayub was posted with the Punjab Boundary Force under Gen. Reese, his old divisional commander in Burma who had relieved him of command.[10] Due to his previous adverse relationship with the force commander, Ayub was unable to deliver either for the teeming refugee columns entering Pakistan or satisfy the political leadership. He was severely criticized by the local politicians, some of whom demanded his removal. This could explain his lasting distrust of the politicians.[11]

To save him further blushes, Iskander Mirza had Ayub transferred to the NWFP to participate in Operation Curzon, under which the regular troops were withdrawn from the forward areas of the province. According to one of his contemporaries, Maj. Gen. Nawabzada Sher Ali Pataudi, Ayub was not up to the mark in higher military studies. He had not read famous books on the art of war, or the personal accounts of great military leaders in detail. During discussions, Ayub would 'deflect the subject from the art of war and revert to issues of basic soldiering – simple, straight forward barrack and battalion stuff'. Pataudi noted that Ayub's main theme was selection boards and issues pertaining to the assessment of a man's character, ceiling and potential. This, according to Pataudi, was due to Ayub having spent much of his time in selection boards during the war.[12]

Others too have commented on Ayub's limited soldiering skills. According to one, 'Ayub's ability as a soldier lay in the direction of organization and administration rather than a commander in battle. He belonged to the school of Carnot rather than that of Napoleon.'[13] In a review of *Friends, Not Masters*, in the *Guardian* on 8 September 1967, Percival Spear, an eminent historian, remarked that Ayub Khan should 'neither be underrated as a politician nor overrated as a soldier'.[14]

Given the setbacks in his career, it was not surprising that Ayub was superseded. At one stage, Ayub sent Pataudi a note saying, 'Sher—am just off to East Pakistan. Have been superseded. Could you do something?... Grateful. Thanks. Ayub.' Sher Ali knew Commander-in-Chief Gen. Frank Messervey of the Pakistan Army well and went to see him to intercede on Ayub's behalf. Messervey gave Sher Ali sound advice which if it had been followed, would have made Pakistan a different place and the Pakistan Army a different army. Messervey told him that 'only correct selection and promotion at this time would ensure that the correct man would rise to the top job when all the British had gone'. He stressed the importance of astute people unburdened with complexes, and without political ambitions heading the army.[15]

Pataudi recounts an interesting incident when he was at the Joint Services Staff College (JSSC) at Latimer, UK, in 1950. Ayub, who had by then been promoted to lieutenant general and was the deputy C-in-C, told Pataudi to do the Imperial Defence College (IDC) course starting in January 1951 as soon as he finished the JSSC, which was unusual. Ayub's reasoning was that Pataudi should finish the IDC course quickly because 'I won't be able to spare you after that. This Army has a much greater and wider role to play than people realize. The C-in-C, in fact, is a more important man than the prime minister in our country as the situation stands today...'[16] Did Ayub have an inkling then that he would be promoted to C-in-C and that the army itself under him would have a greater role in the country?

Army Chief and Dictator

One of the issues in the army was that as a new country, there were a plethora of promotions for a few junior officers who got high military assignments very quickly. The fast pace of promotions meant that these officers did not get the requisite professional grooming at successive levels in higher command.

Despite this, by the end of 1949, the Pakistan government took the decision to appoint a Pakistani as C-in-C of the army. After an intensive examination of possible candidates, Maj. Gen. Iftikhar Ali Khan of Probyn's Horse stood out as the clear choice. The prime minister accepted the joint recommendations of Iskander Mirza (defence secretary) and Gen. Sir Douglas Gracey (C-in-C of the army) to appoint Gen. Iftikhar as the first Pakistani C-in-C of the army. They decided to send Gen. Iftikhar for final grooming to the Imperial Defence College in London.

Unfortunately, on way to England, Gen. Iftikhar's plane crashed and he was killed along with Brig. Sher Mohammad Khan who had also been selected for the Imperial Defence College and was next in line to succeed Gen. Iftikhar. Iftikhar Khan was senior, though Sher Khan was called 'General Tariq' for his successful exploits in Kashmir. This tragedy was a bitter blow to Pakistan because it lost its two best army officers. Their deaths cleared the way for Ayub Khan who at that time was the adjutant general. He was accordingly nominated to succeed Gen. Douglas Gracey in January 1951. Ayub became C-in-C at the age of only forty-two and after only twenty-two years of service.[17] A colonel in 1947, he became the C-in-C of the army, a four-star general, in January 1951, within four years of Pakistan's creation.

In his *Friends, Not Masters,* Ayub wrote that Gen. Iftikhar Khan had not been told that he would be the next C-in-C. Sher Ali, however, contradicts this. According to him, Iftikhar was in Lahore and Sher Ali was with him when he was informed of this decision. Ayub too was in Lahore and since he had never met Iftikhar who was to be the C-in-C, he requested Sher Ali to organize a meeting with him. The meeting, however, never took place because the next day Iftikhar, his wife and only son were killed in an air crash near Karachi.[18]

Ayub described his elevation as C-in-C on 17 January 1951 in the following words: 'After nearly two hundred years, a Muslim Army in the subcontinent would have a Muslim Commander-in-Chief.'

(Mohammad Ayub Khan, *Friends, Not Masters*, London: OUP, 1967, p. 35.)

In the normal course, Ayub Khan should have retired from military service in January 1955 after completing his four-year tenure as C-in-C. Instead, he was granted an extension enabling him to entrench himself in the polity. Prime Minister Mohammad Ali Bogra granted Ayub the extension in 1954 due to pressure from Iskander Mirza, the defence secretary who threatened to resign if the extension was not given. After Ayub's coup, Bogra told Humayun Mirza, Iskander's son, that he had warned Iskander about his misplaced sense of loyalty towards Ayub and that he would live to regret the extension.[19] Subsequently, another prime minister, Firoz Khan Noon, gave Ayub a further extension. This led to a peculiar situation that whereas Pakistan had seven prime ministers between January 1951 and October 1958, the army chief remained the same.[20]

In 1954, Ayub drew up a document titled 'A short appreciation of present and future problems of Pakistan' when he was in London. While it provided an insight into what Ayub was

> thinking, it was not a blue-print for a takeover. After he became minister of defence in 1954, it was considered by the cabinet but since no one thought it contained anything substantive, it was relegated to the archives.
>
> (Altaf Gauhar, *Ayub Khan: Pakistan's First Military Ruler*, Karachi: OUP, 1996, p. xl)

By mid-1958, President Mirza was toying with the idea of declaring martial law. By early October he was convinced of its need and he told the Americans about it. After a meeting with President Mirza, US ambassador Langley reported on 4 October 1958 that: '… he [Mirza] would take over the Government of Pakistan probably within a week and simultaneously proclaim martial law. Mirza says he is taking over to prevent an army seizure of power in Pakistan. The pressures within the army come from officers below Ayub, both Generals and Brigadiers. Mirza says the army will fully support his takeover, despite previous reservations by Ayub that seizure of power by the President could only be successful, if preceded by violence.'[21]

In another 'Top Secret' US intelligence report dated 5 October 1958, Ambassador Langley, quoting President Mirza, says:'He has been urged for at least a year by some within the army (Gen. Umrao for one) to take over, but that he has told them the "politicians must first be permitted to make asses of themselves".' Significantly, the ambassador then makes his own observation: 'Although everyone in Pakistan would agree that this is what the politicians have now done.'[22]

Iskander Mirza confided to Ayub Khan on 5 October 1958 that he had decided not to hold elections in view of the adverse law and order situation. Ayub's reaction was: 'It is unfortunate but if the situation is desperate and action is required to save the country, then go ahead.'[23]

President Iskander Mirza scrapped the 1956 Constitution on 7 October 1958 and declared martial law. He held that the constitution was 'unworkable' and that 'more sacred than the constitution [was] the country'.[24]

What Mirza did not comprehend was that under martial law, power flowed from the barrel of the gun that was in the hands of his supposed friend Ayub Khan. The new government was announced on 25 October and sworn in on the morning of 27 October. Ayub was appointed prime minister. Even though preparations for a coup were on, Gen. Ayub together with his confidant Gen. Burki called on the president in the evening and strolled affably with him in the President's House garden. Later that night Ayub sent three generals—Lt Gen. W.A. Burki, Lt Gen. Azam Khan and Lt Gen. Khalid M. Sheikh—to President Mirza, to advise him that it would be in his interest to step down, in fact to leave the country as soon as possible. Mirza knew that his game was up. He signed on the dotted line of his own resignation.[25]

> The night martial law was imposed, Nawab Akbar Bugti, the defence minister was talking in Balochi on the phone with Sher Baz Mazari, a Baloch politician. Bugti informed him that army trucks were all over the place. Mazari responded that since he (Bugti) was the minister of defence, he should know what the army was up to. Just then a third voice (of the intelligence operative taping their conversation) came on the line saying, '*Urdu mein bolo, ya angrezi mein. Aur zaban hummain samajh nahin aati*. (Speak either in Urdu or English. We don't understand other languages)
>
> (Sher Baz Mazari, *A Journey to Disillusionment*, Karachi: OUP, 1999, p. 86.)

Though Mirza would go into oblivion, it was ironic that Ayub would be paid back in the same coin eleven years later when army chief Yahya Khan declined to implement martial law with Ayub as its head and instead sent him into obscurity.

Following Iskander Mirza's abrogation of the constitution and the declaration of martial law, Ayub asked Chief Justice Muhammad Munir as to how a new constitution could be got approved by the people. Justice Munir came up with an amazing proposal—public acclaim. According to him, in ancient times constitutions were approved in the Greek states by 'public acclaim' and this could be repeated in Pakistan as well. He further explained 'public acclaim' to mean that after the draft constitution had been published in national newspapers, Ayub should address public meetings at venues like Nishtar Park, Karachi, Paltan Maidan, Dhaka, Mochi Gate, Lahore, and Chowk Yadgar, Peshawar. During these meetings, he should display the published draft constitution and seek public's approval. The chief justice was sure that the response of the public would be affirmative. This, according to him, would be construed as approval by 'public acclaim'. The suggestion of the chief justice made those present laugh, with Ayub Khan laughing the loudest. Notes Air Marshal Asghar Khan that though Ayub Khan did not accept the advice of 'public acclaim' for getting the constitution approved, it was not surprising that Pakistan has found it difficult to shake off the spectre of martial law ever since with such advice coming from the judiciary.[26]

Iskander Mirza

Iskander Mirza was a direct descendant of Mir Jafar, the infamous commander who had betrayed Siraj-ud-Daulah to the British in the Battle of Plassey in 1757. He was the first Indian officer to receive the king's commission from Sandhurst's Royal Military College. He was commissioned as a second lieutenant in the Poona Horse, a cavalry regiment. By the time he became a colonel he was transferred to the political service of India. This was apparently due to the reluctance of the British officers to serve under an Indian superior. Mirza served for twenty-five years in the NWFP and was a highly regarded administrator. The governor of NWFP, Olaf Caroe's classic book *The Pathans* is dedicated to him.[27] Later, he was bestowed the honorary rank of major general.[28]

> When Iskander Mirza was the political agent in the NWFP, he hosted a dinner for a group of stubborn tribal leaders. He arranged to mix a strong dose of Jamal Ghota (a vicious indigenous laxative) in their food. That was how he 'liquidated' his opponents at least for a few days.
>
> (Altaf Gauhar, *Ayub Khan: Pakistan's First Military Ruler*, Karachi: OUP, 1996, p. xxi.)

After the creation of Pakistan in 1947, Mirza was Jinnah's natural choice for defence secretary. Here he made his first serious mistake of protecting Ayub Khan from getting court-martialled after he had failed to adequately protect the refugees dislocated by Partition. Mirza had him posted to Waziristan to save his skin.[29] Ayub would repay the favour by easing out and exiling Mirza to become head of the state himself.

After the coup, Mirza and his wife were first flown to Quetta and then on 2 November 1958 to London. They carried with them only their personal belongings while their personal effects were confiscated and shared among the army brass. A US intelligence report dated 3 November 1958 described the indignities thrust upon the former president by uncouth army officers. It noted, 'Baggage they took with them had been packed by the Ispahanis. The Mirzas paid for their own transportation. They were made to pay ten rupees each for their passports.' Such was his plight that Mirza did not even have money to tip the porter or pay for his hotel upon arrival in London. It was the kindness of the Ispahanis that ensured that Mirza was not totally destitute.[30]

In London, Iskander Mirza found permanent accommodation in a small flat in Princes Gate, South Kensington. Ayub, through the British, advised Mirza not to go public about his disputes with Ayub since his first wife Riffat Begum and children were in Pakistan. Mirza spent the rest of his life in London in exile living quietly. He sensed an opportunity of going back when Yahya took over from Ayub. He even wrote to Yahya accordingly. However, he received a curt reply from one of Yahya's staff officers: 'Your application to visit Pakistan is hereby denied.'[31]

Bhutto met Iskander Mirza in London after the 1965 war. When Mirza asked him: 'Zulfi, you know the size of India. Pakistan could not have defeated India; then why did you start this war?' Bhutto's reply was: 'There was no other way to weaken Ayub Khan and remove him.'[32]

In London, Mirza was forced to live modestly since his financial resources were limited. He had two pensions: one that he got from his Indian political service and the other as president of Pakistan. His income was supplemented by remittances from his son Humayun and the generosity of the Ispahanis, Ardeshir Zahedi (then ambassador and later foreign minister of Iran), the Shah of Iran, Lord Inchcape, Lord Hume and other heads of European governments.[33] It was also rumoured that he was made a director at Veeraswamy's, a well-known Indian restaurant on Regent Street.[34]

While in hospital in London, the Iranian ambassador Ardeshir Zahedi visited Iskander Mirza frequently. On one such occasions, as he approached the room, he overheard the former president tell his wife Nahid, 'We cannot afford medical treatment, so let me just die.' The ambassador was so overcome with emotion, that he turned away without visiting his friend.[35]

Mirza died in his sleep on his seventieth birthday, 13 November 1969, 'leaving behind a princely sum of £859 capital cash and £80 in income. After paying taxes an amount of £165 capital and £56 was distributed among his wife and five children as per shariah law.'[36]

Shunned by his own country Pakistan, it was the Shah of Iran who lent dignity to the deceased president by honouring him with a state funeral in he. This is how his son Humayun described the funeral. The Shah's special plane flew the body from London to Teheran, where Ardeshir Zahedi (who had become foreign minister by then), the diplomatic corps in Teheran and chiefs of the armed forces and court ministers received it. After a royal salute, President Mirza's body was taken to the Sepah-Selar Mosque where he lay in state covered by a Pakistani flag. The next day, his body was carried by the Shah's Honour Guard through the grounds of the mosque and then placed on a gun carriage. The procession then weaved its way slowly through the flower-decked streets of Teheran that were lined with people. Members of the Honour Guard led the procession with each carrying a decoration that Mirza had earned during his lifetime and the lead soldier carrying his official picture. His son Humayun and wife followed behind. They were followed by the Iranian cabinet led by Prime Minister Hoveyda and Foreign Minister Zahedi. Behind them were the chiefs of the armed forces, followed by the diplomatic corps in Iran. It was a moving tribute.[37]

Despite the best efforts of the Iranian foreign minister, Iskander Mirza's family still living in Pakistan were detained in Karachi by Yahya's military government. They were allowed to leave Karachi only when it was too late to attend the funeral.

Mirza's body was laid to rest in a mausoleum that had been built for Ardeshir's father, Gen. Zahedi. He had saved the Shah's throne from the communists a few years earlier. There the two graves lie side by side.[38]

Apart from Humayun, the only other Pakistanis present at the funeral were Pakistan's ambassador to Iran and friend S. Shahnawaz Khan and his wife Maliha. Pakistan lost a lot of respect in the eyes of the world by the shameful behaviour of its government towards a former president.[39]

Politics

In the newly created Pakistan, the political capital was in Karachi while the army's general headquarters (GHQ) was in Rawalpindi. This necessitated Ayub making frequent trips to Karachi. This was the period when the affairs of the ruling Muslim League were chaotic. There was considerable infighting in the party and the government. This further reinforced Ayub's impression about politics. Ayub would later describe his experiences in Karachi in the following words: '... the malaise in the political and administrative life of Pakistan was becoming painful. Karachi was a hotbed of intrigues ... Why were people not attending to their work with some honesty of purpose and why could they not evolve some team spirit? Why all the factions, dissensions and disputes? And why all this malice and distrust? They were all busy destroying each other.'[40]

Ayub felt the affairs of the Muslim League, the ruling party, were in a mess. Its decision-making bodies were controlled by a small coterie of men and the party had no organizational structure. There were several other problems like conflicts between the provinces and insistent demands from East Pakistan. He felt that Prime Minister Liaquat Ali Khan had proved too slow to regain the initiative: '... there was nobody who could make up his mind about anything.'[41]

On 28 October 1958, Ayub relinquished the post of C-in-C and appointed Gen. Mohammad Musa Khan, a close confidant, in his stead. By doing so, Ayub lost direct contact with his real constituency of power—the armed forces. Moreover, the good relations that existed between the presidency and the GHQ started to taper off after the retirement of Gen. Musa as C-in-C in 1966. None of the other dictators that followed Ayub Khan made the mistake of relinquishing the post of C-in-C/ chief of the army staff (COAS) voluntarily. Musharraf did so very reluctantly and only when he was forcd to do so.

Musa Khan played excellent hockey as a defender. In the British Indian Army, Dhyan Chand of the Punjab Regiment was the legendary forward. It was said that if anyone could stop him, it was Musa Khan of the Frontier Force.

(Hassan Abbas, *Pakistan's Drift into Extremism*, New Delhi: Pentagon Press, 2005, reprinted in 2007, p. 35.)

Even though Gen. Musa khan was a close confidant, Ayub started feeling insecure after his appointment as C-in-C. He sought Bhutto's advice on how to ensure that he would be superior to everyone else. Bhutto suggested that Ayub should elevate himself to the rank of a field marshal.[42] Ayub liked the idea and acted upon it. Thus, self-appointed Field Marshal Ayub Khan has so far been the only five-star general in Pakistan's military history.

Jamsheed Marker speculates that Ayub promoting himself as Field Marshal could also have been motivated by a Punjab Regimental ceremonial march-past. This was led by Field Marshal Sir Claude Auchinleck who was the former C-in-C of the Indian Army before Partition and Supreme Commander of the Indian and Pakistani armies immediately afterwards. Auchinleck was the Honorary Colonel Commandant of the regiment. During the march-past Auchinleck raised his Field Marshal's baton in salute whilst Ayub, as a General, had to reply from the stand with a hand salute.

(Jamsheed Marker, *Cover Point: Impressions of Leadership in Pakistan*, Karachi: OUP, 2016, p. 71.)

Auchinleck was quite upset at Ayub elevating himself as field marshal. He told Iskander Mirza in London that during his visit to

Pakistan a request was made by one of Ayub's aides to borrow his field marshal's baton. It was duly copied and Ayub declared himself 'Field Marshal'. Since this rank was only awarded for exceptional services rendered during wartime, Auchinleck was annoyed by this misuse of military etiquette. He exclaimed, 'I earned my rank for my efforts in WW II against the Germans in the Middle East and the Japanese in Burma. What battle has Ayub won that he presumes to call himself a "Field Marshal"?'[43]

Western intellectuals and economists like Samuel Huntington lauded Ayub as an 'Asian de Gaulle'—a military leader who was also a statesman with a vision.[44] Samuel Huntington wrote: 'More than any other political leaders in a modernizing country after the Second World War, Ayub Khan came close to filling the role of a Solon or Lycurgus or "Great Legislator" on the Platonic or Rousseauian model.'[45] Not surprisingly, Ayub's ego grew to such an extent that in 1965, at a committee meeting of the Muslim League, Ayub Khan boasted that 'during the past fifty years the Muslims had not seen a greater leader than him'.[46] Some went even further and declared that 'no Muslim since the fall of the Moghul Empire ruled over a wider area in the Indian subcontinent for a longer period or more effectively than Field Marshal Mohammad Ayub Khan did in undivided Pakistan from October 27, 1958 to March 25, 1969.'[47]

At the peak of his power, a fawning politician proposed that Ayub should proclaim a hereditary monarchy in Pakistan and that he should make himself its first monarch.[48] For Ayub, this was a serious enough proposal. He formed a two-man committee consisting of Nawab of Kalabagh and Bhutto to examine it. Within a week the committee advised Ayub Khan to forget the proposal. Ayub Khan's observations were '*behtar sallah*' (good advice) but he added, 'It is not all that senseless.'[49] As a journalist wrote, Ayub Khan 'imagined the genius of the people of Pakistan to be ruled by one man'.[50]

> During Ayub's time, the test of successful journalism in Pakistan came to mean that when he glanced at the morning papers, he should not be upset.
>
> (Herbert Feldman, *From Crisis to Crisis: Pakistan 1962-1969*, London OUP, 1972, p. 280.)

***

> The one astonishing contribution that Ayub made to political science was his statement, 'We must understand that democracy cannot work in a hot climate. To have democracy we must have a cold climate like Britain.'
>
> (Tariq Ali, *The Clash of Fundamentalisms: Crusades, Jihads and Modernity*. New York: Verso, 2002, p. 183.)

Ayub Khan did not speak Bengali. During his visits to East Pakistan he would address public rallies either in Urdu or in English using an interpreter for translation into Bengali. On one memorable occasion in early March 1967, Ayub was addressing a large public rally in Mymensingh. The governor of East Pakistan, Monem Khan, decided that he would translate the President's speech. Ayub's speech lasted almost an hour during which the governor dozed off and even started snoring. After Ayub completed his speech, the governor was woken up. His secretary gave him some notes that he had taken of Ayub's speech. Instead of translating Ayub's hour-long speech, Monem Khan spoke for nearly two hours during which he even sang verses from Tagore, Ghalib and Iqbal, though Ayub had done no such thing.

Later, a mystified Ayub questioned the governor on his two-hour long translation. The governor laughed and gave Ayub some sound political wisdom. He said it did not matter what either of them said. What really mattered was what the public wanted to hear. The village folk didn't come from far off places to hear their lectures. They came for entertainment, for distraction from their drab lives. So, it was entertainment that he gave them. As a result, the public sang when he sang and they laughed when he laughed. And then the governor gave the punchline. He said this was the reason why people concentrated on sex, especially during monsoons, when they had nothing else to do. This was also the reason for the population explosion in spite of the Population Control Centres that Ayub had set up countrywide. According to the governor, the people visited these centres not to procure free contraceptives but rather to get erotic pleasure from hearing about how to use them. Ayub was greatly amused with this explanation of the governor.[51]

In April 1965, Ayub visited Moscow, the first head of state of Pakistan to do so. On 5 April, he and his delegation were taken to a dacha on the bank of the Moscow river for a clay pigeon shoot prior to the resumption of formal talks. The likes of Ayub, Bhutto and some others considered themselves crackshots having devoted a lot of time to prearranged official duck shoots in Pakistan. They were confident of giving the elderly Russians a lesson or two in shooting. In the event, it turned out to be a one-sided affair, with the Russians hitting almost every saucer and the Pakistanis missing almost everything. Gromyko scored nine out of ten, Ayub had one out of ten while Bhutto and the other Pakistani 'sharpshooters' scored a duck![52]

Ayub's regime was rocked by the student agitation during the period from late 1968 to early 1969 that began over a trifling incident in Rawalpindi. However, the agitation had its lighter moments too when the demonstrators started welcoming pro-regime government officials and politicians with chamchas (literally spoons but in a derogatory sense sycophants). How big the chamcha was depended on how important the dignitary thought of himself as well as the discernment of the public about his sycophancy.[53] In one instance, N.M. Uqaili, a minister in Ayub Khan's cabinet, was accosted by demonstrators shouting, 'chamcha, chamcha'. When he asked the assistant commissioner accompanying him about the noise, prompt came the smart answer: 'A mere matter of cutlery, sir.'[54] Another tactic of protest was to paint stray dogs with Ayub on their backs,[55] a ploy that would be followed very effectively against Zia too.

One of Ayub's failings was that he refused to submit to accountability. The motives of anyone who questioned the performance of his government were considered suspect. He expected the people to trust their 'leader' implicitly, no questions asked.[56] Several leaders who followed Ayub, notably Nawaz Sharif, would display similar traits.

The one scandal that rocked Ayub Khan pertained to British model Christine Keeler, the femme fatale at the heart of the Profumo scandal. In 1963, a British tabloid, the *News of the World*, serialized the memoir of Christine Keeler. Keeler claimed that Ayub Khan had frolicked with her in the swimming pool at Lord Astor's Cliveden Mansion in the Buckinghamshire countryside. At the time, Keeler was involved in relationships with the British Secretary of State for war, John Profumo, and a Soviet naval attache, Yvegeny Ivanov, simultaneously. As a result of the scandal Profumo had to resign. The Pakistan government denied the Keeler story and lodged a strong protest with the British government. The Pakistan government also ensured that the news about Ayub Khan's alleged links to the Profumo affair were not published in Pakistani newspapers.[57] Bhutto would observe sarcastically that it seemed 'incongruous for an interesting thing like that to happen to such a very dull man'.[58]

United States

Ayub told the first meeting of his cabinet, 'As far as you are concerned, there is only one embassy that matters in this country: the American embassy.'[59] In this, Ayub was, of course, following in the footsteps of Jinnah. During a meeting with Lord Ismay, Lord Mountbatten's chief of staff in India, Jinnah had examined the possibility of Pakistan after the British left and determined, according to Ismay, that 'Pakistan could not stand alone'.[60] It would need to be friends with a superpower. With the British power on the wane, this could only be the US.

Both American and Pakistani leaders repeatedly testified to the closeness and warmth of the relations. Richard Nixon's first visit to Pakistan was in December 1953 when he was vice-president and he forged a close relationship with Gen. Ayub Khan. After returning from this visit, Nixon expressed his strong interest in providing military aid to Pakistan. On Christmas eve, he briefed the US National Security Council that 'Pakistan is a country I would like to do everything for'.[61] Nixon would later write in his memoirs that 'Ayub Khan was one Pakistani leader who was more anti-communist than anti-Indian'.[62]

Secretary of State John Foster Dulles assured Congress in closed hearings in June 1953 that the Pakistanis '… are going to fight any communist invasion with their bare fists if they have to'. In September 1953, Ayub promised the US State Department, 'Our army can be your army if you want us.'[63] In 1961, on a state visit to the US, Ayub while addressing the joint session of the US Congress said: 'The only people who will stand by you are the people of Pakistan.'[64] With US aid pouring in, it was not surprising that an American assessment contained in a November 1957 dispatch stated that 'the only reason why Pakistan is able to keep going is US aid'.[65]

This was in contrast to the early years of the Pak–US engagement when the Governor General of Pakistan, Ghulam Mohammad, complained in 1951 that US aid to India had left it feeling like 'a prospective bride who observes her suitor spending large sums on a mistress [i.e., India] while she herself can look forward to no more than a token maintenance in the event of marriage'.[66] Such sentiments recurred in 1953, when Pakistan asked for additional US aid in exchange for its alliance with the US with Ghulam Mohammad once again claiming that to do otherwise 'would be like taking a poor girl for a walk and then walking out on her, leaving her only with a bad name.'[67]

In November 1963, Foreign Minister Bhutto had gone to Washington DC to represent Pakistan at the funeral of President John F. Kennedy. During his meeting with Bhutto, the new president, Lyndon Johnson, bluntly told him what he thought of Pakistan's growing links with China, 'I do not care what my daughter does with her boyfriend behind my back, but I'll be dammed if she does something right in front of my own eyes.'[68]

While the US had become of critical importance to it, Pakistan diplomats found getting attention in Washington an uphill task. Amjad Ali was Pakistan's ambassador to the US in the 1950s. He asked the former nawab of Bahawalpur to send him a pair of cheetah cubs from his private zoo. The intention was to walk with the cubs on Massachusetts Avenue, get noticed and be written about. Unfortunately, the nawab sent a fully-grown cheetah that made walking with him dangerous and not the kind of publicity he was looking for. So, he presented the cheetah to the Washington zoo. A plaque was put up, photographs taken but the media did not show interest. His conclusion was, '... in the early fifties, most Americans were not even aware that Pakistan existed.'

(Syeda Abida Hussain, *Power Failure: The Political Odyssey of a Pakistani Woman*, Karachi: OUP, 2015, p. 405.)

***

Following the Indo-Pak war of 1965, Ayub travelled to the US in December 1965. He told Johnson quite plainly, 'If I break with America, I will simply lose my economy, but if I break with China, I may even lose my country.'

Time, 10 December 1965, cited in Mushahid Hussain and Akmal Hussain, *Pakistan: Problems of Governance*, New Delhi: Konark, 1993, p. 36.

***

The close relationship that developed between Jackie Kennedy and Ayub Khan during her visit to Pakistan as the first lady of the US was the talk of the town. Whatever be the truth, the fact was that an autographed photograph of Jackie riding a horse had pride of place in Ayub Khan's bedroom. The photograph contained an extremely affectionate note written in Jackie's handwriting. What fuelled rumours was the fact that similar photographs of other foreign dignitaries presented to Ayub Khan were all kept in the living room. Only this one photograph found a prominent spot in his bedroom.

(Arshad Sami Khan, *Three Presidents and an Aide*, New Delhi: Pentagon Press, 1999, pp. 5–6.)

***

In the summer of 1962, Ayub was on a private visit to Washington DC when he had a chance meeting with Humayun Mirza. Ayub told him that he presented a horse to Jackie Kennedy and he was waiting for the official helicopter to take him to Mount Vernon where he was going riding with her.

(Humayun Mirza, *From Plassey to Pakistan*, Maryland: Timespinner, 1999, pp. 289–90.)

China

Ayub was concerned about border demarcation with China. This was based on Pakistan's discovery of a Chinese map that showed a large portion of Pakistan-occupied Kashmir, including Mintaka and Khunjerab Passes, within China. To pre-empt a border dispute with China, Ayub decided to seek demarcation of their border. Ayub's fears for the future were clear from the *Daily Mail* interview where he said that the Chinese were not immediately ready for any major territorial advances but 'tomorrow they would expand'.[69]

Ayub Khan's visit to China in 1964 took place shortly after the Chinese had tested their first nuclear bomb. The Americans, eager to know details, persuaded the managing director of Pakistan International Airlines (PIA) to put some glue or some similar sticky substance under the wings of Ayub's Boeing aircraft. It was believed that bits of contaminated dust would stick to the glue, which would then have been analysed by the Americans.[70]

End of an Era

Ayub had an attack of pulmonary embolism in January 1968. He was in a critical condition but recovered. However, worse was in the offing. There was altercation between some students of Gordon College, Rawalpindi, and customs officials over purchase of foreign-made goods from Landi Kotal on the Pakistan–Afghanistan border. The students organized a demonstration that soon took on an anti-regime character. Bhutto who was in Rawalpindi that day was prevented from speaking to the students. In the melee, a seventeen-year-old first-year student died on the spot. It was from this accidental beginning on 7 November 1968 that the whole of West Pakistan was soon plunged in a massive student agitation. Three days later, Bhutto and eleven other political leaders were arrested. He was charged with inciting disaffection 'to bring into hatred and contempt the government established by law.'[71]

According to Gohar Ayub, 'At the end of July 1968, Father went on a visit to the UK. He met PM Harold Wilson of the Labour Party, who hinted that Z.A. Bhutto possibly had been given substantial funds by an intelligence agency to destabilize Father's government.'[72]

Faced with the student agitation that was getting out of hand, Ayub summoned a special cabinet meeting in mid-March 1969, which also turned out to be his last. Yahya Khan, the army chief was specially invited to attend. Ayub informed them that talks had failed to find a political settlement. Hence, the only remedy to save the country was imposition of martial law. Yahya agreed but asked to see Ayub alone. The cabinet was adjourned for good.

In their private meeting Yahya specified three conditions: dismiss the provincial governors and the cabinet and dissolve the national and the two provincial assemblies [West and East Pakistan]. Ayub agreed to both. Yahya's third condition was to abrogate the constitution. Ayub realized the implication of this: abrogation of the constitution would make martial law the supreme law and the chief martial law administrator (CMLA) would be the final authority. Ayub's position would be same as that of Iskander Mirza from 7 October to 27 October 1958, when Ayub threw him out of the presidency and sent him abroad into exile for life.[73]

Yahya then went in for the kill. He conveyed that if Ayub headed the martial law it would convey the impression that the army was a mercenary one perpetuating the presidency. Hence, the 'suggestion' made was that Ayub should let Yahya head the martial law while Ayub should proceed on sick leave. Ayub knew his time was up. The drama ended with a significant smile and remark from Ayub: 'I know what you want; all right, let us mutually work out the final arrangement.' So Ayub decided to hand over power to Yahya and the final preparations for the imposition of martial law began immediately.[74] On 25 March 1969 Ayub handed over to Yahya and proceeded on leave. Soon after declaring martial law, Yahya assumed the title of chief martial law administrator.[75]

As per his own constitution, Ayub should have handed over power to the Speaker of the National Assembly instead of to Yahya Khan. The fact that the Speaker was a Bengali may have influenced Ayub's decision.[76] Ayub had a highly patronizing, almost racist, attitude towards the Bengalis. He felt that the people in East Pakistan suffered from 'all the inhibitions of down-trodden races and [had] not yet found it possible to adjust psychologically to the requirements of the new-born freedom.'[77]

On 26 March 1969, Ayub invited his former ministers to a farewell meeting. During his speech, he said: 'We were really able to bluff the world but our own people called the bluff. ... We don't know the value of freedom; left to ourselves, we would go back to slavery. ... I never thought our people would go mad like this. ... I doubt if in our political life we will have a good man for a long time. Thank God, we have an army. If nothing else, I have held this country together for ten years. It was like keeping a number of frogs in one basket. What sort of Pakistan will emerge is anybody's guess. There will be either force or mob rule. I hope we can find some answers between the two.'[78]

Ayub wanted his farewell address to be broadcast and telecast live. Yahya, however, turned down the request.[79] In his recorded 'farewell broadcast', Ayub presented a sad picture of the country that was strikingly similar to the one he had painted when he took over in October 1958. Ayub had then justified the coup on the grounds of what he termed 'total administrative, economic, political and moral chaos in the country'. Astonishingly, eleven years later he had no option but to confess that the country was on the verge of total collapse. As he put it: 'I cannot preside over the destruction of my country.'[80] It was indeed a pathetic ending. What made it worse was that he had to ask the C-in-C, Gen. Yahya Khan, to 'save the country from utter chaos and total destruction'.[81]

On his last day at the President's House, Ayub wanted to speak with Yahya Khan. Yahya, however, declined his call and diverted it to his principal staff officer, Lt Gen. Peerzada (Peeru to Yahya). Ayub asked his ADC to confirm with Peerzada that he had received the Office Leaving Note and the letter he had sent on the twenty-fifth. Peerzada did confirm the receipt but told the ADC to tell Ayub '... if we were to go by his prescriptions and follow his suggestions and advice, then we too would be equally doomed. If he takes my advice, he should immediately vacate the presidential premises and proceed abroad, or at least leave the capital for a while.'[82]

Ayub was stunned and told his ADC that he didn't think that it would be his trusted ones who would desert him like this. He lamented that he could never have known that 'the likes of Brutus and Judas were supping off my table and would one day stab me in the back'. He told his son Akhtar, 'We've seen too much glory in these premises to accept this change, this collapse. This world is a strange place—cruel in many ways. It was in this very house that the country honoured us with great laurels, showering us with love and respect and yet today in less than a week after my stepping down, the subordinates I had nurtured until the last moment are virtually throwing us out.'[83]

The day he stepped down, Ayub and his wife decided to go for a drive on Lahore Road. At one place, Ayub saw garbage in the middle of the market. Stopping the car, he stepped out and asked the public to gather round him and talked to them about cleanliness. Then, as if to check the reaction of the crowd, he hinted that he would be leaving office soon. Interestingly, the crowd's reaction was for him to carry on. As he was leaving the scene, there were loud cheers of 'Long live Ayub Khan' accompanied by loud clapping. Later, in the car, Ayub told his wife, 'I think where I failed myself was in losing touch with the masses! I too should have publicly countered the politicians ganged up against me rather than going for the martial law option. In that, I may have been misled by Yahya for his own designs.'[84]

Ayub's ADC describes his departure from the President's House in the following words: 'There was no formal send-off ceremony; no trombones, trumpets, bugles or bagpipes; no lowering of colours and flags; no Guard of Honour; just tears and convulsed faces; followed by the shaking and waving of hands. With that Ayub, with an escort of one jeep, travelled north into Swat[85] and into his sunset; never to see the dawn of power again!'[86]

His ADC Arshad Sami Khan further lamented that 'as the gates of the Presidency closed behind Ayub Khan, history closed the chapter on him. Ayub's oblivion was so complete that even in

Islamabad, the capital city he founded, nothing of prominence was ever named in his memory.' This contrasted with Zia-ul-Haq who had a mausoleum (commonly referred to as Jabrra Chowk) but there was nothing to show that Ayub Khan ever lived in Islamabad despite being its founder.[87] It was at Ayub's behest that a Greek architect had carved Islamabad out of the Margala Hills in the 1960s. One former American ambassador described Islamabad as 'rather like a New York cemetery; half the size, but twice as dead'.[88]

Several years after he had handed over power and was leading a retired life, Ayub had gone for a walk with his wife. On seeing him, some people gathered around and started shouting 'President Ayub Zindabad'. Ayub became emotional and told them instead to start saying 'Ayub *Kutta* (dog) hai'. Likewise, once he met a few students at a bookshop in Islamabad who said, 'Sir, why don't you come back as president.' Ayub replied, 'No, my son. Ayub *Kutta* has become too old.'[89]

All India Radio was the first to announce Ayub Khan's death on 19 April 1974. (Pakistan Television) PTV and Radio Pakistan merely announced that a former president had died. They did not even have the courtesy to mention his name.[90] However, his funeral was attended by thousands of mourners who defied official restrictions to pay their last respects. The Pakistan Army gave him a funeral with full military honours.[91]

3.2

Ayub Khan II: 1965—A Bridge Too Far

Prequel to War

WHAT PROMPTED AYUB KHAN TO provoke a war? First, in Pakistan's assessment the situation in J&K in 1964 and 1965 was one of turmoil due to several factors. In December 1963, there were riots in Srinagar set off by the holy relic, Mohi-Muqaddas (hair of Prophet Muhammad), being stolen from the Hazratbal mosque. Though it was later recovered, the riots in Srinagar were seen by Pakistan as indicative of discontent in the state. In December 1964 India supposedly added to the existing tensions by applying Articles 356 and 357 of the Constitution of India to Jammu and Kashmir that had the effect of eroding the state's special status in the Indian Union.

On 28 December 1964, in the run-up to the presidential elections in Pakistan, Zulfikar Ali Bhutto announced that the Pakistan government would 'take retaliatory steps to counter the Indian attempt to merge the occupied parts of Kashmir with India'. He also stressed on Pakistan's capacity to respond to the Indian initiative: 'You will see better results in the very near future,' he predicted.[1]

Second, the Pakistan Army interpreted the results of the India–China war of 1962 as India being weak and ineffectual. The Indian Army's capabilities in 1963 and 1964 were assessed to be the same as in 1962.[2] However, Pakistan was aware that after the 1962 war, India had embarked on a massive arms build-up that would upset the existing military balance in the subcontinent. It was assessed that if Pakistan were ever to find a military solution to Kashmir, the time in which to do so was limited.

Against this backdrop, Bhutto wrote to Ayub on 12 May 1965 recommending 'a bold and courageous stand' that would 'open up greater possibility for a negotiated settlement'.[3] He warned: 'At present Pakistan has the advantage of military power which is superior in quality to that of India, but this advantage will fast vanish as India is moving fast to take a lead. 1965 is the year when Pakistan can take advantage of this superiority otherwise it will be too late.'[4] Bhutto also linked Kashmir with Pakistan's raison d'être. 'Kashmir', he wrote, 'must be liberated if Pakistan is to have its full meaning.'[5]

Third, in April 1965 clashes took place between India and Pakistan in the Rann of Kutch. Though more in the nature of skirmishes, they were described in Pakistan as a significant military encounter that had tested the armies and Pakistan had been the clear victor. Ayub Khan later bragged in London that 'a full Indian division would have been destroyed in Kutch but for his express order restraining pursuing Pakistani troops'.[6] In fact, the reports of the military success of Pakistan in the Rann of Kutch were greatly exaggerated. They were also played up in the media to create an impression that the Indians were cowards and could not fight. 'As a result, a false sense of optimism and superiority was engendered within the Pakistan Army concerning its ability to fight a war against India.'[7]

In fact, 'In the popular Pakistani mind, the Kutch operation had quite irresistibly revived and conjured up the images of the historic desert campaign of Mohd bin Qasim in the 8th century.'[8] Gul Hassan, then director of military operations, perhaps succinctly summed up the feeling in army circles in Pakistan when he wrote: 'The high command of our army was intoxicated by our showing and our morale could not possibly have been higher. We were ready for any task that may be assigned to us and without any question.'[9]

Due to the self-created propaganda and hype over the Rann of Kutch skirmishes, Ayub's own prejudices got reinforced that 'the Hindu has no stomach for a fight'. This would colour Ayub's judgement and decisively impact the course of events. For Ayub, Indians were 'a diseased people' and the Indian prime minister 'that little man Shastri'.[10]

Fourth, after the death of Prime Minister Nehru in May 1964 Islamabad was convinced that his successor, Lal Bahadur Shastri, was weak. In an article after Nehru's death, Bhutto wrote: 'How long will the memory of a dead Nehru inspire his countrymen to keep alive a polyglot India, the vast land of mysterious and frightening contradictions, darned together by the finest of threads? ... The key to Indian unity and greatness has not been handed over to any individual. It has been burned away with Nehru's dead body.'[11]

These developments seemed to have convinced Ayub Khan and his advisers, especially Bhutto, that the internal situation in Kashmir was ripe for provoking an open revolt against India. It was Bhutto who made the critical assessment about India. He felt that if the evolving situation was channelled into an insurrection, it would force the Indian government to reconsider its frozen position on Kashmir and allow the possibility of a plebiscite.[12] In fact, Bhutto told a Western diplomat at a new year party on 1 January 1964: 'The time to act is coming.'[13]

The self-created hype about the army was reinforced during a state visit of the Shah of Iran to Pakistan in February 1965. He apparently was so taken up by the Pak Army demonstration

> that he commented on the wide training gap and disparity between the armies of India and Pakistan. C-in-C Gen. Musa readily concurred with the Shah and boasted: 'Your Imperial Majesty, the Pakistan Army is at least five years ahead of the Indian army in training.'
>
> (A.R. Siddiqi, *The Military In Pakistan: Image and Reality*, Lahore: Vanguard Books Ltd, 1996, pp. 79–80.)

The Planning

Ayub wanted to keep the Kashmir situation under watch and so sometime in 1964 he created a Kashmir Publicity Committee. Foreign Secretary Aziz Ahmed was its chairman. Aziz Ahmed seemed to have exceeded his brief and instead of just keeping a watch on the situation, told the committee that the 'president had ordered the GHQ' to prepare two plans, one to encourage sabotage activities across the ceasefire line and the other to provide 'all out support for any guerillas who were inducted into the Indian-held part of Kashmir'.[14] Towards the end of 1964 the Foreign Office and the Inter-Services Intelligence (ISI) Directorate produced a paper that was to become the basis of 'Operation Gibraltar'.[15] When, in mid-February 1965, the plan was presented to Ayub, he inquired, 'Who authorized the Foreign Office and the ISI to draw up such a plan? All I asked them to do was to keep the situation in Kashmir under review.'[16] This would indicate Ayub's initial scepticism towards this operation that was under active consideration by the end of 1964. However, Bhutto and Ahmed kept underlining the favourable situation for Pakistan due to India's weak position in Kashmir. The April 1965 military 'success' in the Rann of Kutch seemed to have buttressed their belief.[17]

On 13 May 1965, a top-level meeting was held at Murree attended by Ayub, Gen. Musa Khan and senior officers from

GHQ, though the naval and air chiefs were not invited. Maj. Gen. Akhtar Malik, GOC 12 Division, made a sand model presentation on Operation Gibraltar, the objective of which was to inject mujahideen into Kashmir to incite a popular uprising against India.[18]

The point of view of the GHQ seems to have been that the launching of Operation Gibraltar would make a general war with India almost inevitable. Gen. Musa, the army chief, claims that he opposed the plan, both verbally and in writing, till he was ordered to implement it, despite his opposition.[19] As K.M. Arif notes, since his professional military advice about war was rejected, the honourable option for Musa would have been to resign. He did no such thing.[20]

Maj. Gen. Akhtar Malik, GOC 12 Division, had initially proposed to attack Akhnur but due to lack of troops had given up the idea. However, during the Murree meeting Ayub put his finger on Akhnur on the sand model presentation and asked: 'But why don't you go for the jugular?' When Gen. Malik said that it would require a lot more men and money, Ayub sanctioned additional funds and told Musa to provide the necessary manpower.[21] Though additional troops were not available, C-in-C Gen. Musa said he would make them available. The scope of operations was thus widened to include Operation Grand Slam—the capture of Akhnur.[22]

What seems to have carried the day at Murree was the assurance of the Foreign Office that India's retaliation would be limited to the territorial limits of Kashmir. The clinching argument was Bhutto's written assurance to Ayub a day before this meeting advising him that India was '... at present in no position to risk a general war of unlimited duration for the annihilation of Pakistan'.[23] Incidentally, the duo of Foreign Minister Bhutto and Foreign Secretary Aziz Ahmed did not take the Foreign Office into confidence which was unaware of Operation Gibraltar.[24] Former foreign secretary Abdus Sattar, who worked as director in Foreign Secretary Aziz Ahmed's office in 1965, maintains that, 'while Foreign Minister Bhutto and Foreign Secretary Aziz Ahmed were involved in the process, the "Foreign Office" was ignorant about Operation Gibraltar. The Foreign Ministry did not get an opportunity to conceive, examine, analyse or plan this operation.'[25]

Thus, there were at least two major assumptions made: one, the people of J&K would rise in revolt at the sight of the Pak-trained infiltrators and, two, that India would not retaliate across the international border. Based on these two assumptions the go-ahead for launching Operation Gibraltar was given in May 1965, soon after the April Rann of Kutch skirmishes.[26] However, according to Gul Hassan, the response of the Kashmiri leadership was lukewarm when they were contacted. Yet, the report sent by Bhutto, as foreign minister, claimed that the Kashmiris were ready for an uprising and only needed support from Pakistan. Based on this, Operation Gibraltar was launched.[27]

Ayub, in spite of his professional background and clear thinking on such matters, came to the conclusion that, 'If the situation in Kashmir could be reactivated by stirring a rebellion in Indian-held Kashmir, then Western powers would be forced to intervene to save the situation. Thus, India could be pressurized to accept mediation.'[28] Ayub wrote in his autobiography that the crucial factor in military thinking was 'capability' because if a country had decisive military capability its intentions could always change.[29] Despite this, he accepted Bhutto's assertion about Indian intentions of not crossing the international border despite having the capability to do so.

Operation Gibraltar

The name 'Gibraltar' is the Spanish derivation of the Arabic name *Jabal Ṭāriq* meaning 'mountain of Ṭāriq', which is named after Tariq ibn Ziyād. He was a famous Arab general who crossed from

North Africa into Spain and then burnt his boats so that no retreat was possible for his force. Gibraltar is a corruption of Jebel [Jabal] (mountain) Tariq.[30]

The overall operational objective of Operation Gibraltar was to provoke the Kashmir Valley into a state of armed rebellion, thus keeping the Indian Army suitably preoccupied. This was to be done by inducting small groups of infiltrators into the Valley from many areas to target '... bridges, ammunition and supply dumps, lines of communication, military convoys. This, it was hoped, would create panic and encourage the people to rise in revolt.'[31] For this purpose, Azad Kashmir (as Pakistan calls Pak-occupied Kashmir [PoK]) units would train guerillas in large numbers. However, their training (about which India obtained details from POWs) appeared to have been poor.

The proposed supplementary Operation Grand Slam sought to capture Akhnur. This would sever the only road link between India and Kashmir, thereby isolating and preventing Indian troops in Kashmir from obtaining further supplies from India.

The initial infiltration took place on 28 July 1965 and the main infiltration began on 5 August 1965 all along the 750-km ceasefire line. The main body was to converge on Srinagar with the aim of proclaiming its takeover on 9 August 1965.[32]

According to Gen. K.M. Arif: 'The infiltrating teams achieved minor gains but because of conceptual flaws and inadequate planning, Op. Gibraltar fizzled out without achieving the aims set by its planners. Indeed, the unachievable goals had little chance of success.'[33] Operation Gibraltar collapsed after the capture of four Pakistani soldiers who disclosed the purpose and plan of the attack in a broadcast on All India Radio on 8 August 1965. This was nearly a month before India crossed the international boundary.[34]

Asghar Khan ascribes the failure of the operation to the fact that the stepping up of the tempo 'was not gradual enough to give it the character of an internal uprising, nor was it controlled sufficiently to keep it within the bounds of Indian political and military acceptability'.[35] According to Altaf Gauhar, 'Operation Gibraltar failed because ... the fundamental difference between commando raids and guerilla operations was never clearly recognized. Personnel were selected without taking into account that many of them knew neither the area nor the language.'[36]

Meanwhile, after approving the launch of Operation Gibraltar, Ayub went off to Swat ostensibly for rest, though according to Altaf Gauhar this was done to fool the Indians about the scope and purpose of the operation. If this was correct, the plan backfired because Ayub became the victim of his own stratagem. By being in Swat and away from the scene of action, he became distanced from the daily developments of the situation in Kashmir. This left the field open to others, especially Bhutto and Aziz Ahmed who took control of Operation Gibraltar, 'not only in the context of foreign affairs, but also in the field of military planning and manoeuvres'.[37]

Once Bhutto realized that Operation Gibraltar was floundering, he, Gen. Musa and Gen. Malik decided to launch Operation Grand Slam and sought Ayub's approval for the same.[38] Bhutto rushed to Swat and on 29 August obtained a directive about the objectives of the operation from Ayub Khan to C-in-C Gen. Musa and himself as foreign minister. Its wording was clearly an afterthought and drafted by Bhutto to save himself from any responsibility for the fiasco that was taking shape.

According to the directive, the political aim for the struggle in Kashmir was '... to take such action as will defreeze Kashmir problem, weaken India's resolve and bring her to a conference table without provoking a general war. However, the element of escalation is always present in such struggles. So, whilst confining our action to the Kashmir area we must not be unmindful that India may in desperation involve us in a general war or violate Pakistan territory where we are weak. We must therefore be prepared for such contingency.

'2. To expect quick results in this struggle, when India has much larger forces than us, would be unrealistic. Therefore, our action should be such that can be sustained over a long period.

'3. As a general rule, Hindu morale would not stand more than a couple of hard blows delivered at the right time and place. Such opportunities should therefore be sought and exploited.'[39]

The wording of the directive was indicative that Ayub did not know that Operation Gibraltar had floundered completely. As K.M. Arif notes: 'After initially putting the country on the warpath, Bhutto inserted a safety valve to escape personal responsibility. The directive placed him in a pre-eminent position to interpret it to his convenience.'[40]

In his briefing to Ayub, Bhutto insisted that, 'the success of the current movement in Kashmir is not only vital and crucial but it will be a decisive factor in the history of Pakistan'. He rejected professional military advice of not escalating by stating: 'I will not ... even consider allowing this movement to die out because from the point of view of foreign policy as well as the requirements of internal politics ... such a course would amount to a debacle which could threaten the existence of Pakistan.'[41]

Operation Grand Slam

The success of Operation Grand Slam hinged on the speedy capture of Akhnur to choke the lifeline of Indian forces in Kashmir and to release the pressure of Indian action in upper Kashmir. However, two factors acted against its success. One was that it was delayed. Second, it was never visualized as a desperate salvage operation after the collapse of Operation Gibraltar. As Altaf Gauhar puts is, 'To go for the enemy's jugular when one's knees were wilting, made no military sense.'[42]

Gauhar also notes that Operation Grand Slam required the Pakistani forces to cross what Pakistan called the 'working boundary' but which India referred to as the international border between Sialkot and Jammu. This was a gamble that Bhutto decided was worth taking.

Pakistan considered the border between the province of Punjab and the princely state of J&K prior to Partition as the 'working boundary'. It was not the result of the ceasefire of the 1947–48 war. Thus, in the Pakistani view, the international border would not be crossed when they proceeded from the point where the pre-Partition border and the ceasefire line met. India, however, did not recognize any 'working boundary' and it held this to be the international border since the Maharaja of Kashmir had acceded to India. Thus, for India, crossing the border from any point was a violation of the international border.[43]

On 24 August, Gen. Malik, the commander on the ground, asked GHQ for permission to launch Operation Grand Slam but it was delayed and the operation was launched only in the early morning of 1 September, more than a week after he had first asked for the go-ahead. It was successful in capturing Chhamb by the early hours of 2 September. The momentum of the offensive had carried the Pakistani troops to the banks of the Tawi river and just six miles short of Akhnur, the key point of the whole operation. Jaurian stood between the Pakistan Army and Akhnur.

Originally Jaurian was to be bypassed and a quick attack launched against Akhnur. However, suddenly, a change in command took place and Yahya Khan was given the command and Iftikhar was relieved and reverted to Murree.[44] Yahya Khan changed the original plan and instead of bypassing Jaurian decided to capture it first before moving towards Akhnur. This change in command and plans cost Pakistan thirty-six hours—critical time that allowed India to regroup. Jaurian fell to Pakistan on 4 September but by then Operation Grand Slam had run aground.

The news about the change in command spread like wildfire in Pakistan, notes Altaf Gauhar. Since fake claims of triumphs and advances had been spread, Gen. Malik was being compared to the great Muslim hero, Tariq, who, as noted earlier, had burnt his boats before he invaded Spain. Malik was reported as being on the verge of inflicting a crushing blow on the enemy. So why had he been relieved of command at such a critical moment?[45]

No one apart from the C-in-C Gen. Musa and Gen. Yahya seem to have known about this critical change. Hassan Abbas calls it a conspiracy between Ayub, Musa and Yahya, '... that if the operation got into trouble, Malik could keep the command and also the blame that would accrue as a result, but that if it held promise of success, Yahya would be moved in to harvest it.'[46]

War

With both Operation Gibraltar and Operation Grand Slam running aground, Ayub finally summoned Bhutto and Musa to know the truth. Musa had to admit that Gibraltar was a complete failure and Grand Slam was halted in its tracks. After some discussion, Ayub decided to cut the losses and wind up the operations. The expectation was that India would get the message and not escalate any further.[47]

At 5.30 a.m. on 6 September 1965, the Indian forces began their attack towards Lahore. So great was the surprise that the soldiers of some of the Pakistan infantry battalions were, in fact, busy doing morning physical exercises as the Indian forces reached the outskirts of Lahore.[48] The belief that the Kashmir operation would remain a localized battle had been so internalized that 10 Division of the Pakistan Army, responsible for the defence of Lahore, was busy hosting a football tournament. The Pakistan Army was in peacetime deployment along the Lahore–India border. There was only a single company of 3rd Baloch Regiment on duty at the border.[49]

According to AltafGauhar, the person most surprised by the Indian attack was Ayub Khan and another person who shared this surprise was no less than the C-in-C of the Pakistan Army. Their assumption was that since Operation Grand Slam had wound down, the Indians would relax. Likewise, the assertions of Bhutto and Aziz Ahmed about Indian military intentions were proved totally wrong.[50] They were equally surprised. It was an air force officer on reconnaissance duty who conveyed the news about the Indian advance towards Lahore to Ayub at 4 a.m. on 6 September. When Ayub questioned Gen. Musa, his reply was that he had also heard the news but was awaiting confirmation!

Both during and after the war, Ayub Khan and C-in-C Mohammad Musa Khan, asserted that they were aware of Indian plans before hostilities began in September 1965.[51] If this was indeed so, it was surprising that Ayub and Musa were surprised at the Indian attack!

Bhutto was also hard put to explain his assurance that India would not cross the international border. He ascribed this at different times to inputs received from the Chinese foreign minister, and from the Australian high commissioner. In a meeting, just before he left for the UN (attended by Altaf Gauhar), he backtracked saying, 'An assurance is not a guarantee; what I conveyed to the President was the advice of the Foreign Office'. When some other participants in the meeting criticized him, he broke down and started weeping bitterly. After he recovered he said, 'This means the end of my political career.'[52] In fact, 'neither Bhutto nor Aziz Ahmed had read domestic conditions within India, and both operated on whims and personal perceptions'.[53]

In Pakistan, the Indian attack on 6 September is seen as a 'surprise' attack and not an intelligence failure. Actually, Pakistan's intelligence was unaware about the Indian attack. According to Ziring, Pakistan's intelligence proved a total failure. Both political and military reporting was deficient. It was neither professional nor in any way related to the reality on the ground.[54] The DG, ISI, Brig. Riaz Hussain, could not inform Ayub about the actual location of India's only armoured division. According to Bhutto, Ayub was furious and gave hell to Riaz Hussain saying, 'The armoured division was not a needle in a haystack.' Brig. Riaz Hussain's defence was that from June 1964, military intelligence had been diverted for political assignments on elections and post-election repercussions.[55]

Bhutto and Aziz Ahmed had received warning of the impending Indian attack and it should not have come as a total surprise. Two days prior to the attack, the Pakistan high commissioner in Delhi, Mian Arshad Hussain, had sent a top-secret cipher message to the Foreign Office through the Turkish embassy in Delhi. The message mentioned an emergency meeting of the Indian cabinet on 4 September at which the decision was taken to hit at Pakistan. The date of the attack on Lahore was also given as 6 September. According to Altaf Gauhar, Bhutto and Aziz Ahmed suppressed the message because they thought that Arshad Hussian, known for his nervous temperament, had panicked as usual.[56] As a result, Ayub Khan did not get to see the telegram. Had Ayub got this information, he would have alerted the army and, in all probability, the army would not have been taken by surprise when faced with the Indian attack on the Lahore border.[57]

A few hours after Indian forces had crossed the Pakistan border, Ayub addressed the nation, 'Now that the Indian rulers, with their customary cowardice and hypocrisy, have ordered their armies to march into the sacred territory of Pakistan, without a formal declaration of war, the time has come for us to give them a crushing reply which will put an end to India's adventure in imperialism. … The Indians will soon know what kind of people they have taken on!' However, by 13 September, two days after the Khem Karan fiasco, Ayub had been saying, 'Pakistan is not against a ceasefire as such but it must be a purposeful ceasefire …'[58]

Post-war accounts in Pakistan portray the attack on Lahore as the initiation of India's effort to undo Partition, or at least occupy Pakistan's part of Kashmir. However, commentators have noted that even at that time, it was clear that the Indian move was motivated by relieving pressure on Akhnur and to put the Pakistan forces on the defensive.[59]

The US ambassador to Pakistan, Walter P. McConaughy, had a loud voice and abrasive manner. He told Ayub, 'Mr

> President, it seems the Indian have got you by the throat; if you want we could relieve the pressure.' Ayub calmly replied, 'Mr Ambassador, we don't know who has got whom by the throat.'
>
> (Altaf Gauhar, Foreword, in M. Asghar Khan, *The First Round – Indo-Pakistan War 1965*, Delhi: Vikas, 1979, p. xv.)

A relatively unknown facet of the war was that like in 1947 once again frontier tribesmen were brought in, expecting them to do a repeat of the 1947 attack on Kashmir. According to Altaf Gauhar, the GHQ invited sizeable groups of tribesmen from the NWFP to the Lahore border for support to the units on the front. Along the route to Lahore, the tribesmen looted whatever shops came their way. The administration, however, ignored these incidents treating them as 'customary exuberance' of tribesmen in pursuit of their foe. Unfortunately for the GHQ, the Punjab border did not have the kind of terrain suited for the tribesmen's traditional skills. They refused to fight in the open where they would be exposed to air attacks and where there was no cover. They, thus, became a serious nuisance and had to be forcibly repatriated to their tribal sanctuaries.[60]

Pakistan's response, code-named Mailed Fist, was launched in the Khem Karan sector on 7 September. Comprising 1 Armoured Division and 11 Division, its objective was to capture the bridges over the Beas river at Harike.[61] So sure was Pakistan of the success of the riposte that provisions were made for administering the East Punjab areas that would come under its control. It was stressed that undue harm should not come to civilians, especially the Sikhs. Diplomatic missions were even instructed on how the Pakistani occupation of Indian territories was to be projected to foreign governments and the media.[62]

Initially, the 1 Armoured Division made a rapid advance and captured Khem Karan on 8 September. Thereafter, the advance lost steam for two reasons: the high sugar cane crops restricted visibility and provided cover for the Indian anti-tank teams; India breached the Madhopur canal to inundate the terrain that bogged the Pakistani tanks down. Mailed Fist thus came to a standstill and was called off on 11 September. Pakistan's entire military strategy had collapsed and effectively, for Pakistan, the war was over.[63] Asghar Khan describes the failure in these words: 'So unrealistic had been the appreciation, so faulty the timing, and so inadequate the preparation that success in the venture would have been, to say the least, most unlikely.'[64]

On the fourth day of the war, Asghar Khan was deputed to Beijing with a letter from Ayub for premier Zhou Enlai seeking Chinese assistance. Ayub wanted fighter aircraft for the Pakistan Air Force (PAF). However, he did not want these to be sent directly but routed through Indonesia from where they should be sent by sea to Pakistan. So as not to upset the US, Ayub felt that it would not be appropriate for China to supply these aircraft directly. Zhou Enlai was surprised at this, saying if Pakistan wanted to use the aircraft in the war, China could have them flown to Peshawar or Sargodha within twenty-four hours. Despite Pakistan's odd attitude, the aircraft were sent via Indonesia.[65]

In Indonesia, the naval chief Martadinata asked Asghar Khan 'Don't you want us to take over the Andaman Islands? A look at the map will show that the Andaman and Nicobar Islands are an extension of Sumatra and are in any case between East Pakistan and Indonesia. What right have the Indians to be there?' He then offered that the Indonesian navy would immediately commence patrols of the approaches to these islands and carry out aerial reconnaissance missions to see what the Indians had there.[66]

On the night of 19–20 September, Ayub and Bhutto went on a secret visit to Beijing and met with Zhou Enlai and Marshal Chen Yi. According to Altaf Gauhar, Zhou Enlai urged Pakistan to fight on and not give up the struggle even if some Pakistani cities were lost. Numerous examples of Chinese experiences of guerilla warfare were given. In response to Ayub asking him how long would China maintain pressure on India, Zhou, looked straight into Ayub's eyes and said, 'For as long as necessary, but you must keep fighting even if you have to withdraw to the hills.' It was clear that if Pakistan wanted full Chinese support it had to be prepared for a prolonged war in which some major cities like Lahore might be lost.[67]

Ayub was flummoxed and was not sure how to respond to this offer of unconditional support. In Ayub's perception, the Indians would not survive a couple of hard blows while Bhutto had never imagined a long-drawn-out 'people's war'. Additionally, the army and air force were totally against protraction of the war. Gen. Musa was disheartened by the lack of ammunition and spare parts, while Air Marshal Nur Khan by the high attrition rate that was daily reducing the number of operational aircraft available to him.[68]

Surprising Tactical Mistakes

In an interview to *Dawn* on 5 September 2005, Air Marshal Nur Khan made the following assertions about the war. (i) The army did not share Operation Gibraltar plans with the other forces. (ii) An assurance was given by both generals Musa and Akhtar Malik that the air force would not be required since retaliation from Indians was not expected. (iii) Except for a small group of top generals, very few in the armed forces were aware of Operation Gibraltar. (iv) Neither the Lahore garrison commander nor the West Pakistan governor, Malik Amir Mohd Khan of Kalabagh, were in the loop. The latter, in fact, had gone to Murree on a vacation.[69]

Nur Khan was critical of the performance of the Pakistan Army saying, 'The performance of the Army did not match that of the PAF mainly because the leadership was not as professional. They had planned "Operation Gibraltar" for self-glory rather than in the national interest. It was a wrong war. And they misled the nation with a big lie that India rather than Pakistan had provoked the war and that we were the victims of Indian aggression.'

Nur Khan was frank enough to call the 1965 war an unnecessary war. He felt that had President Ayub Khan held his senior generals accountable for the debacle and resigned, it would have served as a lesson for the generals who followed Ayub. He said, 'Since the 1965 war was based on a big lie and was presented to the nation as a great victory, the army came to believe its own fiction and has since then used Ayub as its role model and therefore has continued to fight unwanted wars – the 1971 war and the Kargil fiasco in 1999.... In each of the subsequent wars we have committed the same mistakes that we committed in 1965.'[70]

Nur Khan's assertions are borne out by the fact that the operating factors were dismal: 25 per cent of the soldiers were on annual leave;[71] the army was short of two infantry divisions;[72] the army's key strike formation, the 1 Armoured Division, had one regiment's worth of tanks that were out of commission due to mechanical problems.[73]

After a few days of full-scale war, Pakistan began to face an acute shortage of weaponry, spare parts and ammunition. When Ayub asked Gen. Musa Khan how the war was progressing, Musa informed him that the army was running out of ammunition.[74] This was a disaster because major tank battles were developing on the Sialkot front. Worse was to follow. The Pakistan Army desperately needed armour-piercing ammunition but Ayub was astonished to find that GHQ had imported the wrong kind of ammunition. Instead of armour-piercing (AP) ammunition they had stock-piled highly explosive (HE) ammunition that was of little use.[75]

Coordination between the three services was a major issue. As Lt Gen. Gul Hasan noted later, the joint planning with the air force was dismal: 'There had never been any meaningful planning discussions with their representatives. They were invited to some army exercises that bore little similarity to its actual operational plans.' As far as the navy was concerned, he writes that they were aware that 'we had such a service in the country and that it was located somewhere near Karachi. Such a high level of enlightenment ended our knowledge of the Pakistan Navy.'[76]

Thus, militarily, the Pakistan Army was not ready to fight a war in 1965. Hence, it is all the more surprising that it ventured into one deliberately based purely on Bhutto's assessment that India would not cross the international border to launch a counteroffensive.

At the UN, Bhutto waxed eloquent that Pakistan would 'continue to wage this struggle for a thousand years if necessary'. In a dramatic fashion, he then went out apparently to talk to Ayub on the phone. On his return to the discussions, with tears in his eyes, he announced that the president of Pakistan had instructed him to accept the ceasefire. However, Foreign Secretary Sultan Mohammed Khan claimed that as the Pakistani delegation was returning from the meeting, Bhutto was laughing and saying that while Ayub Khan would be furious, the people would put garlands around his neck. Sultan Khan notes, 'By staging a drama about a phone call, Bhutto was distancing himself from Ayub,' something he would do again after Tashkent.[77]

Backlash of the Propaganda War

Propaganda during the war was to play a big part in its aftermath. The focus of Pakistani propaganda was that the army and air force were inflicting crushing defeats on the Indian forces. Highly imaginative stories of outnumbered Pakistani forces causing immense destruction on the Indian forces through superior courage and fighting abilities swept the country. After 6 September 1965, 'Our Patton's will stroll into Delhi' was the popular buzzword of many conversations in Pakistan.[78] The propaganda of Pakistanis defeating India—in the air, on land, and on sea—created the illusion that the Pakistani forces were poised for major advances. Altaf Gauhar writes that few people knew that GHQ had been feeding the press with highly embellished stories of fictional victories against imaginary enemies. 'Within the government there was no arrangement to check or verify these stories. Whether it was an advanced form of camouflage, self-delusion, or prevarication by common consent to boost one another's morale and prospects, conscience had certainly yielded place to wilful fabrication.'[79]

Such propaganda, divorced from reality, was to boomerang severely. For example, it was not surprising that the Tashkent Declaration seemed like an inexplicable surrender. The dilemma for Ayub at Tashkent was that the hype that had been created by Pakistani propaganda meant that anything short of Indian concessions on Kashmir would be seen as a defeat. All that the Tashkent agreement mentioned was agreement on disengagement and this clearly was not enough primarily due to the propaganda.[80]

Anti-Ayub feelings developed in the armed forces and among the civilian population who had lost soldiers in the fighting. Processions of bereaved mothers and wives in Lahore demanding to know why they had sacrificed sons and husbands were an uncomfortable sight. The extent of animosity in the armed forces was revealed when it became known in 1969 that fourteen officers of the Pakistan Navy had been sentenced to life imprisonment for opposing the Tashkent Declaration.[81]

Another part of the propaganda effort was to drive home the point that at last India had set out to do what it had always wanted, namely to undo Partition.[82] Later, the official narrative as prepared in the Foreign Office under Foreign Secretary Aziz Ahmed's supervision became that the war was never about Kashmir, rather it pertained to Indian intentions and aggression to destroy Pakistan. Since India was unable to take Lahore, Pakistan had won. In a nutshell, Pakistan's rulers simply declared victory and described the events to suit their motives.[83] 'In fact, Pakistan failed to achieve any of its objectives, from liberating Kashmir to forcing India to make concessions'.[84]

According to American experts on US–Pak relations, the Pakistan Army had perpetuated the myth of Muslim soldiers being far superior to Hindus. The usual ratio mentioned was one Muslim soldier was worth ten Hindu soldiers. 'In some ways, then, the Pakistan military was the victim of a delusion of its own making.'[85]

Impact

The Indo-Pak war of 1965 adversely impacted Ayub Khan's political persona. Ayub was livid at the failure to achieve their objectives and reportedly proclaimed that never again would Pakistan 'risk 100 million Pakistanis for 5 million Kashmiris'.[86]

Though the then East Pakistan was not involved, the war had a profound impression there. With only one division of troops in East Pakistan, the people felt vulnerable since they were at the mercy of the much larger Indian Army. This sense of insecurity was intensified by Bhutto's statement in the National Assembly that East Pakistan was saved by China. The Bengali reaction was that 'if we really owe the salvation of East Pakistan during the war not to the military strength West Pakistan always boasted about, but only to the fortuitous circumstances of Chinese hostility to India, what need have we of Pakistan'.[87] As *The New York Times* noted, 'enthusiasm for autonomy has grown tremendously since early this year. ...The pressure stems from the feeling of complete isolation from and utter dependence on West Pakistan that gripped East Pakistan during the war with India.'[88]

A bizarre aspect of the whole 1965 fiasco was that soon after the war, GHQ ordered all units to destroy their respective war diaries. The destruction of the war diaries, that contained first-hand source material about the war at the ground level, was an irreparable loss. This ensured that no lessons were learnt from the war. However, it was not only the army that excised all records. After he assumed power, Zia instructed the Ministry of Foreign Affairs (MOFA) to analyse the archival material of the war and scrutinize the role of the major policymakers of the time. However, it was found that even the relevant diplomatic records, including cipher telegrams of the period were missing. MOFA's response was that these papers had (perhaps) been destroyed as a matter of routine. However, there was no note to this effect on record.

Quite likely, the obliteration of the war diaries of the army and the vanishing of the wartime records in MOFA was the result of a deliberate effort to conceal the actions of those who had something to hide.[89]

Tashkent

By mid-September Ayub was putting out feelers to President Johnson to lend his good offices for both countries to stand down without either being humiliated.[90] This is what a Pakistani prime minister would do thirty-four years later in the wake of Kargil intrusions. Ayub visited Washington in December 1965, prior to Tashkent. In their meeting, President Lyndon Johnson unequivocally told him that the US could not influence India on Kashmir and advised Ayub to 'get it out of your system'.[91]

Before going to Tashkent, Ayub had boasted about his proposed meeting with Prime Minister Shastri, saying, 'Oh, I am going to make circles around that little man. I won't even bother to spit on him.'[92] However, in Tashkent, Ayub decided to talk to Prime Minister Shastri as soon as the first day's formalities ended. Bhutto wanted to join them but Ayub shook his head and extended a stern forefinger, making Zulfi back off, writes Wolpert. Ayub's snubs hurt Bhutto because the president met Shastri alone daily while Bhutto had to remain in another room with Swaran Singh, the foreign minister of India.[93]

Interestingly, during the Tashkent summit, Bhutto somehow annoyed the Soviets so much that Premier Kosygin while addressing Ayub sarcastically commented, 'We shall ask your young and clever Foreign Minister to sit with Gromyko [the Soviet foreign minister] and draft an acceptable formulation [for a no-war reference]; that is why we have Foreign Ministers, even if they themselves don't always understand the meaning of their clever drafts.'[94]

On 8 January, Uzbek artists entertained the two delegations to a musical performance. Premier Kosygin sat between Ayub and Shastri. The performances included several Urdu and Hindi songs. The most popular one that drew huge applause was the Hindi song: '*Main kya karun Ram, mujhe budha mil gaya*' (Oh God, I have got hitched to an old man) from the hit movie *Sangam*.

(Altaf Gauhar, *Ayub Khan: Pakistan's First Military Ruler*, Karachi: OUP, 1996, p. 265.)

After he had met the Indian prime minister, Ayub told the Pakistani delegation on 6 January, that it was unlikely that Shastri would be flexible on Kashmir. He recounted that Shastri kept saying that he was answerable to the people. At this Bhutto interjected sharply and said: 'But you too are answerable to the people. You don't have a heavenly mandate.' This, according to Altaf Gauhar, was the first indication of Bhutto's unhappiness with the way the negotiations were proceeding.[95]

After long-drawn-out negotiations, Altaf Gauhar typed a two-page draft of an agreement that Ayub was ready to sign. However, Prime Minister Shastri was not satisfied and asked for a 'no-war' clause. So Ayub 'wrote in his own hand on the typed draft that Pakistan would renounce the use of force in settling disputes with India'. Shastri agreed to the draft.[96]

Bhutto was furious when he read Ayub's insert in the pages. He threatened to return to Pakistan and 'expose' what he called Ayub's treacherous 'surrender'. Faced with Bhutto's hostility, Ayub was forced to delete the insert, even though others in the delegation like Information Secretary Altaf Gauhar, Information and Broadcasting Minister Shahabuddin and Commerce Minister Ghulam Farooq had agreed to it.[97]

This change had to be shared with the Soviets. So, Bhutto immediately called Foreign Minister Andrei Gromyko, who was with Shastri when the telephone rang. According to Wolpert when Bhutto tried 'diplomatically' to explain that Ayub had agreed to 'renounce force' only because India had 'agreed' to a 'plebiscite' in Kashmir. Gromyko's angry reply was 'it is a lie'.[98]

As per the Tashkent agreement[99] both countries agreed to solve their disputes by peaceful means and to withdraw to the positions they had held before 5 August 1965. J&K was only mentioned as being discussed and each side setting forth its respective position. All that the agreement mentioned was agreement on disengagement.

The Tashkent Declaration was signed in a joint ceremony on 10 January 1966. According to Shuja Nawaz, Prime Minister Shastri's last exchange with Ayub was marked by customary civility. *Khuda Hafiz*, (May God protect you) said Ayub. Shastri responded with the same words and then added, '*Achchha hi ho gaya*' (It was all to the good) to which Ayub responded '*Khuda achchha hi karega*' (God will only do good).[100] That was around 9.45 pm. Three hours later, Shastri suffered a massive heart attack and died. Aziz Ahmed walked across to Bhutto's room to give him the news that 'the bastard had died'. Bhutto responded from his room with a loud chuckle. 'Which of the two, theirs or ours?'[101] According to Benazir, Bhutto had 'acidly remarked that he must have died from happiness'.[102]

Ayub Khan was genuinely grieved at Shastri's death. He served as one of Shastri's pall-bearers, a personal act of Indo–Pak friendship.[103] Unfortunately, this gesture of normal courtesy in the tragic circumstances came to be disliked by many in Pakistan. In fact, Tashkent was soon to become an abusive word, used by anti-Ayub politicians to embarrass the government. Bhutto himself started the practice, when he began a movement against Ayub, of hinting about a 'Tashkent secret'—i.e., a secret deal between Ayub Khan and the Soviets in which Kashmir had been sold out —that would be revealed at the proper time.[104] However, that 'appropriate' time never came and Bhutto conveniently forgot all about the 'secret agreement' of Tashkent once the purpose of discrediting Ayub was served.

In 1968, on the third anniversary of the war, in a speech at the village of Burki, near the Indo-Pakistan border, Bhutto said he was ready to accept the responsibility for engineering the war in September 1965. In this, he compared himself with Jinnah who, Bhutto said, had approved the entry of the Pathan tribesmen into Kashmir (in 1947).[105]

Postscript

In August 1966, a Pakistan military delegation visited China. Sultan M. Khan, then Pakistan's ambassador to China and later foreign secretary describes an incredible incident that took place. The Pakistani army officers were quite confused after meeting their Chinese counterparts because their uniforms were neither smart nor did they wear any badges of rank. When the delegation was leaving, a Pakistani general 'asked a modest-looking individual wearing un-pressed trousers and jacket to fetch his suitcase that had been left behind in his room'. Just as the man moved to comply, Sultan Khan stopped him and apologized for the Pak general's mistake. The man who had been asked to bring the suitcase was a lieutenant general in the People's Liberation Army (PLA) and a veteran of the Long March. When informed that he had been sitting opposite the Chinese general for two days during the talks, the response of the Pak general was, 'They all look the same to me! Why don't they do something about wearing badges of rank?'[106]

On the final day of their visit to Beijing, Zhou Enlai received the delegation. He informed them that all the Pakistani requests would be met. However, Zhou said he was unclear about the basis on which the requirements of the quantity of ammunition had been worked out.

One of the generals replied that the requirement was based on fourteen days' reserve supplies. This made Zhou ask, 'And what happens after fourteen days? How can a war be fought in that short time?' The general explained that it was Pakistan's expectation that during this period of fourteen days, the Security Council would meet and urge both countries to observe ceasefire and withdraw armed forces to their respective borders.[107]

Zhou was quite stunned at this and said, 'Please forgive me if I appear to be confused by your reply. But if the outcome of a conflict has been predetermined to be a restoration of the status quo ante, then why fight at all? Why unnecessarily waste human lives and economic resources? Wars cannot be fought according to a timetable, and one has to be ready for a prolonged conflict.' Sultan Khan laments that there was no answer from the Pakistani side.

Zhou Enlai advocated, 'as their friend', the setting up of a 'people's militia' in every village and town in case it became necessary for the people to operate behind the enemy lines.[108] The Pakistani generals were stunned. Notes Sultan Khan, 'The notion of a prolonged conflict involving the citizenry of Pakistan was not part of the defence strategy planned by these professional soldiers. … The military doctrine … was inherited from the British … and did not visualize unorthodox tactics better suited to a country lacking in any military-industrial capability.'[109]

At dinner that night at the ambassador's residence one of the generals pompously said: 'War is a serious business and should be left to the professionals.' He concluded by asking, 'What does Chou En-lai know about soldiering and military affairs anyway?' His ignorance was amazing and Sultan Khan had to remind him that Zhou Enlai had fought in more battles than one could count. For several years, he was a division commander and the chief of general staff of the People's Liberation Army.[110]

4.1

Yahya Khan I: Unsteady Hands

Early Life and Personality

AGHA YAHYA KHAN WAS BORN in Chakwal (Jhelum district) on 4 February 1917. He was the son of a police officer, whose Shia Qizilbash family had migrated from Afghanistan. Although a Persian-speaking Pathan, Yahya also spoke Punjabi.[1]

By all accounts, he was a boisterous person, a hard drinker and had a weakness for unrestrained frolicking. For those who knew him, Yahya had a distinct routine: the daytime was dedicated to the affairs of state but after sunset, especially after 8.30 p.m. or so, to his lively private life.[2] A telling description in the *Time* magazine was that 'between dusk and dawn, Pakistan was ruled by pimps'.[3] There was some truth in this with stories about the power of his close friend Akleem Akhtar alias 'General Rani' dominating the chatter among the glitterati of Pakistan. In fact, Yahya himself made no secret of his preference for the good things in life. In his words, 'I do not present myself as a model of rectitude or piety. As a sinful man there exist many flaws in my personal character for which I seek forgiveness from Almighty Allah.[4]

His behaviour was not hidden from the diplomatic community either. For example, Sir Morrice James, British high commissioner to Pakistan recalls: '... as GOC commanding Pakistan troops in the East Wing, [Yahya Khan] invited me to dinner one evening in his mess. Afterwards there was dancing, and Yahya in a mood of good-humoured tomfoolery took over the regimental bandmaster's hat and baton, and for some time conducted the music.[5]

Given Yahya's penchant for enjoying nocturnal pleasures, Gen. Abdul Hameed Khan, chief of staff of the Pakistan Army had instructed military governors of the provinces to carry out the president's verbal orders only after reconfirming them personally with the president the following morning if they were given after 10 p.m.[6]

One example of Yahya's cavorting was on the eve of Pakistan's defeat in Dhaka. Just before Pakistan's surrender, Yahya threw a party in his newly constructed house in Peshawar. One of the invitees was Mrs Shamim, popularly known as 'Black Pearl', a Bengali beauty who was Yahya's latest partner. Yahya had also appointed her as Pakistan's ambassador to Austria. As the party progressed, it got increasingly nude. When everyone was drunk and naked, except for Maj. Gen. Ishaque, Yahya's military secretary, 'Black Pearl' wanted to go home. Yahya insisted that he would personally drive her home, with both of them stark naked. Notes Hassan Abbas, 'General Ishaque could not save Pakistan, but he did manage to knock enough sense into the sizzled head of a fun-loving president to put him into his pants. Thus coincided the housewarming of the President's House with the surrender in East Pakistan.'

(Hassan Abbas, *Pakistan's Drift into Extremism*, New Delhi: Pentagon Press, 2005, p. 66.)

Yahya Khan was an avid TV watcher. The 6 September 1971 Defence of Pakistan Day formal reception clashed with the performance of Noor Jehan (a famous Pakistani singer) scheduled for that evening on TV. So, he got the information secretary to delay Noor Jehan's programme by an hour so that he could watch it after the reception. What the fiddle was to Nero while Rome burnt, TV became for Yahya at the peak of the meltdown in East Pakistan, and later during the war with India.[7]

Yahya's cavorting on one occasion caused a major protocol issue with the Shah of Iran who was on a state visit to Pakistan. The Shah was getting late for his departure but Yahya would not come out of his bedroom. Finally, his close friend Akleem Akhtar aka 'General Rani' was persuaded to enter the bedroom and get him out. When she did, she found him in bed with a famous female singer. She helped the President dress and brought him out.

(Owen Bennet Jones, *Pakistan: Eye of the Storm*, Lahore: Vanguard Books, p. 258.)

***

One of the idiosyncrasies that Yahya had was about his eyebrows. Make-up men were warned not to touch them if they cared for their well-being. In the Samson mould, whose strength was in his hair, Yahya believed he obtained all his strength from his brows.

(Roedad Khan, *Pakistan: A Dream Gone Sour*, Karachi: OUP, 1997, p. 54.)

Army Career

After graduating from the Punjab University, Yahya joined the Indian Military Academy (IMA), Dehradun. He topped his class.

He was commissioned in 1938 and attached first to the 2nd Battalion of the Worcester Regiment and later to the 3rd Battalion of the Baloch Regiment, where he received his first command. He later served in 4/10 Baloch in Italy during the Second World War; and was taken a prisoner of war by the Germans. After the war, he served as general staff officer-2 in GHQ, India, between 1945 and 1946. In July 1947, he was posted as an instructor to the Command and Staff College, Quetta.[8] After Partition, he opted for Pakistan. He was promoted to colonel and made a signal contribution in the development of the Pakistan Army Staff College, Quetta. Yahya became a brigadier at the age of thirty-four and assumed command of an infantry brigade. He was the youngest officer to be promoted as major general and became Ayub's chief of staff in 1957. In 1962 he was sent to East Pakistan as GOC.[9] In March 1966, Yahya Khan, the 'conqueror' of Jaurian, was promoted lieutenant general and appointed deputy C-in-C.[10]

Yahya's career profile would show that he had held all the key appointments: instructor at the Staff College, Quetta; director, military operation (DMO) at GHQ; division commander and then chief of general staff. His reputation was that of a thorough professional,[11] a solid field commander and staff officer. Early in his career, his annual confidential reports depicted him as 'an intelligent and hardworking officer with a logical mind and a sharp brain – a valuable, all round officer, who was an asset to the army'.[12] He was, however, a novice at political intrigue and allowed his ambitious colleagues to play a major role in political as well as strategic planning.

Yahya found the daily humdrum of government boring and monotonous. As an administrator, Yahya was not very serious. He did not like reading official files and letters except for brief summaries. He used to describe himself as 'part-time' president.[13] Thus, daily decision making was left to key administrators in the central secretariat. Yahya would often tell his audiences: 'I am a soldier.' This was an alibi for his political mistakes.[14]

Ironically, Yahya's main problem was a smooth career with all the prized appointments coming his way before it was his turn. According to Lt Gen. Jahan Dad Khan, 'he became what was termed a "G Type", who would never concern himself with the nitty-gritty of a problem. He was quite happy to delegate authority to his subordinates, leaving it to them to produce results. But he never learnt to give guidance where needed or to take timely action if he was saddled with incompetent and weak subordinates.'[15]

Yahya's great opportunity came during Operation Grand Slam in 1965 (see the previous chapter) to prove his credentials as a decisive field commander. Just as the Pakistani forces were poised to attack Akhnur he was put in charge of the operation due to a sudden change in command on 2 September 1965. Yahya, however, reacted inadequately, showing caution instead of a 'killer' instinct.[16] Rather than bypassing Jaurian and going for the jugular, i.e., Akhnur, Yahya did the reverse, attacked Jaurian allowing India adequate time to bolster Akhnur. This failure to capture Akhnur should have been a blot on his professionalism; instead he was feted as the conqueror of Jaurian.

One reason for this was that prior to becoming C-in-C, Yahya managed to project himself by influencing the making of two documentary films being prepared by the Inter-Services Public Relations (ISPR) on the 1965 war: *Fath-e-Mubeen* (Manifest Victory) and *On to Victory* in Urdu and English respectively. He watched the footages closely and suggested several changes. Key among these were shots of himself taken in the Chhamb area that showed him in command of the situation. Before the film was approved, Yahya ordered the deletion of the shots of his predecessor Maj. Gen. (later Lt Gen.) Akhtar Hussain Malik being decorated by the C-in-C. Yahya suffered in comparison to Akhtar Malik who was tall and slim, and much more impressive.[17]

When the time came to appoint a new commander-in-chief of the Pakistan Army, the incumbent C-in-C, Gen. Musa took to Ayub a list of three general officers. Gen. Sarfraz was the senior-most.

Though he projected himself as the saviour of Lahore in 1965, he rarely ever visited the forward troops. The next in seniority was Gen. Hameed, widely esteemed for his personal and professional qualities but he had come under a cloud for his performance during the war as coordinator of the Khem Karan Operation.[18]

Ayub added a fourth name to Musa's list—Yahya Khan. Musa told Ayub that professionally, Yahya was at par with the other three. However, Yahya's soldiering virtues were overshadowed by his personal shortcoming. Ayub discounted Musa's fears about Yahya. In the event, Musa was overruled and Ayub chose Yahya.[19] The formal announcement was made in August 1966.

Many rued Ayub's choice. One such was the nawab of Kalabagh, the governor of Punjab. He warned, 'Ayub will make the blunder of his life if he appoints Yahya as C-in-C because he is a debauchee and drunkard.'[20] His warning would prove to be prophetic during 1971. Many felt that it was Yahya's antics that made Ayub appoint him as C-in-C—his reputation would be Ayub's best insurance against Yahya unseating him. Unfortunately for Ayub, as things shaped out, Yahya's reputation did not stand in his way when he chose to show Ayub the door.[21]

One of Yahya's contemporaries noted that his highest ceiling was of a divisional commander. His promotion beyond this level was tragic both for the country and unfair to the general who lacked the stamina and the intellectual discipline for the higher appointments.[22]

The shabby manner in which Yahya had treated Ayub after ousting him was to haunt Yahya because he faced worse. After Bhutto replaced him, Yahya was put under 'house arrest' and detained at a rest house in a small, unknown place called Banni near Kharian. According to the family, Yahya was in almost solitary confinement because friends and relatives were not allowed to visit him. The location of the rest house was unhygienic, full of flies, mosquitoes and snakes. Electrical outages in the midst of heat waves, and water shortage were common. Yahya was devastated that his friends had let him down and rued their betrayal. It was only when Bhutto was behind bars that Zia had him shifted to Rawalpindi and released after six years in 'protective custody'.[23]

> During a state visit to the Soviet Union, the Russian leaders tried to play on Yahya's weakness for alcohol. They kept raising their glasses to toast him. Yahya, however, got the better of them when he said, after the fourth toast, 'Mister President, Mister Prime Minister, I feel this is not very fair. I know what you are trying to do, but there are only two of you against me, and that is not fair to you. I warn you that I can easily handle four of you.' At that Prime Minister Kosygin laughed, threw up is hands and promptly put his upended glass on the table.
>
> (Jamsheed Marker, *Cover Point: Impressions of Leadership in Pakistan*, Karachi: OUP, 2016, p. 77.)

Assuming Power

Yahya detected an opportunity for himself when Ayub was faced with the combined opposition parties' movement for his removal. Symptomatic of this was the round table conference that was organized in Rawalpindi in 1969. Sheikh Mujibur Rahman who was in prison for the Agartala Conspiracy Case, was especially brought to Islamabad for this conference. Yusuf Haroon, an Ayub confidant, received Mujib at the Chaklala airport and took him straight to the GHQ to see Gen. Yahya Khan. Ayub wanted Yahya to tell Mujib that the army would back Ayub in order to pressurize Mujib into softening his opposition towards him. But nothing of the sort happened. On the contrary, Yahya told Mujib that the army would be neutral in the tussle between the opposition and the president. Yusuf Haroon was dumbfounded by Yahya's turnaround.[24]

As the opposition to Ayub gathered momentum, Yahya became more confident. One evening, bolstered with spirits, he asked a lady seated next to him at dinner if she was aware whom she was having the meal with? He pre-empted her reply by stating that it was with the future president of Pakistan.[25]

On 24 March 1969 when Bhutto was flying from Karachi to Larkana for his aunt's funeral, the aircraft was diverted to Rawalpindi on some pretext. On landing, he was taken to see Gen. Yahya Khan who told him that Ayub had failed and he would have to take over and asked for Bhutto's views. Bhutto agreed but put three conditions: an independent foreign policy, break-up of 'one unit' and restoration of the four provinces of West Pakistan, and general elections within a year. Yahya agreed to all of Bhutto's suggestions.[26]

With the situation getting out of hand, Ayub saw no option but to hand over power to Yahya Khan on 25 March 1969. The 1962 Constitution was abrogated and Yahya Khan assumed charge as chief martial law administrator. The *Economist* (London) reported the news under the title 'Tweedle Khan Takes Over'.[27] Bhutto called off the protest movement and peace was restored.

Yahya had no qualms about pushing aside Ayub who had been his benefactor. As he put it, 'I claim to be a professional army officer who is nothing if not a soldier. I did not force Ayub to relinquish power in my favour ... but welcomed the chance to take power away from him.'[28]

> Ayub told his son, Gohar Ayub Khan, 'You have served in GHQ and should know that if the Commander-in-Chief of the Pakistan Army gets it into his head to take over, then it is only God above who can stop him.'
>
> (Gohar Ayub Khan, *Glimpses into the Corridors of Power*, Karachi, OUP, 2007, p. 114.)

One basic lesson that Yahya learnt from Ayub's tenure was that he had lost his clout in the GHQ as soon as he stopped being the C-in-C and became an 'elective' president. Consequently, Yahya (and Zia and Musharraf, after him) always retained the post of C-in-C/COAS so as to have direct access to and control over the GHQ.[29]

Ayub in 1958 had pretended to be a 'reluctant' dictator. In 1969, Yahya would echo his sentiments.[30] In his first broadcast to the nation, Yahya said, 'I wish to make absolutely clear that I have no ambition other than the creation of conditions conducive to the establishment of constitutional government.' However, within a month, addressing a gathering of his fellow Baloch Regiment officers at their regimental centre in Abbottabad he said, 'We must be prepared to rule this unfortunate country for the next fourteen years or so. I simply can't throw the country to the wolves.'[31]

US Opening to China

Yahya Khan's finest hour was perhaps the role he played in facilitating a dialogue between the US and China in 1970. During Yahya's visit to the US in October 1970, President Nixon had requested him to act as an intermediary and arrange a secret meeting between his emissary and a Chinese leader, preferably Zhou Enlai. Yahya agreed and kept the request confidential. He did not share it even with the foreign office. This request was conveyed to Zhou Enlai when Yahya visited Beijing on 10 November 1970. After consulting Mao Zedong, Zhou indicated that a special envoy of President Nixon would be welcome in Beijing. Zhou informed Yahya that previously the US had sent similar messages through other sources 'but this is the first time that the proposal has come from a Head [of state] through a Head, to a Head. The US knows that Pakistan is a great friend of China and, therefore, we attach importance to the message.'[32] The stage was set for the first Kissinger–Zhou Enlai meeting through Pakistan that took place in July 1971.

1970 Elections

The most important event domestically under Yahya Khan's watch was the 1970 elections and its aftermath. On 28 November 1969, Yahya announced a detailed plan for the holding of elections to both the national and provincial assemblies under a Legal Framework Order. There was a three-phase political plan: elections, framing a constitution, and transfer of power to the elected representatives. However, the elections led to a civil war and the break-up of Pakistan. Neither by training nor by temperament was Yahya equipped to handle issues of such magnitude.

Yahya created a National Security Cell (NSC) headed by Maj. Gen. Umar to help him assess the evolving political situation and to devise relevant policies. Ayub Khan's collapse had revealed that reports from different intelligence agencies were invariably at variance with each other leaving him confused during the political crisis. So, Yahya ordered that all such reports be routed through the NSC that would examine and analyse them and make an assessment of the political situation. He specifically wanted an estimate of the likely make-up of parliament and the role that the army could play in the new political set-up.[33]

After examining all the inputs, the NSC came to the conclusion that with thirty-three big and small parties in the field there would be a highly divided parliament and no single party would win sufficient seats to form the government. In fact, the NSC predicted that parliament would be hung—a worse scenario than prior to Ayub's takeover of 1958. As electioneering progressed, the intelligence estimates gave Mujibur Rahman's Awami League between forty-six and seventy seats out of the 167 seats in East Pakistan, and gave Bhutto's Pakistan People's Party (PPP) between twenty to thirty seats out of the 144 in the West. Based on such estimates, Yahya was assured that he would be in a strong position to play the role of godfather and the army would continue to retain the real power, manipulating a divided parliament. The report thus recommended that 'free and fair' elections be held.

Yahya followed that advice in letter and spirit. Even the politicians failed to read the political currents. Mian Mumtaz Daulatana's Convention Muslim League, for example, rejected the offer of twenty-nine uncontested seats in East Pakistan from Mujib in exchange for collaboration after the elections.[34]

In fact, Yahya told Henry Kissinger as much when he visited the US in October 1970 to meet Nixon during the UN session. When Kissinger asked him about power of the president after the elections, a confident Yahya said that he expected that a multiplicity of parties would emerge in both West and East Pakistan. He believed that they would constantly be fighting with each other and the president would, therefore, remain the central figure of Pakistan's politics.[35]

The elections were held on 7 December 1970. There is no doubt that they were free and fair. The results, however, came as a shock for the military. The pre-election report prepared by various agencies was massively off the mark primarily because they were so out of touch with the realities on the ground, especially in East Pakistan. The results would also prove to be a disaster for the future of a unified Pakistan.

Instead of the anticipated hung and divided parliament enabling Yahya Khan to emerge as the powerbroker, the elections resulted in the victory of two strong political opponents—one with an overwhelming majority in one province and the other with a dominant vote in the other. Both political parties had a mass support base in two different regions and each of whose leaders wanted to be prime minister. Mujib's Awami League won 162 seats out of 164 in the eastern wing (but none in the west), giving it a majority in the 313-seat National Assembly. Z.A. Bhutto's PPP, which had no candidate in the east, was the big winner in the western wing, winning eighty-one seats out of 138. The election result was an obvious outcome of strong regional sentiments that had been totally misread and misjudged by the intelligence agencies.

> In 1962, with uncanny foresight, Sir Morrice [James, high commissioner to Pakistan 1962–65, and to India 1968–71] wrote, 'the atmosphere in East Pakistan in some ways now resembles that of a colony on the brink of achieving its independence'.
>
> (Roedad Khan, *The British Papers, Documents 1958-1969*, Karachi: OUP, 2002, p. xvii.)

The New York Times of 13 December 1970 headlined the result as 'Vote Jolts Punjabis'. The article described the sentiment of the people in Punjab as being of restiveness and anger. One comment summed it up: 'The Punjab is finished ... We will be ruled by Sindh and Bengal. Our country has gone to the dogs.'[36]

In his memoir, former Pakistani ambassador Jamsheed Marker reveals that the then US national security adviser Henry Kissinger told him (with reference to the 1970 elections), 'Everywhere else in the world elections help to solve problems; in Pakistan they seem to create them.'[37]

The incompatibility in the positions of Mujib and Bhutto put Yahya in a dilemma. Mujib would not compromise on East Pakistani autonomy as per his six-point manifesto and now he had the majority to implement it. Having won the elections overwhelmingly on the basis of autonomy, he could not let down the people by diluting it.

For his part, Bhutto acted as 'the catalyst of separation'[38] during the period between the general elections and the crackdown in Dhaka on 25 March 1971. He took the peculiar stand that the rule of majority did not apply to Pakistan. He ruled out being in the opposition on the grounds that the pledges his party had made to the people could not be redeemed unless the authority at the Centre was shared between the PPP and the Awami League in 'a grand coalition'. It was this that blocked summoning the session of the National Assembly and thereby a peaceful transfer of power from the military to the elected representatives. Bhutto's apprehension was that if the National Assembly session was held prior to an agreement on power sharing, the Awami League would be able to dictate terms, given its majority, including having its own nominee as Speaker.[39]

Addressing a meeting on 14 April 1971 in Karachi, Bhutto stated that it was 'only fair that in East Pakistan, it [prime ministership] should go to the Awami League and in the West to the PPP'. The Urdu newspaper *Azad* reported this speech under the headline: *'Udhar tum, Idhar hum'* (You stay there, we stay here), words that were construed to mean that Bhutto was talking about the bifurcation of the country.[40]

Bhutto also threatened to break the leg of whosoever dared to go to Dhaka to attend the National Assembly scheduled for 3 March 1971 warning anyone who did so should go on a one-way ticket.[41] Ahmad Raza Kasuri, the killing of whose father would lead Bhutto to the gallows, was the only member of the PPP who braved Bhutto's diktat and went to Dhaka.

Bhutto's arguments were not only weak but detrimental to the democratic system itself. He declared that Punjab and Sindh were 'the bastions of power' in Pakistan and since PPP had won a sweeping majority in these provinces, his party's cooperation was 'essential for the formation of the constitution or any Central Government.'[42] He went on to argue that just because East Pakistan had not shared power in the Government of Pakistan for last twenty-three years did not mean that during the next twenty-three years East Pakistan should rule over West Pakistan.[43] In a rejoinder, Awami League's Secretary General, Tajuddin Ahmed, said: 'We are with an absolute majority in the National Assembly and a clear electoral mandate authorizes us to frame the constitution as well as to form the Central Government. Punjab and Sindh can no longer aspire to be bastions of power now.'[44] These exchanges further aggravated the situation.

In effect, it would have required a great deal of statesmanship to resolve the situation created by the elections; else it would be the end of Pakistan as it existed. Yahya was not the statesman who could have crafted a new Pakistan based on the electoral reality.

> At a dinner given for him before he left for Beijing, Kissinger had an opportunity to reproach Yahya for the mess in East Pakistan. 'Everyone calls me a dictator,' bellowed Yahya in his bluff imitation of the Sandhurst manner. 'Am I a dictator?' he asked every guest, American as well as Pakistani, in turn. Everyone protested with varying degrees of sincerity that of course Yahya was not a dictator. When he came to me, I said: 'I don't know, Mr President, except that for a dictator you run a lousy election.'
>
> (Henry Kissinger, *The White House Years*, New Delhi: Vikas, 1979, p. 862.)

On his return to Karachi from Dhaka in March 1971, Yahya met Bhutto for dinner. Nawab of Junagarh, Muhammad Dilawar Khan and his wife—an extraordinarily beautiful woman and icon of sophistication—accompanied Bhutto. The nawab wanted his privy purse to be maintained. During the dinner some progress was made between Yahya and Bhutto over a covert political understanding about the situation. Interestingly, 'Yahya's excited eyes kept focusing on the alluring movements of the attractive Begum Junagarh. She had returned his oozing gaze with more than a hint of approval; making him dribble and drool over her with unconcealed overtures.'[45]

A week later, Yahya went to Bhutto's ancestral home in Larkana ostensibly for a partridge shoot. Discussions were held again about dealing with the situation created by the unexpected verdict in the elections. At one stage during the visit, Bhutto pointed to a beautiful antique musket hanging from a wall as a decoration piece and said, 'Go for it.' The implication was Bhutto would support Yahya were he to initiate military action against the Awami League.[46]

Yahya told Gen. Tikka Khan before leaving Dhaka on 25 March night, 'Sort them out.' Wolpert infers that while the fires were burning in Dhaka 'Yahya was sipping scotch and soda at 40,000 feet over Ceylon (Sri Lanka).'[47] Bhutto remained behind to see what Tikka did. On 25 March 1971, the Pakistan Army launched Operation Searchlight and cracked down on all dissent in the East. The plan had been operationalized by generals Farman (office of the CMLA) and Khadim Raja (GOC 14 Division) on 18 March and cleared by Tikka and Yahya two days later.[48] As a result, thousands and thousands of Bengalis were butchered. The Pakistan Army had the option of putting down dissent with minimal force. Instead it decided to use maximum force.

An interesting sidelight of the talks between Yahya and Mujib in Dhaka was that there was so much distrust between them that Mujib refused to hold discussions in the drawing room of the President's House fearing it was bugged. As a result, their first meeting took place in the bathroom off the main bedroom.

(Ian Talbot, *Pakistan: A Modern History*, New Delhi, OUP, 1998, p. 207.)

As a commander, Tikka Khan strictly followed orders. He had earned the moniker of 'Butcher of Balochistan' for his forceful military action in 1958 against the Baloch who had risen in revolt under Nawab Nauroz Khan. According to Shuja Nawaz, 'Tikka's mind was reportedly unclouded by strategic thinking or complicated vocabulary. He was expected to get the job done in short order.'[49]

A perceptive Kissinger noted that 'Yahya Khan with less than 40,000 troops decided to establish military rule over the 75 million people of East Pakistan, to suppress the Awami League, and to arrest Mujibur Rahman.' He could not comprehend why Yahya took such a thoughtless step since the chance of success was remote. His reasoning was: 'Once indigenous Bengali support for a united Pakistan evaporated, the integrity of Pakistan was finished. An independent Bengali state was certain to emerge, even without Indian intervention. The only question was how the change would come about.'[50]

Bhutto saw Dhaka burning. In the morning on 26 March, he is supposed to have patted Tikka, Farman and Arbab on the back, congratulated them for doing exactly what was needed, and assured them that their future was secure. Bhutto kept his promise. After the 1971 war, Tikka became army chief, Farman became chairman of the Fauji Foundation and Brig. Arbab, despite proven corruption charges, was promoted as major general and later as lieutenant general. On reaching Karachi on 26 March, Bhutto told the people, 'Thank God Pakistan has at last been saved.'[51]

Clearly, Pakistan's military leaders were confronted with events way beyond their understanding. Caught between two ambitious men and a fractured electoral reality, Yahya was not equipped to deal with the precarious situation. As Kissinger put it, 'They had no understanding of the psychological and political isolation into which they had maneuvered their country by their brutal suppression. The result was that never throughout the crisis did Pakistan manage to put forward a position on which it could take its international stand.'[52]

Considerable controversy exists if Bhutto wanted Yahya to execute Mujib or not. Prof. G.W. Choudhury, known to have enjoyed Yahya's confidence, recalls his first meeting with Gen. Zia in March 1979 in these words: 'He (Zia) also asked me about Bhutto's advice to me in September 1971 to urge President Yahya to execute Mujib before Yahya would go to attend the two-thousand-year anniversary of the Iranian monarchy ....' Bhutto's assertion was that Yahya, being a weak person, would capitulate to international pressure and release Mujib or transfer power to him. Therefore, Bhutto wanted Mujib executed before Yahya went to Teheran in late 1971. When Choudhury gave General Zia the evidence of Bhutto's suggestion, Zia was quite shocked.[53]

However, when Mujib was freed in January 1972, Bhutto told him that it was he (Bhutto) who had saved him from being executed because Yahya had been determined to do so. He requested Mujib several times that he should disclose this publicly when he arrived in Dhaka.[54]

Yahya died after a prolonged illness. Zia was president but was away on a tour of Turkey. The question arose about the burial and there was a difference of opinion between the acting CMLA, Gen. Sarwar Khan and the acting president, Chief Justice Anwarul Haq. The former wanted the burial to be with full military honours while the latter advised a quiet and low-key family funeral. This was in view of 'General Yahya Khan's role in the East Pakistan crisis and the opinion expressed about him in the Hamoodur Rahman Commission Report'. Sarwar, however, told Anwarul Haq that Yahya was a highly decorated retired army chief who had neither been tried in a court of law nor convicted of any charge. The clinching argument was that the Hamoodur Rahman Commission report was not a public document and its contents were unknown. Sarwar discussed the issue with Zia in Turkey who approved his decision. Yahya was accordingly given a funeral with full military honours.[55]

Role of Intelligence

The ISI had assessed that Bengali resistance, if any, to the army crackdown would end quickly and the possibility of Indian involvement was remote.[56] Yahya relied on this estimate. As a result, the campaign in East Pakistan did not seem to have any specific aim or strategy. Yahya and his advisers just ordered the army 'to sort out the Bengalis', and thereafter watched events unfold. According to Iqbal Akhund, they 'did not seem to know what to do next or indeed care what happened. The political strategy of the regime seemed to have been based on the puerile belief that a taste of *danda* – the big stick – would cow down the Bengali babu.'[57]

In fact, one reason for Yahya losing his way was the abysmal lack of intelligence about what was going on in East Pakistan. This was hardly surprising given that one morning, during the war, the DG, ISI, told Yahya, 'Sir, Jean Dixon the astrologer of international fame, known for accuracy of her predictions, has said that you have a long life ahead of you as head of State – perhaps ten years or more.' Yahya was thrilled to hear this, not knowing that he would no longer be in the presidency in less than ten days.[58]

Several commentators have noted the reasons for poor intelligence work. Shuja Nawaz, for example, writes: 'The lack of political knowledge and experience of the intelligence operatives continued to hamper their ability to report accurately to headquarters ... Wishful thinking continued to dominate political discourse and analysis in Rawalpindi.'[59] Mushahid Hussain and Akmal Hussain write: 'At almost all crucial moments in Pakistan's politics, the intelligence has been proven wrong, either in their assessments of the popular mood or intentions of the opposition; even in 1988, the intelligence misread the mood in Sindh.' According to them, the intelligence organizations instead of functioning on the same page, have come to represent opposing power structures: the Intelligence Bureau (IB) representing the civilian government and the ISI the military. Resultantly, 'they have worked more as rivals, with overlapping functions and competing roles'. This has also generated hostility. When elected prime ministers were dismissed by presidents as on 29 May 1988 (Muhammad Khan Junejo) and 6 August 1990 (Benazir Bhutto), the IB headquarters was targeted with its offices sealed and records scrutinized, in 'operations' reminiscent of the style of a coup d'état.[60]

The authors also provide two hilarious examples of the ham-handed manner of the IB's approach to collecting intelligence. In 1954 the Communist Party of Pakistan was banned and the communists were being rounded up by the Intelligence Bureau. During one such raid on the house of a prominent communist, the operative said, 'We have come to arrest you because you are a communist.' He replied, 'I am anti-communist.' The Intelligence officer retorted with an air of supreme confidence: 'We don't care what kind of a communist you are, anti or whatever, as long as you are one!' Similarly, when Faiz Ahmed Faiz, Pakistan's left-wing poet laureate was in jail, he could not get a copy of *The Communist Manifesto*. However, when he requested for a copy of Karl Marx's *Das Capital*, it was promptly allowed.[61]

4.2

Yahya Khan II: 1971—How Not to Fight a War

'Defence of the East Lies in the West'

UNDER AYUB KHAN, A MILITARY decision was taken that 'the defence of the East lies in the West'. This decision was based on the principle that if the military was split and stationed equally in both the wings, neither of the wings could resist the strength of the Indian Army. Further, since the bulk of the Indian Army was deployed against West Pakistan it was felt that a bigger portion of the Pakistan Army should be placed in the West. A smaller force could, accordingly, be kept in East Pakistan to defend the border. Hence, the dictum 'defence of the East lies in the West'.[1]

This doctrine had, however, been shattered in 1965 after Bhutto claimed in the National Assembly that it was the Chinese that had saved East Pakistan. This was an eye-opener for the people of East Pakistan who realized that they could no longer depend on the Pakistan Army for their defence.

Situation in East Pakistan

Sahibzada Yakub Khan was posted as commander, Eastern Command, in 1969. (He was later governor for a brief period.) He reorganized and regrouped the troops under his command in consonance with the army doctrine that 'the defence of the East lies in the West'. He conceived a security plan titled 'Blitz', meant to counter any unrest in East Pakistan.[2] In fact, Operation Blitz was formulated much before the 1970 elections and on 11 December 1970, within four days of the elections, Yaqub Khan signed and issued an 'operational directive'. The plan 'authorized the commander, Eastern Command, to relieve the governor of his duties and take control of the entire civil administration of the province. He [the former] was then to implement the plan to restore law and order…[and] was given complete freedom in exercise of his powers[…]'[3]

The Hamoodur Rahman Commission (HRC) set up to inquire into the surrender in Dhaka, in its report confirmed: 'The decision not to hand over power, and the use of a military crackdown codenamed "Operation Blitz" had been prepared well ahead'; and 'the negotiations which were carried on from the middle of March up to this date were no more than a camouflage, it being all along the intention of Gen. Yahya Khan and his military advisers to cow down the Awami League with a heavy hand'.[4]

Faced with the deteriorating situation and possible action, the governor, Admiral Ahsan, relinquished the governorship of East Pakistan on 4 March 1971. In early March 1971, Gen. Yakub too started having doubts about a military operation when he assessed that it would be counterproductive. He, therefore, recommended the search for a political solution. Faced with resistance from the GHQ, Yakub too resigned on 5 March 1971. In his resignation message, he stated: 'Only solution to the present crisis is a purely political one. Only President can take this far-reaching decision by reaching Dhaka by 6th which I have repeatedly recommended.

Am convinced there is no military solution which can make sense in present situation. I am consequently unable to accept responsibility for implementing a mission, namely military solution, which would mean civil war and large-scale killing of unarmed civilians and would achieve no sane aim. It would have disastrous consequences. I, therefore, confirm tendering my resignation.' When he returned to the GHQ, Yahya refused to see him. Yakub was subsequently reverted to his substantive rank of a major general and retired from the army.[5]

Lt Gen. Tikka Khan arrived in Dhaka on 7 March to assume the role of both governor and commander, Eastern Command. The chief justice of the East Pakistan High Court, citing the chaotic conditions, made himself unavailable to administer the oath to the new governor. Tikka Khan could be administered the oath only after the military crackdown of 25 March by the same judge who did not do so earlier.[6]

Gen. Tikka Khan summed up the military situation in East Pakistan on his arrival in an interview with the influential Egyptian journalist Mohamed Hassanein Heikal. He said that they were like 'blind men'. Intelligence officials told him about the refusal of the people to cooperate or give information to their men. 'We were in complete darkness regarding what was happening except where we had troops. This was intolerable. It had never occurred before and it is impermissible. ... This man [Mujib] incited mutiny and a boycott of my troops.'[7]

What Tikka Khan was lamenting about was that the law-enforcing agencies and the East Pakistan Rifles were believed to have been infiltrated. They were thus prejudiced in favour of the Awami League and against the army. With these units compromised, any operation against the Awami League and its leaders had to be handled entirely by the regular Pakistan Army.[8]

There were several examples of this. For one, as Brian Cloughley puts it, the West Pakistan authorities did not have any clue about Mujib's intentions except what he had declared publicly. After he was arrested, inputs about movement or intentions of resistance groups dried up. There were no significant intelligence assets that the government's intelligence agencies had in the Awami League, the Mukti Bahini, or any other element. In the urban areas, the people declined to talk with West Pakistanis. In the rural areas, coupled with resentment, there was no common language with the security forces. Quite literally, the Pakistan army was conducting operations in the dark. At the same time they were quite clueless about Indian thinking.[9]

Army Excesses

The excesses carried out by the Pakistan Army have been very well documented. According to Niazi, who succeeded Gen. Tikka Khan, his predecessor's policy was brutal – killing of civilians and scorched-earth. His order to the troops were: 'I want the land and not the people.' Maj. Gen. Farman and Brig. (later Lt Gen.) Jahanzeb Arbab carried out these orders faithfully. Farman had written in his table diary, 'Green land of East Pakistan will be painted red.' Niazi goes on to say: 'The military action was a display of stark cruelty, more merciless than the massacres at Bukhara and Baghdad by Changez Khan and Halaku Khan, or at Jallianwala Bagh by the British General Dyer.'[10]

Three further examples taken from the account of the then Pakistan foreign secretary Sultan Khan are mentioned here.

In May 1971, Joseph Farland, the US ambassador, met Foreign Secretary Sultan Khan after a visit to Dhaka. He complained that the army had to be curbed in East Pakistan. He revealed that in his meeting with several Pakistan Army officers he was shocked to hear how they openly talked about 'getting a bag of Bengos' (short for Bengalis) or conducting 'search and destroy' mission. He mentioned that the US consul general had also briefed him extensively about the extent of atrocities being committed daily.[11]

In early June 1971, the Canadian high commissioner met the foreign secretary. He said he was bound to 'express his government's deep concern about the treatment of the Hindu minority in East Pakistan and hoped that the action against them would cease'. Speaking with anguish he added, 'There are ten million of them in East Pakistan and it is impossible to get rid of them.'

Even the Chinese reacted to the genocide that the army was carrying out in the then East Pakistan. During Bhutto's visit to Beijing on 9–10 April 1971, Zhou Enlai, speaking with great emphasis, said, 'Please tell the President to hold the army tightly, improve relations with the masses, take impressive economic measures and commence political work.'[12] This was a clear reprimand about the brutality of the army crackdown in East Pakistan.

Several Pakistanis too were horrified at what was happening in East Pakistan. At a conference of nineteen Pakistani envoys from important countries held in Geneva in August 1971, the ambassadors recommended a political rather than a military solution in East Pakistan. However, Information Secretary Roedad Khan, National Security Secretary Maj. Gen. Ghulam Umar and Foreign Affairs Secretary S.M. Yusuf, all based in Islamabad, maintained that the situation in East Pakistan was under control and the present problems would soon be resolved. The proceedings of the conference were tape-recorded but later these tapes mysteriously disappeared from the official records. Clearly, once again those who had something to hide made sure that the records were destroyed.[13]

Sultan Khan noted that these and other similar reports were brought to the attention of the president, but they did not alter the course of events.[14] In September 1971, Sultan Khan again brought the matter of rape, murder and looting by the armed forces to the president's attention. 'To my surprise, the President heard me out in a subdued manner and his comment was, "I know what you are saying. I have sent [Gen.] Hameed to Dhaka to talk some sense into them. I will send him again to talk to Niazi.'[15]

However, Yahya's insensitive attitude was echoed in his interview to *The New York Times*. In reply to a question relating to army atrocities, Yahya said: 'What happened in Dhaka was not a football match. When one fights, one does not throw flowers.'[16]

Lt Gen. A.A. K. Niazi

Lt Gen. Amir Abdullah Khan Niazi took over as commander, East Pakistan from Tikka Khan on 10 April 1971, when the latter relinquished the post and retained that of governor and martial law administrator. He was appointed the martial law administrator of East Pakistan on 3 September 1971 to replace Lt Gen. Tikka Khan. At the same time A.M. Malik was appointed governor. Maj. Gen. Rao Farman Ali was the military adviser to the governor.

By most accounts, Niazi was an inappropriate choice of commander for East Pakistan. According to Lt Gen. Gul Hassan, 'professionally, Lt Gen. Niazi's ceiling was no more than that of a company commander'.[17] The prevailing conditions dictated a mature, intelligent and professional leader who could grasp the problems involved and had the ability to tackle the myriad challenges. By temperament and training, Niazi was not cut out for such a role. By appointing him as commander of the Eastern Command, Yahya demonstrated his own ignorance about the capability of his senior officers. According to Lt Gen. Jahan Dad Khan, the appointment was a grave error of judgement and one of the major factors responsible for the debacle.[18]

Niazi was known mainly for his collection of dirty jokes—'juicy tales and unprintable anecdotes'[19]—in the army. Niazi condoned the army atrocities for reasons of practicality. He is reported to have said, 'One cannot fight a war here in East Pakistan and go all the way to the Western wing to have an ejaculation!' This was thought funny at the time.[20] Niazi was also known as 'Tiger' in army circles—'to the ultimate mortification of that noble animal', writes Hassan Abbas. Before he surrendered, it was reported that he was involved in smuggling betel leaves to his son Habibullah in West Pakistan on official aircraft.[21]

Niazi's attitude is best summed up in two incidents. In a meeting of officers soon after his arrival, Niazi became abusive. Breaking into Urdu, he said: '*Main is haramzadi qaum ki nasal badal doonga. Yeh mujhe kya samajhtey hain*. [I will change the race of this bastard nation. What do they think of me.] He threatened that he would let his soldiers loose on their womenfolk.[22] Niazi's traits were also revealed by his telling comments to the outgoing GOC, 14 Division, who had gone to brief Niazi. Instead of listening to the briefing, Niazi put his hand on Raja's shoulder and said '*Yaar, ladai ki fikr na hi karo, wo to hum kar lenge. Abhi to mujhe Bengali girlfriends ke phone numbers de do.*' [Don't worry about the war, we'll manage that. For now, just give me the phone numbers of your Bengali girlfriends.][23]

Pakistan's Strategy

Yahya was convinced that the Indian objective was to capture a portion of territory to install the Bangladesh government on its own soil.[24] During his interrogation in India after the war[25] Gen. Niazi confirmed this and said that Pakistan's strategy was centred on the premise that India had 'planned only a limited action' for establishing Bangladesh government in East Pakistan. On the basis of this assessment, Pakistan deployed her forces thinly all along the border spread out over 2,500 miles and ordered them to hold on at any cost. As a result, Pakistani troops were pinned down at the periphery. This enabled the Mukti Bahini to expand their sway inside East Pakistan.

What the Pakistani leadership did not realize was that their grip on East Pakistan lay in Dhaka and that the defence of Dhaka should have been the priority. It was only when the Indian forces bypassed Jessore city and raced towards Dhaka that Pakistan realized that their assessment of Indian intentions had been misplaced. The Indian objective had not been capturing a chunk of territory—even if it was, it had been modified. However, by then it was much too late for Pakistan to change course and rectify its strategic mistake.[26]

In fact, the army leadership in Pakistan contravened a basic principle of war of concentration of force and maintenance of reserves. By spreading themselves too thin, Pakistan would pay heavily for violating this fundamental rule of war.[27]

On 9 July 1971, Henry Kissinger arrived in Islamabad en route his secret trip to Beijing. During the discussions with Yahya, he realized that 'Yahya … fundamentally was oblivious to his perils and unprepared to face realities.' Kissinger informed Yahya and his advisers that the chances of war with India were 'two in three'. However, he found they were convinced that India would not do so—but, if India did start a war, they were convinced that 'they (Pakistanis) could win'. How Pakistan would do so without air support, and faced with the hostility of the local population, however, had not been thought through. When Kissinger asked as tactfully as he could about the Indian advantage in numbers and equipment, Yahya and his colleagues answered with bravado about 'the historic superiority of Moslem fighters'.[28]

On his return to the US, Kissinger briefed the National Security Council on 16 July 1971 that India was determined on a war with Pakistan and that Yahya 'lacked the imagination to solve the political problem in time to prevent an Indian assault'. He thus recommended that the US should prepare for an 'evolution that would lead to eventual independence for East Pakistan'. Unfortunately, this was not likely to happen in time to head off an Indian attack.[29]

Air Marshal Asghar Khan recounts an interesting conversation he had with Gen. Gul Hassan, chief of general staff, at a social function in October 1971. The conversation revealed what the junta was thinking about the situation. In response to Asghar Khan asking him what was the answer to the grim situation in East Pakistan, Gul Hassan replied, 'The only answer is to start a war.' A surprised Asghar Khan asked him why. 'In order to have a ceasefire', Gul Hassan replied. According to Asghar Khan, Gul Hassan was articulating the thoughts of the junta and Yahya Khan. He assessed that 'in the desperate situation they had got themselves in, they had begun to believe that should open hostilities start with India, they would be bailed out by the United States. Yahya felt that the least that President Nixon could do was to pressurize the Indians to cease hostilities, and bring India and Pakistan on to the conference table.' In this regard, Yahya's TV broadcast, prior to the outbreak of war created the perception of his hoping that the world powers would intervene to stop any hostilities. In his TV appearance, Yahya Khan had rolled up his sleeves and said, 'I put the world on notice, we will fight.'[30]

Situation in West Pakistan

Even though the situation in East Pakistan was rapidly deteriorating, Yahya prevaricated in opening the western front as per the army's own dictum of 'defence of the East lies in the West'. He had to be 'dragged' to the GHQ operation room on 23 November to explain the ground conditions and to get a decision to open the western front. Even then, Yahya delayed matters first promising a decision by 27 November, then agreeing on 29 November to open the western front but without setting a date and finally the decision was conveyed to the forces on the front only on 2 December that troops would be launched on 3 December.

When Yahya left the President's House to go to the Air Command Centre on 3 December 1971, an unusually large vulture appeared from nowhere and landed a few metres

> ahead of his jeep, blocking the driveway to the exit gate. The vulture refused to move even when Gen. Hameed slowly moved up the jeep; blew the horn; or when Yahya tried to scare it away with his baton. Instead, it just stared back with greater defiance. It was only when a nearby gardener shooed the bird with a large sickle that it finally cleared the road with an ominous gait allowing the jeep to pass.
>
> (Arshad Sami Khan, *Three Presidents and an Aide: Life, Power and Politics*, New Delhi: Pentagon Press, 2008, p. 172.)

The Pakistani plan of attack pivoted around a pre-emptive air strike against Indian airfields. In all, thirty-two aircraft out of an inventory of 278 fighter planes took part in the initial strike that started between 5.09 and 5.23 p.m.. The PAF strikes were not successful. Only the Amritsar airfield was blocked and a radar target was destroyed. Pathankot could not be attacked because of poor visibility.[31]

The objective of the air strikes was to target the runways of Indian airbases. However, the platforms used, i.e., F-86s, for this purpose were inappropriate. According to Arshad Sami Khan, the F-86 was a multi-role aircraft but the one role it was not very accurate at was bombing, especially high-level bombing. The release the two 1,000-pound bombs required climbing to 10,000 feet, going into a 45-degree dive and releasing the bombs by about 4,500 feet at speeds of 460 knots. So, most of the bombs did not hit the targets. Moreover, the damage to runways even from a direct hit could be repaired in a few hours.[32]

The limited Pakistani attack was surprising. The chairman of the Joint Chiefs of Staff Committee (JCSC) of the US, Admiral Thomas H. Moorer, told the Washington Special Action Group (WASAG) meeting on 3 December (held just three hours after the PAF raid) that he was 'surprised that the Paks attacked at such a low level. In 1965, they moved much more strongly.' Henry

Kissinger, the chair of the group, added: 'These aren't significant fields. That's [a] helluva way to start a war.' Moorer filled in the details: 'One field had only 12 helos [helicopters] and 17 Gnats [fighter aircraft] ... There was a field not too far away with 82 aircraft on it, including 42 MIG-21s. They didn't go for them.'[33]

The confused state of higher-level decision making in Pakistan was revealed by the fact that even the defence secretary and the head of the ISPR, the official mouthpiece of the regime, were unaware of the imminence of the war on 3 December. The latter was informed via a telephone call at his residence from the defence secretary about an announcement he had heard over Radio Pakistan that India had invaded West Pakistan. Radio Pakistan announced the news at 5 p.m. as did PTV. The statement was so worded as to convey that it were the Indian forces that had attacked West Pakistan at 'various points'. According to Shuja Nawaz, 'The thinking behind this subterfuge was to invoke US help, based, among other things, on the aide memoire of 6 November 1962 to Ayub Khan in which US ambassador McConaughy had promised to assist Pakistan "in the event of aggression from India against Pakistan".'[34]

Yahya addressed the nation on 4 December and made a stirring speech, very much like what Ayub Khan had done on 6 September 1965. Yahya brought in a religious touch too: 'The Indian aggressor should know that they have to face 12 crore *mujahids* of Pakistan, imbued with the love of God and the Holy Prophet. The Indians know that in 1965 our brave forces had smashed them into pieces. But this time, God willing, we shall hit the enemy even harder than before.'[35]

Speeches were, however, no substitute for strategy. Brian Cloughley succinctly sums up the disastrous campaign: 'Poor planning, indecision, ... hasty and countermanded regrouping, inadequate or even non-existent coordination between formations, inability to seize the moment for exploitation, bungling of movement control procedures – the list of failures is long.' He asked, 'Had nothing been done in the years 1965–1971 to hone the skills of the Pakistan Army? It certainly seemed so.'[36]

A day after the war began, Brigadier Gul Mawaz went to see Yahya, his close friend. He found him and Hameed, his chief of staff, inebriated. Yahya told Gul Mawaz that as commander he had launched his armies. Now it was up to his generals. While they were talking, Yahya received a call from Japan from Noor Jehan, the famous Pakistani singer. After telling the brigadier who the call was from, Yahya asked her to sing him a song.

(Hassan Abbas, *Pakistan's Drift into Extremism*, New Delhi: Pentagon Press, 2005, reprinted in 2007, p. 67.)

War in the East

Though Niazi waxed eloquent about his prowess and about not surrendering, the reality was just the opposite. One of his colleagues, Gen. Rao Farman Ali, told the Hamoodur Rahman Commission that Niazi's morale had collapsed as early as 7 December. As evidence, he cited a meeting between Niazi and the governor, A.M. Malik, who was to be briefed on the military campaign. According to Farman Ali: 'The Governor had hardly said a few words when General Niazi started crying loudly. I had to send the bearer out. The Governor got up from his chair, patted him, and said a few consoling words.' This was the decisive moment that prompted the governor to repeatedly urge Rawalpindi to agree to a ceasefire.[37]

With the war in East Pakistan going badly, A.M. Malik, the governor of East Pakistan, sent a distress signal to the president of Pakistan on 9 December 1971. In it he depicted a hopeless situation and requested a political solution of the crisis. In reply, Gen. Yahya passed on the decision to the governor saying that he was taking all measures internationally but due to their isolation from each other he would leave decision about East Pakistan to the governor's judgement. He added he would approve of any decision the governor would take. 'Whatever efforts you take in your decisions to save senseless destruction of the kind of situation you have mentioned, in particular the safety of our armed forces, you may go ahead and ensure safety of armed forces by all political means that you will adopt with our opponent.' Yahya had mentally written off East Pakistan and was clearly passing the buck to a subordinate for accepting the onus of surrender.[38]

In the event, Dhaka fell without a fight. Barely twenty-four hours earlier Niazi had defiantly told BBC that the army would fight to the last man. Niazi had also boasted that the Indians would only capture Dhaka over his dead body. Instead of any heroics, Lt Gen. Niazi surrendered to Lt Gen. Aurora of the Indian Army on 16 December and tamely signed the instrument of surrender in a formal public ceremony.[39] The main thrust of Niazi's defence of his actions has been detailed in his book. He holds that he had decided to fight till the end but he was forced to surrender by the Pakistan high command in West Pakistan. The reason was that the war in the west, despite near parity of forces, was not going well. As such, Yahya was not willing to risk losing the west to save the east. Pakistan's strategy that the defence of the east lay in the west had boomeranged.[40]

> The generals responsible for Pakistan's humiliation in 1971 reminded Roedad Khan of Wellington's famous observation on the eve of the battle of Waterloo. He said. 'Really, when I reflect upon the character and attainment of some of the General officers of this army, and consider that these are the persons on whom I am to rely to lead my columns against the French Generals, and who are to carry out my instructions into execution, I tremble;' and as Lord Chesterfield said of

> the Generals of his day, 'I only hope that when the enemy reads the list of their names, he trembles as I do.'
>
> (Roedad Khan, *Pakistan: A Dream Gone Sour*, Karachi: OUP, 1997, pp. 33–34.)

Defeat

The people of Pakistan heard the news of the surrender through the Indian prime minister's broadcast, over All India Radio. The announcement of surrender was soft-pedalled by Radio Pakistan in its 5 p.m. news bulletin in these memorable words: 'Following an arrangement between the commanders of India and Pakistan, fighting has ceased in the eastern theatre and the Indian troops have entered Dhaka.'[41]

Yahya confirmed the surrender in East Pakistan in a radio broadcast at 7.15 p.m. on 16 December 1971 that was heard by a stunned nation in tragic silence.[42] Yahya tried vainly to bolster morale of the country by saying that the war with India would continue; Pakistan had only lost a battle but the war would carry on. Earlier in the year, he had boasted that if India declared war on Pakistan, 'I will shoot my way out of it.'[43] With false swagger, he had even announced a national mission: Crush India, a slogan that appeared on bumper stickers throughout the country. However, on 16 December 1971, a chastised Yahya justified the ceasefire stating: 'I have always maintained that war solves no problem.' Writes Robert Jackson, 'the victors in Dhaka knew otherwise'.[44] In his testimony before the Hamoodur Rahman Commission, Yahya was back to his blustering ways saying, 'No military historian would call this a military defeat. It was nothing but a treachery of the Indians.' He also added that he would have continued to fight in the west had the UN General Assembly not asked for a ceasefire.[45]

In the context of the war in the west continuing, when Roedad Khan raised the matter with Yahya and told him that nations do not fight wars by halves, Yahya retorted that he was not going to endanger West Pakistan 'for the sake of Bengalis'.[46] This was very much like Ayub Khan saying at a cabinet meeting after the 1965 war that never again would Pakistan 'risk 100 million Pakistanis for 5 million Kashmiri'.[47]

> If Niazi lost the will to fight at Dhaka, those directing the war from Islamabad did no better. In fact, when Gen. Yahya was told about the Indian attack he said, 'What can I do for East Pakistan? I can only pray.' With one sentence Yahya had absolved himself of all his responsibilities and duties as the head of state and supreme commander of the armed forces.
>
> (A.A.K. Niazi, *The Betrayal of East Pakistan*, Karachi: OUP, Preface.)

Following Indira Gandhi's unilateral offer of a ceasefire in the west, the Emergency Committee conveyed Pakistan's unconditional acceptance. However, such was the unreality of the situation that, according to Roedad Khan, 'Nobody raised any objection to the substance of the draft but a heated and animated discussion followed on how the timings of the ceasefire was to be described, in terms of IST, GMT, or PST; and if PST, in terms of West Pakistan Standard Time or East Pakistan Standard Time. The implications in each case were discussed threadbare.'[48]

Several elements were responsible for the worst military defeat suffered by Pakistan till then. The first was clearly the lack of coordination. Shuja Nawaz points to the astonishing lack of coordination between the army, navy and air force. Being located at different cities made matters worse. The naval headquarters was in Karachi, the air force in Peshawar, and the army in Rawalpindi. Neither the Joint Chiefs of Staff Committee (JCSC) nor the Joint Warfare Directorate were actively involved in making decisions. The only JCSC meeting since July 1964 (a year before the 1965 war with India) had been held in August 1967. The Defence Committee of the Cabinet, headed by the president and consisting of ministers involved in defence planning, existed only on paper. It had only met twice in the five years prior to the 1971 war with the last meeting being in November 1968. The Secretaries Coordination Committee on defence planning that enabled civilian input in the coordination of defence strategies had brought out a war book that was largely pro forma; it was last updated in 1970.[49]

Such was the state of affairs that the naval chief was not informed about the air strikes directly but he found out from a Pakistani radio broadcast. Pakistani naval ships at sea heard about the attack also from the radio.[50] On the eastern front, Lt Gen. Niazi learnt of the air strikes while listening to the BBC world service.[51] The chief of Pakistan Navy also alleged in an interview that air cover was unavailable during the Indian attack on naval ships despite frequent appeals. Similarly, on 8 December, when the Indian Navy and the Indian Air Force attacked Karachi and sunk two Pakistani ships, air cover was not forthcoming, leaving the Karachi port at the mercy of the Indian forces.[52]

This led Richard Sisson and Leo Rose to comment: 'The war was planned and pursued with a lack of co-ordination and foresight not dissimilar to that of 1965 – but in a different set of circumstances and with a woefully different outcome.'[53]

A major reason for this was Pakistan's inability to learn from its own mistakes. An authentic account of the 1947–48 Kashmir operations was never compiled. The result was that the mistakes made in 1948 were repeated in 1965. Likewise, since Yahya refused, despite Ayub Khan's orders, to allow an accurate documentation of the 1965 war, the mistakes of 1965 were repeated in 1971 with disastrous consequences. Notes Altaf Gauhar, '… unless the facts of 1948, 1965 and 1971 are made public, our people will go on living in a false world, imagining victories against fictitious adversaries.'[54]

Second, the Pakistan Army leadership was a house horribly divided. The chief of staff (COS), Gen. Hameed, did not get along with the principal staff officer (PSO) Gen. Peerzada who did not get along with chief of general staff (CGS) Gen. Gul Hassan who, in turn, did not get along with the COS Gen. Hameed. Neither were the three constantly available nor were they mentally on the same page. Thus, Gul Hassan, as the CGS of the Pakistan Army was unaware about Operation Searchlight, the army action on the night of March 25/26 in Dhaka until Yahya told him on his return to Karachi from Dhaka. In fact, when Yahya spoke to him, Gul Hassan thought Yahya was speaking from Dhaka. Gul Hassan was also unaware how East Pakistan, if attacked by India, was going to be defended, and how the political crisis was going to be resolved. He was also unaware of the movements of the COS, Gen. Hameed, who kept them secret as far as Gul Hassan was concerned. Even the appointment of Lt Gen. A.A.K. Niazi as commander, Eastern Command, came as a surprise for Gul Hassan. Yahya told him that he (Gul) was being promoted because 'we are promoting Niazi who is junior to you. So, we have to give you the next rank.'[55]

Gen. K.M. Arif noted that there were also communication gaps between the eastern command and the headquarters of the chief martial law administrator (HQ CMLA) and the general headquarters (GHQ). HQ CMLA and GHQ functioned at separate places, and frequently one was unaware of what the other did or failed to do. The army's chain of command did not function smoothly. Quite naturally, the lack of communication between different power centres in combat was an invitation to disaster.[56]

Gul Hassan later admitted in his memoirs that he did not think that the GHQ had ever been so ineffective as it was in the months prior to the outbreak of the war with India in 1971. 'Events buffeted us mercilessly owing to the absence of direction and a sense of cohesion in the nerve-centre of the Army. The only person who could make amends and guide us was General Yahya Khan, but he was by then a remote figure to us in the GHQ.'[57]

Clearly, all was not well in the inner army circle surrounding Yahya. This had to be one of the major reasons for Pakistan's debacle.

> Gohar Ayub Khan describes a chance meeting on board a flight in August 1971 with CGS Lt Gen. Gul Hassan who told Gohar that after a visit to East Pakistan he felt that only a miracle could save them there. 'Does the Chief [Yahya] know this?' I asked him. 'Will you discuss your report with him?'
>
> Gul Hassan closed his eyes and said. 'Gohar, I do not get to see the Chief for three months at a stretch.'
>
> 'You're not serious!' I exclaimed
>
> 'Believe me, I have to fight my way in to be able to see him, and it is not all pleasant.'
>
> 'God help us,' I sighed. We were heading towards a disaster, and that too, with our eyes wide open.
>
> (Gohar Ayub Khan, *Glimpses into the Corridors of Power*, Karachi: OUP, 2007, p. 128.)

The responsibility for this state of affairs clearly rested with Yahya. As the supreme commander of the armed forces, the responsibility of planning and implementing strategies for the complete readiness for war rested on his shoulders. Yahya, however, was too caught up in his presidential and CMLA roles and neglected the critical role of the army chief. The latter was delegated to Gen. Hameed who was hesitant to take major policy decisions. As a result, operational plans were not updated and important operational decisions were either delayed or not given. The best example of this was the lack of decision on launching the army strategic reserve in Bahawalnagar sector. Even the senior commanders were unaware about GHQ policy and plan of action.[58]

The air of unreality was also demonstrated by the fact that there was no safe underground operations room in the GHQ in Rawalpindi. Notes Sultan Khan, 'With the Indian aircraft striking almost daily at Rawalpindi, the old thatched roof ramshackle GHQ complex could have been easily destroyed in a single strike. Attending nightly briefings there, often with air-raid sirens blowing, gave one an eerie feeling of potentially being a helpless victim.' Even the President's House had a hastily dug pit in his garden with sandbags on its roof by way of an air-raid shelter. Twice Sultan Khan shared it with Yahya when they discussed important foreign policy issues.

(Sultan M. Khan, *Memories and Reflections of a Pakistani Diplomat*, London: The Centre For Pakistan Studies, 1997, p. 369.)

Impact

The surrender in East Pakistan and the creation of Bangladesh was a devastating event for West Pakistan, the aftershocks of which continue to this day. Along with the physical fall of Dhaka, Pakistan was also defeated psychologically. The two-nation theory that Muslims of the subcontinent formed a separate nation, was demolished. Pakistan is still searching for a rationale for the dismemberment. Roedad Khan probably summed up the sentiments in West Pakistan well when he wrote: 'Our surrender in Dhaka was a travesty, a clownish exercise in self-humiliation. Never in my life had my spirits been so low.'[59] Imran Khan, like others in Pakistan, had swallowed the official propaganda of the state television that branded 'the Bengali fighters as terrorists, militants, insurgents or Indian-backed fighters – the same terminology that is used today about those fighting in Pakistan's tribal areas and Balochistan'. He writes: 'Then, as now, Pakistan fought symptoms rather than addressing the root cause of the violence – our failure to address the legitimate aspirations of Pakistan's many ethnic groups.'[60]

The agony of defeat, and the dismemberment of Pakistan, badly damaged the prestige of the Pakistan military. All the more so because, like the propaganda in the 1965 war, the army's public relations office had been spreading fabricated stories of stunning victories over the Indians while the reality was just the reverse. As Gohar Ayub admitted, 'In the past if any officer was asked what his dream was, he would say it was to hoist the Pakistani flag on the Red Fort in Delhi. ... And after 1971, the most anyone would be willing to say is that we could fight a defensive war for a short period against India.[61]

Over the years, Pakistani generals had operated on the assumption that the Indians were too cowardly and ill-organized to offer any effective military response, which could pose a threat to Pakistan. Ayub Khan genuinely believed that ' ...as a general rule, Hindu morale would not stand more than a couple of hard blows at the right time and place'. Now 79,700 of Pakistan's regular soldiers and paramilitary troops were prisoners of war in Indian hands, along with 12,500 civilian internees. Moreover, the army had failed to fulfil its promises of fighting until the last man. The eastern command had laid down arms after losing only thirteen hundred men in battle. In West Pakistan, too, twelve hundred military deaths had accompanied a lack-luster military performance.

5.1

Z.A. Bhutto I: Picking Up the Pieces

Developments in the UN

IN VIEW OF THE OUTBREAK of war with India in December 1971, Yahya Khan directed Bhutto to fight Pakistan's case in the UN. Bhutto left for the UN on 8 December but instead of showing urgency, he broke journey in Teheran and Frankfurt, reaching New York on 10 December.[1]

On 14 December 1971, Poland tabled a draft resolution in the UN Security Council calling for a peaceful transfer of power to the legally elected representatives of the people of East Pakistan. It suggested a temporary ceasefire, the withdrawal of Pakistani armed forces to preset locations and the simultaneous withdrawal of the Indian forces from the eastern theatre of war.

Yahya became aware of the Polish proposal only through media reports. Neither the Pakistan delegation in the UN nor the Foreign Office informed Yahya about it. Worse, it took more than twenty-four hours to get an official copy of the resolution. Immediately after getting it, Yahya ordered its acceptance in principle. Due to the critical situation in East Pakistan, Yahya decided to give verbal instructions to Bhutto in New York to accept the resolution. Bhutto was unavailable. Efforts to get him on the telephone were unsuccessful; both Pakistan's permanent representative to the UN, Agha Shahi, and the Pakistan ambassador to the US, Gen. Agha Mohammad Raza, were unable to trace Bhutto.[2]

Later, when Yahya finally got hold of Bhutto in New York on the phone, he told him that the Polish resolution was suitable and 'we should accept it'. Bhutto replied, 'I can't hear you.' Yahya repeated himself several times, and Bhutto kept saying, 'What? What?' The operator in New York finally intervened and said, 'I can hear him fine,' to which Bhutto replied, 'Shut up.'[3]

Dhaka fell on 16 December before the resolution that Pakistan had ultimately accepted could be implemented.[4]

Bhutto made a lengthy intervention in the Security Council on 15 December. He said, 'I find it disgraceful to my country and to my person to remain here ... legalize aggression, legalize occupation ... I will not be a party to it ... we will go back and fight. The object of the UN had been to permit the fall of Dhaka ... Why should I waste my time here? I will go back to my country and fight.'[5] He then dramatically tore up some papers and stomped out of the meeting.

With Dhaka collapsing, Yahya asked Bhutto to return to Pakistan. After his last address in the Security Council on 15 December, Bhutto stayed in the US for three additional days. He met Chiao Kuan Hua, leader of the Chinese delegation to the UN, on the night of the surrender in Dhaka.[6] Later, he flew to Florida to meet with President Nixon on the yacht of his wealthy friend 'to clear his path to power with Nixon ... explaining to him that he was not anti-US'.[7] He was assured that the US would back him once he had taken over from Yahya.[8]

En route to Islamabad Bhutto halted at Rome. It had been arranged in advance that he would return only after he got an all-clear signal from his confidant Ghulam Mustafa Khar to return home without fear. It was only then that he returned to Pakistan, but not before meeting with the Shah of Iran in

Teheran. Bhutto's apprehension was that Yahya could arrest him on arrival.[9]

After he arrived in Islamabad on 20 December, Bhutto went to meet Yahya at President's House. He found Yahya sitting alone in the verandah in an inebriated state. He was behaving in a frenetic manner, crying one moment and laughing the next. This, according to Bhutto made him take over immediately or else there could have been a complete collapse of law and order.[10] He was accordingly sworn in as president and the first civilian chief martial law administrator (CMLA) of Pakistan.

Army Revolt

Meanwhile, major trouble was brewing in the army. In Gujranwala, Brig. F.B. Ali and six other officers took charge of the troops and placed three generals in 'protective custody'. Gujranwala was important because a substantial portion of the army that had not been deployed in the war was located there. Brig. Ali had a solid reputation for integrity and professionalism. Resentful of the manipulations of the GHQ generals to hang on, he sent two officers—Colonels Aleem Afridi and Agha Javed Iqbal—with an ultimatum to Yahya and his generals that if they did not quit, he and his troops would march on Rawalpindi.[11]

Colonels Afridi and Javed Iqbal met Lt Gen. Gul Hassan, the chief of staff (COS), on 19 December and asked him to deliver Brig. Ali's ultimatum to Yahya. Gul Hassan discussed the gravity of the situation with Air Marshal Rahim Khan, C-in-C of the air force. Later they together met with Yahya. That evening 'a disgraced and dispirited president of a distraught nation addressed the people of Pakistan and surrendered his office'.[12]

With the senior leadership of the army discredited, Bhutto asked Lt Gen. Gul Hassan Khan, to take over the army. One of the conditions Hassan imposed was that he would continue to serve as Lt Gen. though the C-in-C was always a four-star general. Gul Hassan wanted to set a personal example and allay the criticism that the army was top-heavy. Another condition was that Bhutto would not interfere in the army's internal affairs, nor would he seek to deploy it in internal security duties.[13] Bhutto agreed but in his address to the nation he claimed credit by saying: 'I have asked Gen. Gul Hassan to be acting C-in-C ... but he will retain the rank of Lt Gen. We are not going to make unnecessary promotions.'[14]

Relations between the two became strained when Hassan demurred at Bhutto's request that the army put down labour unrest. They further deteriorated when the army chief overruled an order for army intervention by Bhutto's newly appointed national security adviser, retired Maj. Gen. Akbar Khan (of the 1951 Rawalpindi Conspiracy fame) to put down a police mutiny in Lahore and Peshawar. Gul Hassan became apprehensive that Bhutto was 'hell-bent on wrecking the army' due to his plans to put the military under the scanner of civil intelligence agencies. Hassan stood his ground and so was summarily removed.

The way Bhutto asked for and got the resignations of Gul Hassan and air force chief Rahim Khan (3 March 1972) was nothing short of dramatic and executed with military precision. The resignations were typed out and kept ready. Gul Hassan was called to Bhutto's residence on the pretext of a briefing, along with the air chief. Bhutto spelt out his complaints with the army and the air force due to their non-cooperation with the government. Gen. Gul Hassan defended his actions of not accepting government demands. However, he also offered to resign. This was the moment Bhutto was waiting for. The two pre-typed resignation letters were immediately produced. After they had signed on the dotted lines they were taken to the waiting car of Ghulam Mustafa Khar, governor of Punjab. The governor, accompanied by two of Bhutto's ministers, took the newly retired chiefs to Lahore. They were released the next day after their successors were announced.

'Even for Pakistan', notes Hassan Abbas, 'this was a novelty. Two of its armed forces chiefs were virtually kidnapped on the orders of the president of the country!'[15]

Three other elements of the plan were executed simultaneously. To ensure that the army did not get suspicious, Bhutto ensured that its relevant officers were kept engaged. Thus, when Gul Hassan and Rahim Khan were in President's House, the chief of general staff, the director of military operations and the director of intelligence at the GHQ were summoned for a sham meeting in another building. They were kept waiting till the resignations of the two chiefs were secured. Likewise, police contingents were deployed at sensitive locations like the TV and Radio stations in Rawalpindi to prevent a 'possible' coup attempt. Finally, when Gul Hassan and Rahim Khan were being driven to Lahore, Mubashir Hasan, a minister in Bhutto's cabinet, flew Lt Gen. Tikka Khan from Sahiwal to Rawalpindi in a special plane. Tikka Khan was promoted to the rank of general and appointed as COAS.[16] When Nawaz Sharif sacked Pervez Musharraf in October 1999 he would have done well to have studied how Bhutto got rid of Gul Hassan.

For Bhutto, the dismissal of Gul Hassan and Rahim Khan, and the manner of it, would at best be a temporary victory. In the long run, writes Arshad Sami Khan, it would be a disaster because he lost trust of the armed forces at a time when they were smarting due to the humiliating defeat. The army never forgot the disgrace suffered by its chiefs nor would they forgive him. The army would get its revenge by making Bhutto pay in blood.[17]

Bhutto did try to make amends. Shortly after easing them out, he appointed both Gul Hassan and Rahim Khan as Pakistan's ambassadors to Greece and Spain respectively. It was during the Pakistan National Alliance (PNA) agitation that these two would get their own back on Bhutto. In a concerted move, on 13 April 1977, Gen. Gul Hassan resigned as ambassador to Greece and Air Marshal Rahim Khan as ambassador to Spain. Rahim Khan charged Bhutto with having 'made a mockery of democracy in Pakistan.

... You have not honoured your pledges. ... The previous regime held fair and free elections but you have imperiously ignored that fine precedent and allowed them to be rigged instead. I cannot sit idly by and see the country being dragged into another civil war by power-hungry men. I am, therefore, resigning in protest against your oppressive and dictatorial regime.'[18] Gul Hasan wrote substantially the same thing.

They followed this up by giving extremely critical press conferences in London against Bhutto. They also wrote to the army chief Gen. Zia (with a copy to the PNA leadership) not to carry out 'illegal and undemocratic' orders from a 'fascist' Bhutto. The widely publicized actions of the two former military chiefs damaged Bhutto's international image at a time when he was domestically under pressure from the PNA. Another cause of worry for Bhutto was the impact that their actions would have had on the armed forces because both were highly regarded in the services.[19]

Hamoodur Rahman Report

On 24 December 1971, Bhutto ordered the formation of a commission of inquiry, to be headed by Chief Justice Hamoodur Rahman and with justices Anwarul Haq and Tufail Ali Abdur Rahman as members to probe the events leading to the break-up of Pakistan. The terms of reference were to inquire into and find out 'the circumstances in which the Commander, Eastern Command, surrendered and the members of the Armed Forces of Pakistan under his command laid down their arms and ceasefire was ordered along the borders of West Pakistan and India and along the ceasefire line in the state of Jammu and Kashmir'.[20]

It was widely believed that Bhutto's motive in establishing the commission with restricted terms of reference was meant to mask his own role in the national tragedy. Instead of an all-embracing charter, covering internal and external factors that led to the separation of East Pakistan, the aim was clearly not to carry out a detailed probe into the reasons that led to the break-up of the country. The objective appeared to be to pacify the inflamed sentiments of the people at the loss of half the country and divert their attention from the real reasons for the traumatic developments. Thus, the scope was limited to military operations in the eastern theatre, without factoring in the overall war strategy. There was no mention of political responsibility or the action of politicians and military leaders that had led to the disaster.[21] Since, the two key actors in the debacle, Bhutto and Tikka Khan, were firmly in power, they managed to manipulate developments. The latter was completely exonerated, not even being mentioned in the report.

The Hamoodur Rahman Commission (HRC) submitted its preliminary report in July 1972 and its final report in November 1974. After reading the report, Bhutto ordered all copies to be destroyed but he kept one copy with him, reportedly under his mattress. This remaining copy was found in 1978, when Zia's men raided Bhutto's house Al Murtaza.[22] Roedad Khan claimed that he was privileged to have had the HRC report in his custody for eight long years.[23]

In his book, *The Betrayal of East Pakistan*, Lt Gen. (Retd) A.A.K. Niazi makes the following points about the HRC.[24]

First, Niazi cites an article in the *Dawn* (23 and 26 July 1986) by T.A. Chaudhri, a journalist of repute, who wrote: 'Justice Hamoodur Rahman is believed to have pleaded for the enlargement of the terms of reference to enable him to look into the "totality of the situation" before the traumatic fall of Dhaka. But he was firmly directed not to burn his fingers with the political nettle. The implication was clear.' According to Chaudhri, the chief villain, Yahya, was spared because his trial would have opened a Pandora's box and unmasked those who manipulated him from behind.

Second, it had been decided that all Bengalis were to be repatriated to Bangladesh. Justice Rahman was a Bengali who should have been repatriated but he did not want to go. Hamood's son, a major in the army who wanted to go, was not allowed to leave for Bangladesh—perhaps the only instance of a Bengali being retained in the Pakistan Army. Such leverages were applied to obtain a favourable report

Third, a parallel internal army committee, under Lt Gen. Aftab, was appointed to inquire into the military operation. It interviewed officers to assess their state of mind. Only those found in sync with GHQ's line were allowed to appear before the HRC. Those found conflicting with the official policy were 'persuaded' to change their statements using intimidation, allurements, etc.

Fourth, Bhutto did not issue the report because he was heavily involved in the political manipulations prior to the dismemberment of the country. Even the PPP cabinet was not allowed to examine the 'Top Secret' parts. Only a cabinet subcommittee consisting of confidants like J.A. Rahim, Khan Qayyum Khan (a coalition partner) Hafeez Pirzada, Gen. Tikka Khan, Aziz Ahmed, Rafi Raza and Ghiasuddin were permitted to have a look and they recommended against releasing it since the political section did not reveal the true picture.

Fifth, the commission announced in court that the president issued orders for laying down arms on 14 December. Despite Niazi's return signal—'My decision to fight it out stands'—he was informed by COS Gen. Hamid to lay down arms and further by the president to surrender. Given this sequence of events, the commission accepted that it was the president who had given the orders for surrender.

Sixth, there were eighteen pages in the report about Bhutto's activities that made him furious. He ordered all copies of the report to be taken into custody. Thereafter, the pages with the adverse remarks were changed and the registrar of the Supreme Court was asked to authenticate the replaced pages. The registrar, however, refused to do so. Bhutto had him locked up in a room without food and water. He was freed only after the intervention of Hamoodur Rahman.

Seventh, after the report was submitted, Bhutto asked the judges to hand over their personal notes to him, which they did. The Federal Security Force (FSF) searched the commission's office and the residence of the HRC staff and others and confiscated relevant papers.

Niazi asserts that all the original copies were destroyed and only one copy of the amended report remained that was not authenticated. So, according to him, in reality, there is no Hamood report and if there is, its contents are largely fabricated. If the amended version of the report was published it would have become obvious that statements had been altered. Wali Khan, in an interview published in an Urdu newspaper pointed out that when he saw the typed version of his statement it had been tampered with. He even corrected the draft and sent it back after retyping. He claimed that a photocopy of the corrected draft was still with him.

Bhutto later tried to lure Niazi with several job offers including that of commander, civil armed forces of Pakistan and a diplomatic assignment. The catch was that Niazi would have to publicly say that East Pakistan was a military and not a political defeat. When Niazi refused, Bhutto 'fixed him' by removing him and his chief of staff Brig. Baqir Siddiqi from service and deprived them of pensions. The others were all rewarded with promotions or diplomatic assignments. For example, Gen. Yahya Khan got two pensions and was honoured with a military burial after his death; Gul Hassan became COAS; Sahibzada Yakub Khan was given an ambassadorship; Tikka Khan later became COAS.[25]

The Pakistan Army's review of the war, which began on 29 December 1971, focused on purely military aspects of the operations on the western front. Maj. Gen. Azmat Baksh Awan, then commandant of the Command and Staff College, Quetta, headed it and had a team of eight officers (including one from the air force).[26] The review held that 'the war in the west was initiated too late to influence the battle of East Pakistan. When started on 3 December 1971, India had already established itself in East Pakistan, obliterated the Pakistan Air Force there and paralysed communications. Had a more broad-based policy formulation machinery existed, a timely and correct decision may have been taken which may have helped either to avert total disaster in East Pakistan or may have put us in a better bargaining position.'[27] The conclusion was: 'The causes of the disaster vary from running down of Army's professional efficiency by years devoted [to] involvement in martial law duties at the cost of military training, to inadequacy of resources, faulty policy formulations and unsound judgement and untimely decisions.'[28]

When he appeared before the Hamoodur Rahman Commission, Yahya was asked about his affairs with numerous women. Lt Gen. (R) Altaf Qadir asked him whether it was true that he had been involved in the accounts they had just presented to him. Without batting an eyelid, Yahya smoking a cigarette said, 'Toffee – (this was Altaf Qadir's nickname in the army) – I never called any one of them; their husbands brought them to me. How is it my fault?'

(Gohar Ayub Khan, *Glimpses into the Corridors of Power*, Karachi: OUP, 2007, p. 153.)

***

On another occasion he said, 'Of course, Pakistan broke when I was at the helm of affairs. Of course, the Pakistan Army was defeated when I was its C-in-C. However, much more than myself, it is Zulfikar Bhutto who is responsible for the defeat and disintegration (of Pakistan).'

(A. Basit, *The Breaking of Pakistan*, Lahore: Liberty Publishers, 1990, p. 127, cited in K.M. Arif, *Khaki Shadows: Pakistan 1947-1997*, Karachi: OUP, 2001, p. 100.)

Simla Summit

Bhutto went to Simla in June 1972, taking Benazir with him. On the flight to Chandigarh, Bhutto told her, 'Everyone will be looking for signs of how the meetings are progressing, so be extra careful. You must not smile and give the impression that you are enjoying yourself while our soldiers are still in Indian POW camps. You must not look grim, either, which people will interpret as a sign of pessimism. They must have no reason to say, "Look at her face. The meetings are obviously a failure. The Pakistanis have lost their nerve. They have no chance of success and are going to make concessions."'[29]

Prior to the summit, Tikka Khan forwarded the army's views on the main issue involved to Bhutto on 11 June 1972. On the subject of recognition of Bangladesh, the army's position was that it should not be recognized until there were solid international guarantees for the withdrawal of troops to the international border/ceasefire line; return of POWs; no trials of the alleged war criminals; proper treatment of Biharis[30] and pro-Pakistan elements in East Pakistan; future relationship between East and West Pakistan to be decided in future meetings.[31]

In an interview before the Simla summit, Bhutto described Indira Gandhi thus to the Italian journalist Oriana Fallaci: 'With all her saris, the red spot on her forehead, her little smile, she'll never succeed in impressing me … a mediocre woman with a mediocre intelligence… a diligent drudge of a schoolgirl, a woman devoid of initiative and imagination.' He added that the idea of meeting her, of shaking her hand, filled him with acute disgust. Indira Gandhi was so furious on reading the interview that she almost changed her mind about meeting Bhutto at Simla.[32] For her part, Indira Gandhi had described Bhutto as '… not a very balanced man …' who, 'when he talks, you never understand what he means'.[33]

Even after four days of hectic negotiations Bhutto and Indira Gandhi failed to come to an overall agreement. On 2 July, Bhutto decided to call it quits and prepared to return to Pakistan. On his farewell call on Indira Gandhi that day, he spoke non-stop for half an hour offering a way out of the impasse. Indira Gandhi was non-committal, saying she would give an answer at dinner that Bhutto was hosting for the Indian delegation prior to his departure from Simla the next day. After dinner the negotiations continued.[34]

The Pakistan delegation had devised a code to enable each other to know how things were going. 'If there is an agreement, we'll say a boy has been born. If there is no agreement, we'll say a girl has been born.' At 12.40 a.m. '*Larka hai, Larka hai*! (it's a boy, it's a boy) rang out through the house.[35]

While both leaders had initialled the draft agreement, it was necessary to draw up the final accord. However, there was no electric typewriter at Himachal Bhawan (where Bhutto was staying and had hosted the dinner). There was a scramble to get one from the Oberoi Clarkes Hotel. For their part, the Pakistani delegation realized that the official Government of Pakistan seal had been sent back with their heavy luggage that afternoon. So, both sides did not put their official seal on the document.[36]

Faced with the choice given by Indira Gandhi of returning either the POWs or territory, Bhutto chose territory. He later told Benazir, that prisoners were a human problem, in this case the enormity of it was increased because there were 93,000 of them. India could not keep them indefinitely—it would be both inhuman and pose practical problems to continue housing and feeding them. 'Territory, on the other hand, was not a human problem. Territory can be assimilated. Prisoners cannot. The Arabs have still not succeeded in regaining the territory lost in the 1967 war. But the capture of land doesn't cry out for international attention the same way as prisoners do.'[37]

Bhutto returned triumphantly to Lahore on 3 July. A special session of the National Assembly unanimously approved the accord. Bhutto claimed that his role in finalizing the Agreement was even more difficult than the one played by Count Tallyrand at the 1815 Congress of Vienna (after Napoleon's defeat at Waterloo).[38]

Like what Bhutto had said about a 'secret' of the Tashkent Agreement in 1966, Ghulam Mustafa Khar, Bhutto's confidant, told journalists in 1988 that he was the only person who knew 'the true story' of the separation of East Pakistan and the birth of Bangladesh. He said the country and the subcontinent would be shaken once he spoke out. To do so, he wanted 'only 15 days of freedom [from incarceration; he was on parole then] to speak out'. Since then, Khar has been out of jail for decades but, like Bhutto before him, has not revealed the 'true story'.[39]

Was there a side agreement at Simla about making the LOC the international border? This issue has aroused much speculation on both sides of the border. According to V. T. Joshi, former prime minister A.B. Vajpayee revealed in a press conference in New York in December 1993 that during the Simla summit, Bhutto had, in fact, given an assurance that the LOC would be made the international border with minor adjustments. He averred that as external affairs minister in the Janata government in the 1970s he had seen the records regarding this. However, domestic political compulsions did not allow Bhutto to honour that commitment. Nevertheless, when Vajpayee was asked at the same press conference, if his party would accept a settlement on the basis of the LOC he replied: 'It is a hypothetical question. Let Pakistan propose it and we will respond.'[40]

After he signed the Simla Agreement, Bhutto made many contradictory statements. At a press conference, he was asked how he could reconcile them. 'What can I do, I am a product of this subcontinent,' he exclaimed and disarmed the media with a smile.[41]

Bhutto's concern, or the lack of it, for the 93,000 POWs was revealed when Sultan Khan called on him a day before he left for Washington as ambassador. When Sultan Khan sought instructions for the assignment Bhutto made no mention of the POWs. 'When asked if their early repatriation should also be an important task for me, Bhutto thought for a while, and said without much enthusiasm, "There is no harm if you try to enlist support on their behalf."'[42]

In one of her first political campaign speeches in Faisalabad in 1977 when Bhutto was imprisoned, Benazir Bhutto said: 'When I was in India with my father during the negotiations with Indira Gandhi, my father refused to sleep in his bed but slept on the floor. "Why are you sleeping on the floor?" I asked him. "I cannot sleep in a bed in India," he answered, "when our prisoners-of-war have nothing to sleep on in the camps but the ground." The crowd responded appreciatively.

(Benazir Bhutto, *Daughter of the East*, London: Hamish Hamilton, 1988, p. 103.)

The 93,000 prisoners of war were released in 1974 after Pakistan recognized Bangladesh. The special train carrying the POWs reached Wagah in the early hours of 30 April 1974. Niazi describes what happened. First, he was asked by one Brigadier Anjum not to make any statements to the media. 'Then he produced a piece of cardboard about four inches square on which "No 1" was written. He told me to stick it on my chest so that I could be photographed. I asked if this was only for me, or for others as well. He said it was for other generals as well. I asked him whether anyone else had been photographed. He said no one else had been photographed. It was General Tikka's orders. Even in India we had not been subjected to such humiliation.'[43]

The best tribute to Bhutto in the days after the 1971 debacle was by Henry Kissinger who wrote of Bhutto in this period: '... in the days of his country's tragedy, he held the remnant of his nation together and restored its self-confidence. In its hour of greatest need, he saved his country from complete destruction. But his courage and vision in 1971 should have earned him a better fate than the tragic end his passionate countrymen meted out to him and that blighted their reputation for mercy.'[44]

5.2

Z.A. Bhutto II: The Arrogance of Power

Early Life

ZULFIKAR ALI BHUTTO (HENCEFORTH BHUTTO) was born on 5 January 1928, the son of a Sindhi feudal landlord Shahnawaz Bhutto and his second wife, a Rajasthani Hindu dancing girl Lakhi Bai. In 1924, Shahnawaz had fallen in love with Lakhi Bai who converted to Islam to marry him and changed her name to Khurshid. The nikah(wedding) took place at the residence of Nawab Bahadur Aazam Jan of Kalat in Quetta. Khurshid bore three of Shahnawaz's children: two daughters, Manna and Benazir and his youngest Zulfiqar.[1]

Shahnawaz named his son Zulfiqar after the sword of Hazrat Ali. The sword of Ali has been long seen as a symbol of fight against tyranny.[2]

Khurshid had Bhutto's horoscope made by an old astrologer in Bombay. He predicted many things about Bhutto, including his marriages, his success and power, but only till the age of fifty. Beyond this the astrologer declined to say any more, telling Khurshid, 'I don't know what I see.'[3]

Bhutto's early life and education were far removed from Larkana, the family home of the Bhuttos in Sindh. In 1934, when Bhutto was six years old, his parents relocated from Karachi to Bombay. His father joined the Bombay Presidency's legislative council. Consequently, Bhutto's childhood and adolescence, schooling and early friendships were strongly influenced by Bombay. He did his Senior Cambridge from the Cathedral and John Connon School at the second attempt. As a fellow student, Piloo Mody (later a member of the Lok Sabha) remarked, Bhutto 'did not show much promise' at this stage.[4]

In 1947, Shahnawaz Bhutto took up appointment as minister in the council of the ruler of Junagarh Sir Mahabbat Khan Rasul Al Khanji. Junagarh was a a princely state on the Gujarat coast. A few months later he was appointed Divan.[5] Bhutto, however, stayed back in Bombay.

Bhutto was a big fan of the Indian cricketer Mushtaq Ali. Bhutto may also have had a teenage crush on Nargis, the famous Indian actor. Nargis remembered him as 'very charming and likeable' but always smelling of gin and perfume. As she recalled: 'Bhutto as I knew him was the feudal landlord with princely pleasures – drinks, *shikar* and dancing with a new girl every night.'[6]

In September 1947, a month after the creation of Pakistan, Bhutto left India for the US. There he pursued further education at the University of Southern California in Los Angeles. It was only in September 1949 that he first visited the newly created state of Pakistan during holidays. He would finally return to Karachi in November 1953 after completing his education in Berkeley, Oxford and Lincoln's Inn. With such an eclectic education, it was not surprising that Bhutto could hardly speak any Urdu or Sindhi. He was an urbane, English-speaking Bombayite with very little trace of a Sindhi.[7]

At the age of thirteen, Bhutto was married for the first time to Shireen (later renamed as Amir Begum), the only child of a distant uncle. Shireen was much older than Bhutto. According to his biographer, Stanley Wolpert, Bhutto made it clear to his second wife Nusrat Bhutto on the eve of their marriage that his first marriage was 'purely for property'.[8] Bhutto told Italian journalist Oriana Fallaci about his first marriage, 'I didn't even know what it meant to have a wife, and when they tried to explain it to me I went out of my mind with rage, with fury. I didn't want a wife, I wanted to play cricket.'[9] Shireen Amir Begum would outlive Bhutto by twenty-four years. She visited him just prior to his hanging and attended his funeral in Larkana.

Personality Traits

By all accounts, Bhutto was a complex personality. Most of Bhutto's biographers like Stanley Wolpert, Shahid Burki and Salman Taseer have highlighted the impact of his mother on his psyche. Khurshid's humble origins made the feudal Bhuttos shun her and they resisted the union for a considerable time. According to Salman Taseer, even as a young boy, Bhutto was conscious of the opposition towards his mother and her suffering made a deep impression upon him. He never forgot his mother's humiliation by the family. 'Poverty was her only crime,' he once said, and even attributed his own egalitarian attitudes to his mother's patient endurance of the injustices of the feudal system.[10]

Others, who had personal experience of his mother, have commented that Bhutto suffered from an inferiority complex concerning his maternal parentage. For example, Haji Maula Buksh Soomro (a Sindhi politician) told Zia in August 1977 that Bhutto treated his mother with considerable contempt and harshness. The mother had told Soomro's wife. 'May God's curse be on my son.' Soomro's wife was stunned to hear such words from a mother regarding her own son. Soomro was convinced that her cries would be heard and that God would punish Bhutto for maltreating his mother.[11]

His inferiority complex was also apparent when after A.Q. Khan had agreed to return to Pakistan, Bhutto banged his fist on the table in his usual style and said, 'I will see the Hindu bastards now!'[12]

Whatever the reason, Bhutto was a complex personality, enthralled by his own sense of grandeur. Despite being a democratically elected mass leader, he had a strong dictatorial streak, making him intolerant of any opposition. Not surprisingly, Sir Morrice James, Britain's high commissioner in Islamabad wrote about Bhutto in his *Pakistan Chronicle*, 'I believe that at heart he lacked a sense of dignity and value of other people, his own self was what counted. I sensed in him ruthlessness and a capacity for ill-doing which went far beyond what is natural.[13]

> Instances abound of Bhutto's authoritarian mentality, insecurity, suspicious nature and megalomania. Convinced that there were enemies everywhere, he wrote a memo in 1973 to Mustafa Khar, then governor of Punjab, stating dramatically, 'There are pistols to the right of us, pistols to the left of us, pistols all around us. This seems to be the motto of the party.'
>
> (Christina Lamb, *Waiting for Allah: Pakistan's Struggle for Democracy*, New Delhi: Viking, Penguin Books, 1991, p. 80.)

The *Guardian*, probably summed him up well when it wrote on 7 March 1977: 'There is a fatal flaw in the character. He is a total cynic ... he does not believe in political parties, least of all his own, and he believes that a corrupt instrument is better than an honest one, because he can use it more easily. ... When faced with an independent institution or social group – whether it was big business, the judiciary, the Press, the Balochi aristocracy, the Punjabi middle class, or even his own party – Mr Bhutto's instinct has been either to take it over, or, if that was not possible, to destroy it.'[14]

Foreign Secretary Sultan M. Khan, and his deputy Mumtaz Alvie had gone to see Bhutto soon after he took over as president and CMLA. While waiting for Bhutto to finish his meeting with Wali Khan of the National Awami Party, Alvie mentioned to Sultan Khan that Bhutto should be careful since these were experienced and seasoned politicians. Later, during their meeting, Bhutto looked at Alvie and said, 'Don't worry about seasoned politicians. I have their measure.' According to Sultan Khan, that was the first time that the ante-room at the President's House had been bugged. Thereafter, everyone who visited the President's House was watched and recorded.[15]

Bhutto's insecurity was also reflected in the establishment of a national documentation centre in April 1976, the sole purpose of which was to compile information on important political personalities. The introductory note to the dossiers elucidated their purpose: 'It is hoped that for working purposes the material contained in these dossiers will be of some use at the time when the nation is going to the poll.'[16] Zia's government issued Volume III of the 'White Paper on the Performance of the Bhutto Regime', in January 1979. It summed up the dossiers in these words: 'The pen picture makes very depressing reading. The details are unsavoury and sordid. A sizeable majority of the National and Provincial Assembly members, in the fold of Mr Bhutto's party, are revealed as licentious, lecherous and harbourers of criminals, goondas and smugglers. At least a dozen of them have been shown to be sexual perverts.' According to K.M. Arif, 'Many pieces of information contained in the dossiers, prepared with painstaking care and a sadistic pleasure, giving insight into the personal lives of political leaders, are unprintable.'[17]

A few days after Bhutto became president, he summoned Justice Feroze Nana, a highly respected judge of the Sindh High Court. Bhutto first made him wait for about half an hour and then had him shown into his office but did not acknowledge his presence for a few minutes. He then raised his head and asked if Nana knew why he had been sent for. When Nana replied in the negative, Bhutto said, 'I

> have sent for you to remind you that your father was my father's enemy.' Nana was shocked and replied that they may not have been on good terms but they were certainly not enemies. 'Oh no,' Bhutto said. 'They were enemies and if I do not take revenge from you, your children will take revenge from my children. Do you understand? That is all. You can go.' As a result of this exchange Justice Nana suddenly resigned.
>
> (M. Asghar Khan, *We've Learnt Nothing from History, Pakistan: Politics and Military Power*, Karachi: OUP, 2005, p. 220.)

Bhutto's arrogance and obsession with maintaining an aura of invincibility was so intense that on several occasions, on his personal instructions, several of his jailed political opponents were subjected to severe sexual humiliation.[18] In fact, he would not even spare those who had been loyal and devoted over the years. The worst example of this savage brutality was the treatment meted out to senior federal minister Jalaluddin Abdur Rahim, the man Bhutto had himself described as his 'mentor and guru'. Bhutto had created a portfolio of Presidential Affairs for Rahim. Every paper for the president passed through him showing how completely Bhutto trusted Rahim and his advice.[19]

On 2 July 1974, Bhutto had invited Rahim and other senior leaders of the PPP to a dinner at the PM's house at 8 p.m. Bhutto, however, failed to show up. By midnight the seventy-plus-year-old Rahim had had enough. He put down his empty tumbler and said in an irritated, clearly audible voice, 'You bloody flunkies can wait as long as you like for the maharaja of Larkana, I am going home.' Hafiz Pirzada informed Bhutto of Rahim's outburst when he finally made an appearance. Later that night, the chief of the prime minister's security went to Rahim's residence and thrashed him senseless. Rahim's son Sikander who tried to intervene was also beaten mercilessly. The two of them were then thrown into a jeep and taken to a police station. This was Bhutto's reply to Rahim's taunt about the maharaja of Larkana and sent a clear message to all PPP members that no one was immune from Bhutto's rage.[20]

This wasn't the end of Rahim's travails. Almost two years later, on 2 May 1976 Rahim and his son were again thrashed senseless and even tortured with cigarette burns. His son was sodomized. Jam Sadiq Ali, a Sindhi politician, organized this brutality on instructions from Bhutto.[21]

Jam Sadiq Ali was one politician who seemed to have escaped Bhutto's wrath. One evening, Jam Sadiq Ali walked past Bhutto without acknowledging his presence. A peeved Bhutto asked him, 'Without a salaam, Sadiq? Don't you remember your father, when he attended my father's kutcheri, used to sit on the floor?' Jam Sadiq stood for a moment and said, 'Yes Sahib, I remember. But he sat there because that was the best seat to watch Lakhi Bai's (Bhutto's mother) dance.[22]

Bhutto had a series of love affairs and dalliances that he claimed were part of his inherent romanticism: 'I am a romantic,' he told Orina Fallaci, the Italian journalist, 'I don't think you can be a politician without being a romantic – and as a romantic, I think there is nothing so inspiring as a love affair. There's nothing wrong with falling in love and conquering a woman's heart – woe to men who don't fall in love!'

(Salman Taseer, *Bhutto: A Political Biography,* New Delhi: Vikas, 1980, p. 200.)

A must on Bhutto's calendar was the annual hunt he hosted in Larkana to celebrate his birthday. His guests would include the Sheikh of Abu Dhabi and the Shah of Iran, as well as Pakistan's presidents Ayub Khan and Yahya Khan. Bhutto was reputed to hold one of the best and largest private collection of hunting rifles in Pakistan.[23] He also had in his library thousands of first edition volumes on Napoleon, one of the largest private collections in the world.[24]

> Bhutto believed in palmistry and astrology. Once he sent his palm print to the famous palmist of Pakistan, M.A. Malik, through a friend. After seeing Bhutto's palm print, Malik made several predictions though he did not reveal everything. Years later, when Bhutto was in jail facing trial for murder, Malik showed the print to Kausar Niazi and told him, 'This man's brain will lead him to the gallows.'
>
> (Kausar Niazi, *Zulfiqar Ali Bhutto of Pakistan: Last Days*, Delhi: Vikas Publishing House, 1992, pp. 66–67.)
>
> ***
>
> During his visit to Sri Lanka, Bhutto sought a meeting with the official astrologers of Prime Minister Sirimavo Bandaranaike. He asked the astrologers to tell him about the outcome of the elections that he had fixed for 7 March 1977. Interestingly, all the astrologers kept quiet, as if stunned. After Bhutto persisted in knowing, the senior-most astrologer said, 'Now when you have already announced the date what opinion can we give?'
>
> (Kausar Niazi, *Zulfiqar Ali Bhutto of Pakistan: Last Days*, p. 67.)

Mass Leader

Despite his many faults, Bhutto had an uncanny ability to relate to the people. With his gift of eloquence, he could whip up the crowd. He combined populism with an incisive intellect. According to James Farwell, he was 'equally at ease attired in expensive suits strutting about in foreign capitals and in the awami (people's) shalwar-kameez and Jinnah cap haranguing working people. A celebrity, Bhutto cut a dashing figure in the media. He inspired pride in ordinary Pakistanis.'[25]

Once in Larkana, his hometown in Sindh, farmers and activists complained to him about the unkept promises he had made to them and about the lack of implementation of reforms. Bhutto heard them out patiently and in the end just asked, 'Now tell me this and be completely honest. Can you think of any other prime minister who would have met you and sat quietly listening to your complaints?' The peasant leaders laughed and cheered and the meeting came to an end.[26]

As a Pakistani taxi driver in New York commented about Bhutto, '*Sahib, iss nay humein zabaan dai dee*' (Sir, he has given us a voice).[27]

It was well known that Bhutto was fond of his drink. At public meetings, he invariably carried a silver flask that contained whiskey that he would mix with water and sip. At one such meeting, a group of Islamists sought to embarrass him by shouting the minute he mixed his drink, 'What are you drinking?' To the amusement of the crowd, Bhutto held up the glass and said 'Sherbat' (a soft drink). The Islamists, however, persisted and told the crowd that Bhutto was drinking sharab (liquor) not sherbet. Not a person to be cowed down, Bhutto retorted back, 'Fine, I am drinking sharab. Unlike you sister f…rs, I don't drink the blood of our people.' This brought the crowd to their feet and they chanted in Punjabi, 'Long may our Bhutto live, long may our Bhutto drink.'[28]

Similarly, when accused of womanizing, Bhutto would reply: 'Yes, I womanize, but I don't go after little boys like my opponents do.'[29]

Bhutto's tragedy was his imagining that his connect with the people made him infallible, and this made him his own worst enemy.

The Media

Opponents apart, the press had to bear the brunt of Bhutto's offensive. He was determined to hammer them into submission.

Among those targeted were the chairman of the National Press Trust, Gen. Habibullah Khan (Retd), who was dismissed, put in prison and humiliated by being handcuffed like a common criminal in public; editor-in-chief of the *Pakistan Times*, Z.A. Suleri, who was dismissed; the editor of *Dawn*, Altaf Gauhar, who was arrested; the printer, publisher and editor of *Urdu Digest*, *Zindagi* (Urdu), and *Punjabi Punch* (English) who were arrested; Shorish Kashmiri of the weekly *Chattan*, who was jailed; the newspapers *Hurriyat* and *Jasarat* that were banned and their editors Anwar Khaleel and Salahuddin, imprisoned; the *Mehran* which was banned while Iqbal Burney's weekly *Outlook* was forced to shut as was the daily *Sun*.[30]

The media would, however, get their back on Bhutto. In a press conference held in Governor's House, Lahore, Bhutto had announced a ban on liquor and gambling. While reporting it, BBC Urdu mentioned that 'when Mr Bhutto was announcing a ban on liquor, he was smoking a cigar'. In Urdu, the translation was 'cigar *pee rahe the*' ('he was drinking a cigar'.) In Urdu since the word used for 'smoking' is 'drinking' there was a lot of confusion among the people about the step he had taken. In the common man's perception, a cigar was also some kind of liquor that Bhutto was 'drinking' even while announcing a ban on it![31]

The Showman

Sultan Khan, then foreign secretary, narrates a fascinating insight into Bhutto's craving to demonstrate that he was in total control and of his showmanship.

Soon after he assumed power, Bhutto took the Islamabad-based ambassadors and their spouses to Larkana for a duck shoot and a cultural programme. The diplomats boarded a luxury special train from Rawalpindi in the evening. They were provided with well-appointed coupe's with 'fine rugs, bed linen and a cabinet full of the best wines and liquor'. The catering was done by Intercontinental Hotel and there was a very attentive staff. Larkana railway station was decked up to give the impression of receiving a royal wedding party, complete with a brass band belting out Sindhi tunes.

The dinner was hosted on the residence grounds in a huge tent with musicians providing the entertainment. When the popular Sindhi tune '*Hay Jamalo*' was played, Bhutto gestured to two or three of his cabinet ministers to dance, followed by the chiefs of the army and air force. Much to his disappointment, however, none of the ambassadors joined the dancing.

After the dinner, the Soviet ambassador told Sultan M. Khan, 'We are all very fortunate to be here, and grateful for such lavish hospitality. To be entertained by Cabinet Ministers, a provincial Governor and two Chiefs of Staff is indeed a great privilege.' Sultan Khan writes that rarely had he felt so humiliated. Bhutto clearly used those who served him as pawns. The event also signalled to the ambassadors that Pakistan may have been dismembered but he was in control now, something that the diplomats would no doubt convey to their governments.[32]

Sense of Humour

When he was in prison a reporter asked Bhutto how he was passing the time. Bhutto, replied. 'I'm reading a lot of Napoleon to learn how he kept his generals in line when I couldn't control mine.'[33]

Diplomats at the UN had realized that Indo-Pak relations were a minefield that was best avoided completely or else approached with a lot of caution. Once, an annoyed European delegate told Bhutto, 'We are tired of you Indians and Pakistanis constantly snapping at our heels.' The vintage Bhutto response was: 'Be careful. Next time we may aim higher.'[34]

Prem Bhatia, the renowned Indian editor, had interviewed Bhutto for *The Indian Express* in Calcutta, when he was the foreign minister in the early 1960s. The newspaper's cartoonist who accompanied Bhatia sketched Bhutto while Bhatia did the interview. Later, the nervous cartoonist asked Bhutto to autograph his work. A balding Bhutto looked at the cartoon and quipped, 'I've got more hair around my private parts than he's given me at the top of my head.'[35]

During the election campaign of 1977, Asghar Khan claimed that Bhutto was such a bad Muslim that it was only now that he was learning to pray five times a day. Bhutto's retort to this was when a reporter asked him why the PLO leader Yasser Arafat was coming to see him, 'He is coming to teach me prayers.'[36]

Nusrat Bhutto

In 1951, Bhutto married India-born Nusrat Ispahani, the daughter of an Iranian businessman who shifted from Bombay to Karachi. At that time, he was still a student in Oxford. However, later Bhutto fell in love with Husna Sheikh who was known as 'Black Beauty'. After a fight over his infidelity, Bhutto even threw Nusrat out of the house in 1962. Ayub Khan was appalled by such behaviour and gave Bhutto a choice: take Nusrat back or quit the cabinet. Faced with such a choice, Bhutto took Nusrat back. Husna later left her husband and moved to Karachi from Dhaka. Bhutto got her a furnished house in Clifton, a short distance from his own 70 Clifton.[37]

Bhutto quit Ayub's government in June 1966. Due to his ceaseless criticism of the Ayub regime he was arrested on 13 November 1968 and imprisoned in Mianwali jail. He was released in February 1969. During his incarceration, it was Nusrat who confronted the regime. Sitting in a tonga (a two-wheeled horse-drawn carriage), she would drive through Lahore leading the protestors.[38]

Just before Ayub Khan arrested Bhutto, Nusrat Bhutto was warned about the impending arrest. She remarked, 'But that is just what he would like to happen right now.'[39]

Bhutto's Indian Connection

Bhutto's Hindu origins would haunt him for a long time. After his estrangement with Ayub, the government put out documents showing that Bhutto had considered himself a citizen of India till 1958.

Prior to Partition, Bhutto's father, Shahnawaz Bhutto, had sold a house in Bombay for Rs 140,000 (about £10,000 at the prevailing rate of exchange). The property was in Bhutto's name and as he was a minor, the sale proceeds were left in the custody of the court. Due to Partition and his departure for the United States, he was declared an evacuee by an order issued on 6 July 1949. According to the arrangements made between the two countries he could get the money only through an application to a Pakistani court.[40]

While challenging the order with the Custodian of Evacuee Property, Bhutto contended that he had left India on an Indian passport and visited Karachi in 1949 'as an Indian national'. He was, therefore, not an evacuee when the order was made. In his petition of 1949 he said: 'Things are so nebulous that I cannot say where I shall settle down when I return after finishing studies.' In another statement in 1955, he said he was thinking of settling 'permanently' in England. In 1956, he said that 'merely because the applicant's parents resided in Karachi and the applicant's marriage took place there ... it could not be concluded that the applicant's home was also in Karachi at any relevant time'. In a nutshell, he refuted having become a Pakistan citizen, else his applications would be immediately unsustainable. It was only on 3 November 1958, some weeks after he became a minister, that he accepted that he had settled down in Karachi, and so withdrew his appeal pending before India's Supreme Court.[41]

Simultaneously with his extended legal battle in India, Bhutto also tried to recover the Bombay court deposit through legal processes in Pakistan as a citizen of that country. The Indian minister for rehabilitation stated this in the Rajya Sabha on 19 November 1965, in reply to a call attention notice. The issue was also discussed in the Pakistan National Assembly on 30 June 1967. Replying to a question, Information Minister Khwaja Shahabuddin said that relevant Indian documents showed that 'till 1958, Mr Bhutto was claiming in Pakistan citizenship of Pakistan and in India he was claiming citizenship of India'.[42]

The motivation was clearly to dent Bhutto's position. However, Bhutto's Indian connection did not adversely affect his political career or rising popularity.[43]

Bhutto's Politics

Bhutto's approach to politics was best expressed by his statement in an interview: to succeed in politics 'one must have light and flexible fingers to insinuate them under the bird sitting on its eggs in the nest and take away the eggs. One by one. Without the bird realizing it.'[44]

Bhutto's entry into politics was fortuitous. It was the death of his elder brother Imdad Ali that made Bhutto heir to his father's political legacy. At that stage Bhutto was keen to become a member of the Sindh provincial assembly. However, in the 1958 elections he had to cross another hurdle, that of overcoming the political clout of another Sindhi politician, Ayub Khuro, in his hometown of Larkana. Bhutto hated Khuro. One reason was the slight that Khuro had inflicted on him and his father Sir Shahnawaz when they had called on him when he was the chief minister of Sindh. Khuro not only made them wait for half an hour but later, when they were seated in the drawing room, he again slighted them by drinking tea without offering them any. Khuro listened to Shahnawaz's request for a position in the foreign service for his son and asked for a written application. He then dismissed them derisively, with a wave of his hand.

Bhutto was not one to forget. He got his back as soon as he became chief martial law administrator (CMLA). One of his first acts was to have the walls of Khuro's house at Larkana razed to the ground.[45]

Bhutto's initial political advancement was through the association of his wife Nusrat Bhutto with Naheed Mirza, the wife of President Iskander Mirza. Both were of Iranian descent. It was through this association that he gained entry into the President's House.[46] Bhutto assiduously cultivated this relationship and won over Iskander Mirza's affection through hospitality and sycophancy. He liberally used the time-tested Sindhi feudal tradition of hosting shikars (hunting trips) for Mirza, added to which was a liberal dose of downright flattery. Iskander Mirza had made Bhutto a member of the Pakistan delegation to the Law of the Sea Conference in Geneva in April 1958 from where Bhutto wrote to Mirza saying, 'When the history of our country is written by objective historians, your name will be placed even before that of Mr Jinnah. Sir, I say this because I mean to, and not because you are the President of my country.'[47] This reveals the level of sycophancy and obsequiousness that Bhutto could descend to for his personal ambitions. Was this why he succumbed to the flattery of Gen. Zia-ul-Haq later in life?

Given Bhutto's contacts with Mirza, it was not surprising that he was inducted into the cabinet (as minister of commerce and industries). At that time Bhutto was a complete unknown. So much so that in a press report on the cabinet's swearing in, he was called 'Zulfiqar Ali Bhutta'.[48]

Pir Pagara also played a role in the early part of Bhutto's career. The Pir hired him as a legal adviser and even urged President Iskander Mirza to include the young Bhutto in a delegation to the UN. However, the relations between them became strained and they became rivals after Bhutto's career took off. According to the Pir, when Bhutto came to power he telephoned his erstwhile patron and threatened, 'I will now deal with you.' The Pir was charged with sedition and his associates were imprisoned. The Pir kept his peace and prevented the Hurs (his followers) from provoking Bhutto.[49]

The Pir got his revenge when he became one of the pre-eminent leaders of the Pakistan National Alliance (PNA) movement that had been formed to overthrow Bhutto. When the time came for Bhutto's execution the Pir advised Zia against clemency arguing that 'to show mercy to the wolf amounts to tyrannizing the sheep: the sooner riddance from it is secured the better'. Zia-ul-Haq took the Pir in his fold because of the latter's influence in Sindh and his own fight with Bhutto. According to Emma Duncan, the Pir, happy to use and be used, called himself 'the GHQ Pir'. Zia-ul-Haq, Junejo and Pir Pagara 'were described as the Father, the Son and the Holy Ghost – though nobody was quite sure which was which'.[50]

Bhutto and Ayub Khan

A strong bond developed between Ayub Khan and Bhutto so much so that Bhutto was the declared fifth son of Ayub.[51] In August 1963, Ayub Khan awarded Bhutto the 'Hilal-i-Pakistan'—Pakistan's highest civilian award. For his part, Bhutto lost no opportunity in reciprocating Ayub's appreciation by eloquent and flattering public tributes on the floor of the National Assembly, elsewhere and in print. These were to cause him great embarrassment in later years. For example, writing in the *Pakistan Annual* of 1961, Bhutto wrote of Ayub Khan: 'This man of history is more than a Lincoln to us, for he has bound the nation together by eliminating the fissiparous tendencies without violence; more than a Lenin, because he has set the country's economy and social objectives on a high and glorious pedestal without coercion. He is our Ataturk for like the great Turkish leader, he restored the nation's dignity and self-respect in the comity of nations. And above all a Salahuddin [Salauddin Ayubi was the first sultan of Egypt and Syria and founder of the Ayyubid dynasty], for like the great Ghazi-ul-Islam, this heir to the noble heritage has regained a hundred million people's pride and confidence, the highest attribute of life, without which a people are soulless.'[52]

Relations between the two, however, broke down after the Tashkent summit when Bhutto sensed that he had an opportunity to go it alone. After Ayub Khan sacked him in June 1966, Bhutto left Rawalpindi by train. At the Lahore railway station, the next morning, his party workers raised slogans and carried him on their shoulders. From the railway station Bhutto went to Governor's House asking for a room for a few hours for some rest. As a former foreign minister, he was allowed to use the guest room.

The Urdu press reported that the handkerchief that Bhutto used to wipe his eyes at the Lahore Railway Station was sold later for Rs 10,000.

(Salman Taseer, *Bhutto: A Political Biography*, Delhi: Vikas Publishing House, 1980, p. 77.)

When the governor, the nawab of Kalabagh, came to know, he told his military secretary, 'This is a drama to send Ayub the message that we both have ganged up against him.' Later Bhutto had lunch with the governor. As expected, Bhutto's lunch with the governor became headline news creating the impression that it was the nawab who had invited Bhutto to lunch and they had plotted against Ayub. In one stroke, Bhutto succeeded in sowing doubts in the mind of Ayub about the loyalty of the governor who, in fact, was one of his pillars of strength.[53]

Soon Bhutto's differences with Ayub over policy deteriorated into bitter personal acrimony. Bhutto once observed, 'This bloody Field Marshal has the mind of a Sargeant Major.'[54]

Pakistan Peoples Party

In November 1967, Bhutto launched the Pakistan Peoples Party (PPP). Its inaugural convention was held in Lahore. Its political credo was presented in the form of four slogans: 'Islam is our faith; Democracy is our Polity; Socialism is our Economy; and All Power to the People.'

The name PPP was not an original one. Immediately after Partition, Ghaffar Khan, had formed a secular opposition party called the PPP. The first PPP, however, did not last long. It disintegrated after the brutal shooting of the Red Shirts in Babra in 1948.

(Salman Taseer, *Bhutto: A Political Biography*, Delhi Vikas Publishing House, 1980, p. 88.)

The press did not pay much attention to PPP's inaugural convention. Some papers like the government-controlled *Pakistan Times* wrote mockingly: 'The so-called People's Party launched by Zulfikar Ali Bhutto last week, has stirred hardly a ripple. Unfortunately, like other Opposition parties, it had only a string of slogans to offer.'[55] *Dawn*, stressing on the contrast between Bhutto in office and out of it, wrote: 'He can shift his ground faster than a fox and, unlike a leopard, can change his spots from year to year.'[56]

Bhutto had decided as early as in 1969 to form a new organization called the People's Guard. To test the suitability of members of this organization he prescribed a simple test. A match would be lit and the flame held under a volunteer's finger for a few seconds to judge if the volunteer could bear the pain. According to Bhutto, the PPP was a 'militant' party and such an organization was therefore necessary.

(M. Asghar Khan, *We've Learnt Nothing from History–Pakistan: Politics and Military Power*, Karachi: OUP, 2005, p. 82.)

Bhutto seemed determined to get into power, by hook or by crook. Two revealing incidents testify to this. On one occasion, Bhutto told Asghar Khan in 1970,'We can rule together.' When Asghar Khan asked about his programme after coming into power, Bhutto chuckled and his reply was honest, though shocking to the air marshal. He said, 'The programme is to rule. The people are stupid and I know how to fool them. I will have the "danda" in my hand and no one will be able to remove us for twenty years.' Asghar Khan writes that he was grateful for Bhutto's frank views but made up his mind to take a different path.[57]

On another occasion, in the middle of 1970, Bhutto suggested to Yahya Khan he should forget about elections. Instead, Yahya Khan, the soldier, and Bhutto, the politician, as a team could run the country together. Yahya's response was that this suggestion made some sense but he wanted to know what Bhutto proposed to do about East Pakistan? Pat came Bhutto's reply: 'East Pakistan is no problem. We will have to kill some 20,000 people there and all will be well.' When Yahya narrated this incident to Asghar Khan, the air marshal asked him about his reaction to Bhutto's suggestion about East Pakistan. Yahya just shrugged his shoulders and said, 'What can one say to such a suggestion?' Asghar Khan notes that what had appeared absurd prior to the elections of 1970 had by February 1971 become worthy of serious consideration.[58]

In Power

Bhutto was sworn in as both president and chief martial law administrator (CMLA) on 21 December 1971. He would also hold two other offices, president of the constituent assembly and chairman of the PPP.[59] He told his first cabinet meeting, 'Gentlemen, we are here for twenty years.' As part of this vision, he ordered new crockery and cutlery for the PM's house. Interestingly, the engraving on the new crockery and cutlery was the PPP symbol of the sword rather than the crest of the prime minister of Pakistan. Consequently, after he was removed, these expensive items had to be stored.[60] Likewise, his special plane displayed two flags—his personal standard and his party colours. The Pakistan flag did not figure anywhere.[61]

Bhutto amended the constitution to declare Ahmadis non-Muslims. After parliament had passed the amendment, Bhutto left in an open car, acknowledging the appreciation of the crowd. He claimed credit for 'solving' a problem that had troubled the Muslims for the previous ninety years. The Ahmadis felt betrayed since they had strongly supported Bhutto in the 1970 elections. When he declared them non-Muslims, many supporters claimed that he had stolen a march over the mullahs who had been clamouring for such a measure for decades. Others, however, felt that the mullahs would now be encouraged to press for more similar measures. Rafi Raza, who observed the developments closely, maintains that Bhutto had '… lost sight of what was the fundamental principle of whether the religious issues can or should be settled in a political forum'.[62]

Mohammad Abdus Salam, the Nobel prize–winning physicist, serving as science adviser to the government and overseeing the development of the nuclear weapons programme since 1972, resigned to protest the amendment. He was an Ahmadi. While accepting the resignation, Bhutto asked Salam to continue to provide informal advice saying, 'This is all politics. Give me time, I will change it.' When Salam asked if Bhutto would write this down in a private note, he politely declined.[63]

Once entrenched in power, Bhutto systematically moulded state institutions to his will. In the process, they were badly damaged and the state suffered the consequences. As Jamsheed

Marker notes, the judiciary was made subservient, the powerful civil service was ruined with the introduction of the Lateral Entry Scheme that brought in party activists. 'God willing and Waqar living, I will finish this bloody CSP' (Civil Service of Pakistan) was an oft-quoted Bhutto war cry. 'He nationalized industries, banks and even education, so that Pakistan became unrecognizable from the state that had previously existed.'[64]

The net result of the trajectory that Bhutto put Pakistan on was best articulated by a South Korean vice finance minister. He told a Pakistani diplomat in the 1970s that they had replicated Pakistan's First Five-Year Plan when Pakistan was South Korea's role model on what to do. He added, playfully, that Pakistan was still their model; 'But on what not to do!'[65]

Bhutto and the Army

Bhutto had a hide-and-seek relationship with the army. On many occasions, he deliberately provoked the army. For example, after his arrest in 1967 and knowing that his cell was bugged, he would tell his lawyer Mahmud Ali Kasuri: 'General Musa's days as governor of West Pakistan are numbered. We'll dress him in a skirt and make him dance on the streets like a monkey.' This, according to Tariq Ali, was one of the few insults that were printable.[66]

Bhutto did dismiss the army and air chiefs, Lt Gen. Gul Hassan and Air Marshal Rahim Khan, respectively, but this proved to be, at best, a temporary victory.[67] The army would never forget or forgive the humiliation its chief suffered at the hands of Bhutto. The action scarred the psyche of the army and henceforth he lost the trust of the armed forces that was never regained. The seeds were sown for revenge and Bhutto would pay for this with his life.

After he got rid of Gul Hassan Khan, Bhutto made Gen. Tikka Khan the army chief. Tikka Khan later became the minister of defence. He was described by his cabinet colleague, Kausar Niazi, as a man who 'considered licking the shoes of Mr Bhutto to be the straight path to salvation'.[68] Bhutto would replace Tikka Khan with Gen. Zia who also displayed all the necessary signs of complete obsequiousness.

Bhutto was very critical of Gen. Sher Ali Khan Pataudi, the information minister in Yahya's cabinet. His barbs against Sher Ali provoked a group of retired defence service officers to issue a statement condemning Bhutto for being disrespectful towards his seniors. The statement ended with the unforgettable quip: 'The General was in uniform when Bhutto was only in liquid form!'

(Salman Taseer, *Bhutto: A Political Biography*, New Delhi: Vikash, Publishing House, 1980, p. 109.)

Against the backdrop of the defeat in the 1971 war and after Bhutto came to power, scandals about the nocturnal affairs of generals began to appear regularly in the media. The term 'fat and flabby' became associated with the generals. The common refrain was that the generals had failed the country and had dishonoured the uniform they wore.[69] This was Bhutto's way of denigrating the army and destroying its 'mystique'[70]

The United States

Much has been written about Bhutto's anti-Americanism. However, when he needed something from them, he could be extremely charming.

Bhutto visited Washington DC for the first time as foreign minister in October 1963 when he met with President Kennedy in the White House. A famous exchange took place

> between the two men. As President Kennedy shook his hand before leaving, he remarked, 'If you were an American you would be in my cabinet.' Bhutto was quick to respond, 'Be careful, Mr President, if I were American, I would be in your place.' At this they 'both laughed heartily'.
>
> (Stanley Wolpert, *Zulfi Bhutto of Pakistan: His Life and Times*, New York: OUP, 1993, p. 76.)

Sherbaz Khan Mazari had hosted a dinner in July 1969 in Karachi where both Bhutto and Hank Ramsay, the US consul general, were present. During the conversation, Bhutto told Ramsay (in the presence of the host), that people assumed that he was anti-American. In reality, he wasn't. He insisted that Ramsay should inform his government that 'his statements were simply politics and not his personal views', adding for good measure that his personal views were just the reverse. With the air cleared, Bhutto then made a request for the admission of his daughter Benazir in Radcliffe College as a big favour. When Ramsay inquired about Benazir's school grades, Bhutto looked sheepish and said they were not particularly good. That is why he, as a former foreign minister of Pakistan, wanted this admission as a special favour from the State Department. He implored the consul general, 'Please do ask your people to help me out on this one.' Ramsay promised to speak to his superiors in Washington and convey the request.[71]

A lot of controversy surrounds the supposed threat made by Henry Kissinger that Bhutto would be made a 'horrible example' of, if he continued to pursue the nuclear programme. There are, however, different versions of this story. Bhutto had claimed in his memoir, *If I Am Assassinated* written in his death cell, that Henry Kissinger had warned him, during his visit to Pakistan in August 1976, that unless he desisted on the nuclear question, 'We will make a horrible example out of you.'[72]

An article in the Pakistani financial paper *Business Recorder* cited an unnamed senior Pakistani foreign official (on condition of anonymity) present on the occasion in support of Bhutto's assertion. According to this unnamed official, Kissinger told Bhutto that the US had serious reservations about Pakistan's nuclear programme. Therefore, Bhutto had no choice but to accept what he was saying. Bhutto, however, smiled and asked what if he refused? At this Kissinger became very serious and stated, 'Then we will make a horrible example of you.' Bhutto retorted that Pakistan could live without the US and now the Americans would have to find another ally in the region.[73]

Henry Kissinger told Iqbal Akhund that neither he nor the CIA had anything to do with the Bhutto's overthrow. During the meeting with Bhutto in Lahore in 1976 he had cautioned Bhutto on the nuclear issue that he would find the going far more difficult under a Democratic presidency than under the Republican administration. When Akhund specifically asked about his alleged threat that the new administration would make a 'horrible example' of Bhutto, Kissinger was quite emphatic, 'No, no, that language is much too strong.' Kissinger was of the view that Bhutto had really overthrown himself by calling for early elections. He did so to steal a march on Indira Gandhi who, Bhutto said, was always conceited about India's democracy. Despite this, Akhund felt that a threat or warning had been uttered during the Lahore talks.[74]

Stanley Wolpert, writing about the August 1976 meeting, says that when Bhutto refused to back down, Kissinger diplomatically promised another few hundred thousand tonnes of US wheat for Punjab that had been struck by floods. After the meeting, Bhutto told the press that he was 'satisfied' with his meetings with the Secretary of State. It was only later that Bhutto insisted that Kissinger had 'threatened' to make 'a horrible example out of you'. However, in November 1976, Bhutto wrote to Kissinger after the Democratic victory in the presidential elections: 'The termination of your present high office saddens me. ... I shall always cherish my association with you as a friend with esteem and affection.'[75] However, in a turn-around seven months later, Bhutto told the Canadian ambassador to Pakistan that in their August 1976 meeting Kissinger had warned that 'the prime minister would have to pay a heavy price' if it went ahead with the nuclear programme.[76]

Rafi Raza, a close associate of Bhutto, has strongly argued that no such threat was ever made. The clinching argument is, of course, as Hassan Abbas puts it, that if the US had conspired with Zia to overthrow Bhutto to halt the programme, it would be highly unlikely that Zia, after he seized power, would have continued with the programme, which he certainly did.[77]

One day before the 5 July 1977 coup, American ambassador Arthur W. Hemmil met Bhutto on the intervening night of 3–4 July 1977, around 1a.m. Nobody knows what transpired between the two. However, it is said that the ambassador hinted at a coup. Bhutto, however, rejected this offhand, dismissing it as yet another threat from the American side.[78]

1977 Elections and the PNA Agitation

Under the constitution, the term of the National Assembly was due to expire on 14 August 1977. However, on 7 January 1977 Bhutto announced holding of national elections on 7 March. Bhutto's PPP was expected to win the elections comfortably, though a landslide victory was difficult to predict.

One reason for early elections was a fifty-three-page position paper on the elections prepared by the ISI in October 1976. It recommended early elections and was so full of blatant flattery that it would be embarrassing to any reader. For example, it held that Bhutto's '... leadership proved to be a breath of fresh air in the acrid and suffocating political atmosphere, a dawn of hope in the dark days of economic chaos, a shot in the arm for the revival of the spirit of [the] Pakistan Movement. He has given back the "soul" to the people and gave them direction to follow in the new constitution.'[79]

Bhutto's pre-election campaign included distribution of thousands of little red-cover books clearly modelled on the little red books of Mao Zedong's thoughts. They were titled: 'Bhutto Says: A Pocket-Book of Thoughtful Quotations from Selected Speeches and Writings of Chairman Zulfikar Ali Bhutto'. The book was also translated into Urdu, Sindhi and Pashto. In his 'message', Chief Minister Ghulam Mustafa Jatoi of Sindh wrote: 'His great achievements have brought new life to a half-dead nation.' Even a new postage stamp depicting Bhutto's face was brought out with the message, 'Economic well-being of the people is the real strength of the country.'[80]

Approximately, seventeen million out of thirty-one million eligible voters cast their ballots on 7 March 1977. The PPP got about 60 per cent of the vote and 75 per cent of the National Assembly seats – 155 out of 200. The PNA won 35 per cent of the vote but only 17 per cent of the seats.[81]

> So convinced was Bhutto about his 'unopposed' victory in the 1977 elections that in January 1977, two months before the actual elections, the Ministry of Information 'advised' the Pakistani press to publish his photographs with the caption 'The Supreme Leader, the Undisputed Leader, the Great Leader.'
>
> (Sultan M. Khan *Memories and Reflections of a Pakistani Diplomat*, London: The Centre for Pakistan Studies, 1997, p. 457.)

Bhutto was determined to win a two-thirds majority,[82] quite possibly to amend the constitution. To fulfil this ambition, the elections were rigged. In fact, they started to go awry from the outset. It began with Bhutto determined to be elected unopposed from his constituency, NA 163–Larkana 1. The opposition PNA, however, was averse to give him a walkover. They nominated Jan

Mohammad Abbasi, Naib Amir, Jamaat-i-Islami (JI), Sindh, to contest against him. Abbasi resisted official pressure not to file his nomination papers. Consequently, DSP, Larkana, kidnapped him on 17 January 1977 and kept him in wrongful confinement till the time for filing nominations was over. He was released on the evening of 19 January after Bhutto had been declared elected unopposed.[83]

Kausar Niazi confirms that the elections had been rigged. According to him, two days after the Pakistan National Alliance (PNA) had rejected the election result and launched its agitation, Bhutto asked Hafiz Pirzada how many seats were rigged. The reply was around thirty to forty. Bhutto then asked if it would be possible to ask the PNA to have their candidates elected with an assurance that the PPP would not contest them.[84]

Bhutto's catchy slogan of *Roti, Kapda aur Makan* was countered by the religious parties with their own slogan: '*Socialism Kufr hai. Muslim millat ek ho*' (Socialism is a heresy. Let's us unify the Muslim people).

(Christophe Jaffrelot, *The Pakistan Paradox: Instability and Resilience*, Delhi: Random House, 2015, p. 217.)

***

Some tactics of the PNA were quite dubious. For example, the head of the JI told one rally in a rural area that a vote against the party was a vote against God. A vote for the Pakistan National Alliance (PNA) was equal to 100,000 years of prayer.

(Benazir Bhutto, *Daughter of the East*, London: Hamish Hamilton, 1988, p. 72.)

It was the shared antipathy of the smaller political parties towards Bhutto that brought them together in an alliance called the PNA. On 16 January 1977, Maulana Mufti Mahmood was elected PNA president. The speed with which the alliance was formed perplexed Bhutto because his intelligence agencies had briefed him that such a possibility was remote. What the alliance implied was that opposition votes would not get split. The rigged elections became the glue that kept them together. However, the fact that the PNA itself was a divided house, both politically and on sectarian lines, was very much in evidence on the first day of their detention after Zia's coup. When Mufti Mahmood got up to lead the maghrib prayers, several other detained leaders lined up behind him. However, Maulana Shah Ahmed Noorani announced that he could not pray behind a Deobandi and went elsewhere to pray. Asghar Khan opted to follow Noorani, the Barelvi maulana.[85]

During their agitation, the PNA announced a long march to Islamabad from different parts of the country. This alarmed Bhutto so much that he had a large contingent of the Sindh police airlifted to Islamabad on an emergency basis instead of depending on the Punjab police that protected his official residence. The contingent of the Sindh police stayed in the city for a while but was not called upon to act.[86]

The envoys of the countries in the Middle East played an important role in trying to defuse the PNA agitation. The Saudi ambassador Sheikh Riaz Al-Khateeb even acted as a mediator between the two sides. He met the detained PNA leaders in the Sihala rest house that had been converted into a temporary jail, and the PNA leader Mufti Mahmood in the Combined Military Hospital on several occasions, as well as Prime Minister Bhutto. Others who played an active part by visiting both sides and conveying messages from their leadership for negotiations were the foreign minister of the United Arab Emirates, Ahmed Khalifa Alswedi, Libya's foreign minister, Ali Abdussalam Al Tariqi, foreign minister of Kuwait, Sheikh Sabah Al-Ahmed Jabar Al-Sabah, foreign minister of Iran Hoshang Ansari and special envoy of the PLO chairman Yasser Arafat, Hani Al-Hassan.[87]

Bhutto was so desperate to quell the PNA agitation that at one stage he even tried to fool them by raising an external threat. He directed DG ISI, Maj. Gen. Ghulam Jilani Khan to brief Mufti Mahmood, the PNA leader, with the help of charts and maps on the alleged foreign threat. In his briefing, Jilani explained to Mahmood that an abrupt grave situation had 'developed'. Elements of this threat were that Sardar Daoud, the President of Afghanistan had concentrated troops on the border at Torkhum and Darra and was preparing to attack; India too was preparing for a massive attack near Lahore. Even the Iranians were amassing their army at Zahedan. Based on this imaginary threat scenario, Bhutto appealed to Mufti Mahmood that for the sake of national security the PNA should show its patriotism and come to an agreement with the government. Mufti Mahmood, however, saw through the game and insisted on fresh elections.[88]

Karachi was especially disturbed during the PNA agitation. Despite the curfew, a ghastly incident took place in Pathan Colony when an enraged crowd set fire to the house of Habibur Rehman, president of the PPP's ward committee. In the fire, fourteen occupants were burnt alive.[89] In another Karachi neighbourhood, a PNA candidate sprayed a poster of Bhutto with automatic gunfire that killed a young child who was standing by.[90]

An interesting sidelight of the PNA agitation was that a special contingent of lady police was drafted to deal with the PNA lady workers. This force consisted of ladies of the night from Lahore and the PNA gave it the name of '*Nath* Force' (*Nath* is the nose-ring worn by women).

(Faiz Ali Chishti, *Betrayals of Another Kind*, Delhi: Tricolour Books, 1989, p. 44.)

In a speech in the National Assembly on 28 April 1977, Bhutto alleged that the PNA agitation was an international conspiracy. As evidence, he cited that a lot of foreign currency was available in the country and a dollar was available for less than six or seven rupees. 'Money is being showered on the people to sound the azan from mosques; they are being paid to go to jails. This is not a conspiracy hatched by the PNA but it is an international conspiracy – the blood hounds are after me.' According to him, the PNA leaders did not have the intelligence or the capability to raise the agitation to this level. It was all the doing of international manoeuvring.[91]

> During the PNA agitation, every time Mark Tully the BBC correspondent came on air, it would send a cheer through the audience, particularly when he gave details of the PNA demonstrations. He was nicknamed *Mar Talli'* (ring the bell) [sic].
>
> (Gohar Ayub Khan, *Glimpses into the Corridors of Power*, Karachi, OUP, 2007, p. 175.)

Bhutto's Execution

Nawab Mohammad Ahmed Khan, the father of Ahmed Raza Kasuri, then a member of parliament, was shot dead by unknown assailants at Shadman Chowk, Lahore, while returning home after a wedding ceremony in October 1974.[92] Raza Kasuri, one of Bhutto's outspoken critics, escaped. The FIR of the case was registered on 11 November 1974 and included the name of Zulfikar Ali Bhutto as the main accused. Initially, nothing was done in the case. After Zia's coup, Kasuri's widow appealed to the martial law government for justice. Ahmed Raza Kasuri requested the Lahore High Court to hear the case. It was when the director general of the Federal Security Force, Masood Mahmood, turned approver that the case took a serious turn. On 3 September 1977, Bhutto was arrested on murder charges at Karachi. The court proceedings began on 11 October 1977. Bhutto did not present any witness. He boycotted the proceedings from 9 January 1978 and refused to engage any counsel.

Ironically, Bhutto had brought on the statute book a law that banned foreign counsels from taking part in the proceedings of Pakistani courts. Quite possibly, this was done to protect illegal detentions under his regime. However, as a result several prominent foreign lawyers, including the French law minister, Robert Badinter, who was a friend of Bhutto's, were unable to appear on his behalf in the case.[93]

On 18 March 1978, the five-judge bench of Lahore High Court headed by Justice Maulvi Mushtaq Hussain sentenced Bhutto and four others to death. They had been charged with murder, attempted murder and conspiracy to murder Nawab Mohammad Ahmed Khan Kasuri. The Supreme Court upheld the sentence on 2 February 1979 by a split verdict of 4:3. The three judges who did not uphold the high court verdict were one each from Sindh, the NWFP (now KPK) and Balochistan while the four who did were from Punjab. All the five justices of the Lahore High Court who had given the verdict were from Punjab. The element of provincialism was evident in the verdicts.

Once, in his arrogance, Bhutto told the then chief editor of *Dawn*, 'You must know that courts do not figure in my book.' Ironically, it were the courts that sent him to the gallows.

(Altaf Gauhar, *Ayub Khan: Pakistan's First Military Ruler*, Karachi: OUP, 1996, p. xxvi.)

In the last week of March 1979, the mother of Abida Hussain asked Gen. (Retd) Jehanzeb Arbab what Zia was going to do with Bhutto's mercy petition. She hoped that he would grant clemency. Gen. Jehanzeb, however, told her that Zia would reject all appeals for mercy. The reason was that Zia had sent a message to Nusrat Bhutto through Jehanzeb that if she and Benazir left the country, he would spare Bhutto's life and confine him in some rest house. Nusrat, however, had refused saying she could not trust Zia to keep his word. Gen. Jehanzeb concluded, 'I know Zia well enough to know that he will now get the verdict of the court implemented.'[94]

Strangely, on the day Bhutto's death sentence was announced, one of his poodles died suddenly. Perfectly fine one minute, he was dead in the next. The next day the female poodle died, again for no seeming reason. Benazir's Siamese cat died too, on the third day. According to Benazir, some Muslims believed that animals sometimes deflected danger to the master of the house by dying in his stead.[95]

Bhutto was hanged on 4 April 1979. As per the official press note, 'The funeral in Larkana was attended by relatives, including his two uncles, Nawab Nabi Baksh Bhutto and Sardar Pir Baksh Bhutto, his first wife Sherin Amir Begum, friends and residents of the area.'[96]

According to Bhutto's sister Munawwar Begum, NAP leader Wali Khan had warned Bhutto when he was at the height of his power that if he went on as he was doing, 'You won't return to Larkana on your two feet.'

(Iqbal Akhund, *Memoirs of a Bystander: A Life in Diplomacy*, Karachi: OUP, 1997, p. 342.)

***

In fact, Sir James Morrice, British high commissioner to Pakistan (1962–65) and high commissioner to India (1968–71) wrote with uncanny prescience when, in an assessment of Bhutto he sent to London, he said, 'It seems to me that he was born to be hanged.'

(Roedad Khan, *The British Papers, Documents 1958-1969*, Karachi: OUP, 2002, p. xvii.)

According to Murtaza Bhutto, Bhutto's elder son. 'ZAB was never hanged. We saw the marks on his body, his face was like that of a young child. The eyes hadn't bulged, the lips had not turned purple. The back of the skull had been cracked by a pistol butt.'[97] An army officer who was present at the hanging, Col Rafi-ud-Din, revealed in his Urdu book, 'Bhutto's Last 323 Days': 'A photographer, who had been sent by an intelligence agency, took some photographs of Mr Bhutto's private parts because the authorities wanted to confirm if he had been circumcised in the Islamic manner. After the photographs were taken, it was confirmed that he was circumcised in the Islamic manner.'

'No dignity permitted, not even in death,' was Benazir's comment.[98]

The legacy of Bhutto's term continues to remain indelibly imprinted in Pakistan's body politic. Undoubtedly, he was the most popular and effective leader that Pakistan has seen till date. However, it is equally true that due to his arrogance and inability to tolerate dissent, he turned Pakistan from a fledgling democracy into a personal fiefdom where the rule of law was the greatest sufferer. In the process, he earned the hatred of a section of the population. As a result, his execution polarized the country and left a deep scar across the collective memory of the nation. For his followers, Bhutto would always be the 'shaheed', martyr; for his opponents and those at the receiving end of his brutality, 'Bhutto had to be pursued even after his death, in the vilification and persecution of the daughter.'[99]

6

Zia-ul-Haq: A Chess Player in a Nation of Cricketers

Early Life and Personality

ZIA WAS BORN IN 1924, the son of a clerical officer in the army from Jalandhar, in what later became part of Indian Punjab. Zia's early education completed, his father put together the resources to get his son admitted to St Stephen's College, Delhi. In later years, Zia would warmly recall his stay there.[1]

By most accounts, Zia was not very intellectually inclined and many speculated about where he had obtained his knowledge of international affairs. In fact, Maj. Gen. Fazal-e-Haq, commanding 7 Infantry Division told Gohar Ayub Khan, 'Gen. Zia-ul-Haq is not very bright. If you have to make a point, say it slowly and never repeat less than three times.'[2] In May 1988 the mystery was resolved when Zia confessed that he had been addicted to *Reader's Digest* for the last forty years. Apparently, one of his former commanding officers had advised Zia to read it to develop his intellectual and literary capabilities. Zia faithfully followed the advice. Writes Mazhar Ali Khan: 'Perhaps it was understandable that, as a young subaltern, *Reader's Digest* was chosen as digestible reading material; but since he was promoted to, or acquired, higher office it would have been good for the General, and for everyone else, if he had improved on his sources for knowledge and style.'[3]

Perhaps the best description of his personality was that Zia was a shrewd tactician, 'a chess-player in a nation of cricketers'.[4] Others too have held him to be a tactician and a strategist. He remained unruffled under fire and was seldom provoked to anger, except when he chose to do so as a tactic. Several rivals became victims because they did not realize he was the master of the saying 'don't get mad, get even'.[5]

There was a marked change in Zia's personality and appearance after he staged the coup to topple Bhutto. For example, in 1976, when Roedad Khan saw Zia for the first time at the Islamabad Club at a wedding, he looked very ordinary—physically at least. There was a marked contrast with his two predecessors, Ayub and Yahya. However, when he addressed the secretaries on 6 July 1977, a day after the coup, 'Zia was not the man I had seen earlier at the Islamabad Club. He was now impressively clad in the dashing cavalry uniform; with his jet-black hair, eyebrows and moustache, and his steely eyes, he radiated strength and self-confidence and appeared to be in total command.'[6] During the meeting, he outlined his views on the functioning of the government, its inadequacies, etc. He was particularly critical of the Ministry of Religious Affairs and Haj Arrangements. This was a clear signal of what his priorities were going to be.[7]

Finally, when Zia entered the cabinet room for the first cabinet meeting after Bhutto had been executed, Roedad Khan remembered 'how he stalked forward, in total command. On that day, the realization came to all present that, with no one left to challenge his authority, Zia was going to be around for a long time.'[8]

Zia allowed himself to be underestimated, perhaps deliberately, by everyone, leading to recurrent miscalculations about him. His style was always that of an 'unambitious soldier'. He used to listen attentively and, as a habit, he always said 'Good idea' to any suggestion, never saying 'No', even giving the impression that he agreed, but then he would do exactly what he wanted to do.[9] Another ploy would be to walk his guests to the door, shake their hands warmly, see them into their car and give his farewell smile and bow as the guests were driven away.[10]

Zia had several peculiar traits for an army officer. For one, he was hopeless at following schedules or keeping appointments. At times, he frustrated his staff by forgetting appointments set up days earlier.[11] For another, he was late to bed and late to rise. Throughout his military career Zia struggled to commence his day early in the morning.[12]

Another peculiarity was his dislike for staff work, though he revelled in command assignments. He avoided reading pages of files and approving orders on the cases submitted to him. Worse, he was lazy about writing the annual confidential reports (ACRs) of officers and was invariably late in completing them. For example, the military secretary, Lt Gen. Faiz Ali Chishti, while preparing the papers for a selection board found that the annual reports of officers serving under Gen. Zia had not been received; in some cases, they were overdue by two years.[13] When it used to be pointed out to him that the absence of the ACRs would adversely affect the promotion and career planning of the officers, Zia would put his right hand on his chest and remark, 'I will personally protect their interests in the army selection boards.' However, due to his sudden death in an air crash, he left behind dozens of incomplete ACRs that required his remarks.[14] Some of these had not been endorsed for years. Consequently, the careers of affected officers suffered since he was not alive to protect their legitimate interests in the army selection boards.

Due to Zia's dislike for file work, official mail used to accumulate in his study 'for days, weeks, months and in some cases for years'. Rather than dispose of his mail periodically, Zia used an unconventional technique of getting his office room extended to make place for the new files. His office room was so extended twice but even then the files were piled up on the floor. There was just enough space for one person to move around trying to find the file which needed immediate attention. To make matters worse, Zia loathed anyone disturbing the files in his office. Consequently, the office, according to Gen. Arif, 'resembled a junkyard rather than the office of the president of a country'.[15]

Despite his idiosyncrasy about file work, Zia insisted that his staff prepare neat and error-free drafts for his signatures. Typos and spelling mistakes annoyed him. He would sarcastically admonish his lower staff: 'Isn't there a dictionary in your office?', or 'It helps to be awake while typing,' or 'Perhaps you need a proofreader?'[16]

Zia and his wife Shafiqa Zia Begum, whose favourite Indian film star was Nargis,[17] had five children—two sons and three daughters. The youngest daughter, Zain Zia, was a 'special child'. Zia could not say no to her demands. On one occasion, she wanted to be decorated in an investiture ceremony at a function held at the presidency. Accordingly, immediately after the formal closure of the official investiture ceremony, Zain Zia walked up smartly to the dais and received a fake decoration from her father.[18] A doting Zia would even let her dress up in the uniform of a colonel or general and take her along on formal occasions, reception of dignitaries and inspection of guard of honour.[19]

Abida Hussain provides an interesting insight about Zia's wife Begum Shafiqa Zia-ul-Haq. Once Begum Shafiqa asked Abida Hussain about the fidelity of her husband, Fakhar Iman, asking if she was not concerned about leaving her husband alone, especially in Multan because 'Multani women are very dangerous'. To this, Abida replied that if her husband was going to desire another woman over her, 'then to hell with him'. Shafiqa nodded in agreement saying that when the army wives told her not to let Zia travel alone, she said the same thing. 'If my man is stupid enough to prefer a woman over the mother of his children, then it will be his loss and he will come to regret it and, like you I also say, then to hell with him.'[20]

At a press conference in Karachi, a journalist drew Zia's attention to a critical comment made by India's prime minister Rajiv Gandhi. Zia smiled and said,'There are only two options on all such occasions. Rajiv and I should either chase each other with a broomstick or ignore it. It is pointless to follow the first course and I choose the second option,' much to the amusement of the assembled gathering.

(V.T. Joshi, *Pakistan: Zia to Benazir*, New Delhi: Konark Publishers Pvt. Ltd, 1995, p. 92.)

***

Zia developed a fancy, if not an obsession for bathrooms and toilets. He would not share them with anybody. He made sure there was one exclusively for his own use wherever he was likely to stay.

(Faiz Ali Chishti, *Betrayals of Another Kind*, Delhi: Tricolour Books, 1989, p. 108.)

Zia had lost two front teeth while playing cycle polo. He wore a denture after this incident. For a while he got into the habit of removing his dentures and adjusting them again with his tongue. This was quite unpleasant for his audience. Fortunately, in the later stage of his life he got out of this habit.[21]

Army Career

Zia completed his basic military training in the Officers Training School, Mhow, and was commissioned into the Indian Army on 12 May 1945. He was posted to 13 Lancers, then serving in Burma during the Second World War. He saw action in Burma, Malaya and Indonesia. He opted for Pakistan at the time of Partition.[22]

Once, on the occasion of Eid, young Zia went to the JCOs mess of his unit wearing shalwar-kameez. The British commanding officer regarded this as unacceptable, 'un-officer-like misconduct'. As punishment, he was posted to 6 Lancers, which took him to Java and Malaya. Quite possibly, this embarrassment made him insist later in life that government officials wear the national dress for work and official functions.[23]

In September 1950 Zia joined the Guides Cavalry where he stayed for a decade. He went to the US for advanced training. He had been promoted to the rank of lieutenant colonel when the 1965 war with India broke out. He commanded a tank regiment, 22 Cavalry, during the war. Promoted to brigadier in May 1969, Zia commanded 9 Armoured Brigade in Kharian and later he commanded the 1 Armoured Division (1972–75) and subsequently a corps.

Zia did a stint in Jordan, thanks to Lt Gen. Gul Hassan Khan. Zia had been detailed to attend the 1970 war course at Quetta. Due to his dislike for staff work, Zia got cold feet and through one Col Pir A. Shah approached Gul Hassan. Gul, under whom Zia had served, requested Gen. Yahya Khan to change the assignment. Yahya, though reluctant initially, agreed to do so after some urging. He asked Gul if Zia would like to go to Jordan. Gul's reply was that Zia 'would be prepared to go to hell as long as he did not have to go for the war course'.[24]

In Jordan, Zia developed excellent relations with the king. However, he ran afoul of his commanding officer Nawazish Ali

Khan and got a confidential report stating, 'he is not fit to be an officer in the Pakistan Army'. Luckily for Zia, his stars were strong and favourable. On Gul's intervention, Yahya Khan quashed the report.[25]

Zia headed the military court that tried those accused in the 1973 Attock Conspiracy Case, so called because the trial was conducted at Attock Fort. It was an attempted military coup against Bhutto and senior army generals organized by a group of middle-ranking army and air force officers headed by Brig. F.B. Ali and Col Aleem Afridi. The conspiracy was detected and the officers court-martialled. For Zia, the trial opened a direct channel to Bhutto for he wanted regular briefings on it. Bhutto was grateful to Zia for keeping him posted about the trial's progress and the conviction of those involved.[26]

Towards the end of the trial came the time for the officers to make statements in their own defence. According to F.B. Ali, Major Saeed Akhtar Malik in his address to the Attock court martial movingly expressed the feelings of the young officers who had taken such a drastic step. His speech brought tears to the eyes of many present in the court. It was a damning indictment of the army high command. He said:

> When the war became imminent, I took leave from the PMA [Pakistan Military Academy] and joined my unit. The next day the war started. But instead of glory, I found only disillusionment. The truth was that we were a defeated army even before a shot was fired. This was a very bitter truth. With each corpse that I saw, my revulsion increased for the men who had signed the death warrants of so many very fine men. Yes, fine men but poor soldiers, who were never given the chance to fight back, because they were not trained to fight back. When they should have been training for war, they were performing the role of labourers, farmers or herdsmen, anything but the role of soldiers. This

> was not shahadat[martyrdom]. This was cold-blooded murder. Who was responsible for this? I was responsible! But more than me someone else was responsible. People who get paid more than me were responsible. What were some of these men, these callous, inhuman degenerates, doing when their only job was to prepare this army for war? Were these men not grabbing lands and building houses? Did it not appear in foreign magazines that some of them were pimping for their bloated grandmaster? Yes, generals, wearing that uniform (he pointed at the court's president) pimping and whore mongering.[27]

On his first day in office, Zia gifted wristwatches to the soldiers constituting the guard of honour that he had inspected in GHQ calling it a goodwill gesture. Thereafter, as COAS, whenever he went out on a visit, he would ask the accompanying personal staff to take some currency notes in sealed envelopes and gifts like shirts or suit lengths, wristwatches, etc., for the personnel of the unit to be visited. After inspecting different establishments, he would ask the personal staff to distribute the gifts to the other ranks and non-commissioned officers responsible for the maintenance of the unit.[28]

Zia's attitude towards selection boards is revealed in the case of the promotion of an officer to the rank of general. The officer was from the armoured corps who, in normal course, should not have reached beyond the rank of a lieutenant colonel. Zia, however, had helped him to become a brigadier. When he was being considered for promotion to a general, Zia saw his dossier and remarked: 'How life passes. It seems only yesterday when this officer's daughter was just a little girl, and only last week I attended her wedding. Next!'[29] On the basis that life passes so quickly, the brigadier was promoted to major general. Under Zia's watch, Maj. Gen. Akhtar Abdul Rehman became a four-star general without ever commanding a corps, while Maj. Gen. Arif was promoted to the rank of a four-star general without the command of either a division or a corps.[30]

While Zia's long-term legacy in Afghanistan is disputed, a big blot was clearly Siachen. His dismissive reply to a question about Siachen being 'just a pile of rocks where not even a blade of grass can grow' was, in fact, trying to brazen out a military failure. It was left to his successor as army chief, Gen. Aslam Beg, to admit that due to Indian occupation of Siachen, Pakistan had lost 70 km of common border with China and three important passes to the Saltoro glacier region.[31]

How Zia Became Army Chief

Zia managed to ingratiate himself with Bhutto in several ways before Gen. Tikka Khan's successor as army chief had to be selected. On one occasion, when Bhutto was on a political tour in Multan (where Zia was the GOC), Zia went without an appointment to the prime minister's camp. Bhutto, however, had a demanding schedule and did not want to see Zia. However, Zia was not one to give up easily. He waited in the military secretary's room to take his chance. After a long wait and due to several requests of the embarrassed military secretary, Bhutto finally saw Zia. All Zia said was that he had come to personally present to the prime minister a copy of the Holy Koran and to swear loyalty to him upon it.[32] The megalomaniac that he was, Bhutto would no doubt have loved this abject submissiveness.

On another occasion, when Bhutto was visiting the strike corps in Multan, Zia got the wives and children of the garrison to line up along the road and shower flower petals on Bhutto's motorcade. Later, during a meeting of garrison officers, a junior officer questioned Zia about the justification of Bhutto's route being lined by the military families. Not surprisingly, the officer found his military career running into rough weather.[33]

During another Multan visit, Bhutto met with his inner party circle in the conference room of an army mess. Zia, duly attired in full army regalia, waited outside. When Bhutto queried about what he was doing there, Zia said it was his duty to personally guard the leader.[34]

In early 1974, in his role as the colonel commandant of the armoured corps, Zia installed Bhutto as the colonel-in-chief of that corps. Such an honour was normally given to senior officers holding the rank of general. In the Pakistan Army, though, this was not the first occasion such an appointment was made, but it was unprecedented because a civilian with no association with the armoured corps was so honoured. Zia even tried to persuade Bhutto to don the uniform of the colonel-in-chief to be worn at a military parade.[35]

The ceremony to install Bhutto as the colonel-in-chief was held at the Kharian cantonment where 6 Armoured Division was located. According to Gul Hassan, to baptize Bhutto into the corps, he was taken to the tank firing ranges to fire the main gun of a tank. The target was a cluster of barrels filled with petrol that would go up in flames when hit and make Bhutto feel good about himself. The gun had been laid on target earlier and all Bhutto had to do was press the trigger. Despite this, as a standby precaution an officer sat in a trench near the target to ignite a small charge under it, should the newly installed colonel-in-chief happen to miss. The whole show was 'meticulously contrived and executed with rare precision. Acres of ground all around the tank were soaked with oil, to ensure that no dust was raised by the blast of the gun.'[36]

Did the Americans have an inkling about Zia becoming the chief? According to Kausar Niazi, six months before Gen. Tikka Khan was to retire as army chief, one Col Ballatay was posted as military attache in the US embassy in Islamabad. One day while playing golf, Col Ballatay told an air force officer in Peshawar: 'Your next chief of the army staff will be Gen. Zia-ul-Haq.' The air force officer repeated this to the air chief, Air Marshal Zulfiqar Khan who just laughed it off. Those days the top three names floating around for the post were Gen. Shariff, Gen. Majid Malik and Gen. Izzat Buksh Awan. Col Ballatay retired from service during Zia's tenure. Later, when he returned to Pakistan in 1985 on a private visit, Zia hosted a party for him at President's House.[37]

Tikka Khan completed his tenure as army chief in February 1976. As his successor, he recommended Muhammad Akbar Khan who, like himself, was thoroughly loyal to Bhutto and implemented orders with no hesitation. Tikka's second choice was the senior-most lieutenant general, Muhammad Shariff. Bhutto appointed Shariff to the newly created post of chairman, Joint Chiefs of Staff Committee. For army chief, however, he reached past six senior lieutenant generals to select the junior-most: Mohammad Zia-ul-Haq, then fifty-two. According to Wolpert, the 'pen picture' of Gen. Zia sent to the prime minister by his private secretary was of 'a capable officer who owes a lot to Gen. Gul Hassan ... ambitious ... quiet and watchful... A clever and reasonably good professional ... Doubtful reliability'.[38]

Bhutto wanted an army chief who had unquestioning loyalty to the prime minister and Zia had undoubtedly demonstrated the same through his servility. Bhutto even confided to Princess Ashraf Pahlavi, the elder sister of the Shah of Iran, who was on a visit to Pakistan, that Zia 'is in my pocket'. Writes Gen. K.M. Arif, 'Bhutto, like most other politicians and analysts in Pakistan, greatly underestimated the shrewdness and the political acumen of Zia.'[39]

Interestingly, when Zia took over as COAS in 1976, even other officers in the army knew very little about him. He was seen as a rather ordinary personality, and he never quite became popular or much respected either in the ranks or among the officers. In the country, he was virtually unknown.[40]

Benazir met Zia for the first time on 5 January 1977 at a dinner hosted by Bhutto at their residence, Al Murtaza, in Sukkur. She noted in her autobiography that Zia was reported to be a petty thief. She was astonished to see him because unlike the childish image she carried of a soldier as tall and rugged ... 'the General standing before me was a short, nervous, ineffectual-looking man whose pomaded hair was parted in the middle ... He looked more like an English cartoon villain than an inspiring military leader.' Zia also came across as being obsequious, repeating to her how honoured he was 'to meet the daughter of such a great man as Bhutto'. She felt her father could have found a more commanding chief-of-staff.[41] Later Benazir would call him 'Zia-ul-Muck' or 'Cobra Eyes'[42] and spoke of him as 'the devil'.[43]

Zia and Bhutto

Bhutto could never read Zia and instead felt a sense of superiority by humiliating him and making him the object of public derision. For example, Bhutto often would shout at him from the head of the dinner table: 'Where is my monkey general? Come over here, Monkey!' He would make a play of pulling Zia on an invisible string, introduce him to a foreign dignitary and dismiss him, even before the ever-smiling Zia had finished bowing. Sometimes Bhutto poked fun at Zia's 'funny' teeth. Zia apparently did not take offence at such humiliations, treating them as 'jokes', and smiling, would thank his prime minister for 'your such kind attentions, Sir!'[44]

Bhutto could not fathom whom he had appointed as army chief until it was too late. 'Like Bhutto, Zia forgot no insult, no social slight, no attack on his izzat, no challenge to his faith, his God or himself,' writes Wolpert. However, given his modest background, Zia had learnt to be cautious and patient.[45]

Though he often humiliated Zia, Bhutto allowed Zia's entire family to go abroad (all expenses paid by the state) for the treatment of Zia's 'special' child. In fact, when Zia launched his coup, his family was still in the US, thanks to Bhutto's personal kindness.[46]

During the early days of the Pakistan National Alliance (PNA) agitation, Zia defended the Bhutto government. From March to July 1977, military force was used to quell the political agitation. This, however, put the army under great strain. The troops were uncomfortable at the thought of using force against their own countrymen, especially in Punjab. This became obvious when they fired their weapons in the air instead of at the anti-Bhutto agitators. For example, in Multan, forty-two bullets were fired from twenty-five yards away but only two people were hit. Forty-three bullets were fired in Anarkali, Lahore, and again only two people were hit. Where did the rest of the bullets go? It was obvious that the orders to shoot were being subverted by making them ineffective. The ominous implication was breakdown of army discipline and cracks in the army.[47]

In fact, Zia cautioned Bhutto at the height of the PNA agitation: 'If the agitation does not end, it can erode the army's discipline and cause divisions within the ranks.'[48] The situation became precarious when three brigadiers, Niaz Ahmed, Ashraf and Ishtiaq Ali Khan, employed on martial law duties in Lahore had to be relieved of command for refusing to order firing on the PNA demonstrators.[49] These incidents undoubtedly created great unease in the top ranks of the army and would have been a factor in Zia's coup.

On 27 April, chairman, Joint Chiefs of Staff Committee and the three chiefs issued a joint declaration pledging loyalty to the government. Zia held that he had never issued or agreed with any such declaration. It appears that it was Gen. Tikka Khan who, on Bhutto's directives, prepared and issued the declaration to the press as if the chiefs had issued it. However, the chiefs did not object to it.[50]

In August 1977, a month after the coup, Zia was in Multan addressing army officers. He was asked a question about Bhutto who then was not under arrest on murder charges. Zia responded with a smile and pointing at two of his staff officers, Brig. Mian

Afzal and Brig. Ilyas said: 'Why should I kill Afzal myself when I can make Ilyas do it.'[51]

By January 1979, Zia felt confident enough to tell an envoys' conference in Islamabad that also included a number of other high civil and military officials that he could have done away with 'the Bhutto problem' on the very first day of the military takeover. However, he decided to let the law take its course. 'As if the significance of this statement was not clear enough, the General went on to make a slip of the tongue."When we engineered the case, er ... I mean when we instituted the case against Mr Bhutto ..."' He then went on to say that anyway it was a case based on a private complaint and apart from necessary assistance in investigation and prosecution, the government was not involved.[52] However, the point had been made.

There is some controversy about the summary regarding Bhutto's mercy petition. According to Roedad Khan, the joint secretary (law), Irshad Khan, and the chief of staff (COS) Gen. Arif took the summary to Zia. According to Irshad, Zia rejected the mercy petition without even reading it. Arif, on the other hand, says that the president read it carefully. In any case, Zia returned the file with the fateful remarks: 'petition is rejected'.[53]

Did Zia have a choice in rejecting the mercy petition or accepting it? According to K.M. Arif, exercising caution, Zia did consult with the military brass in deciding Bhutto's fate and discussed all the options. The 'entire military team, except for one single voice, supported his decision. This lone general officer backed the punishment awarded but recommended the final decision being left for the next government to take.'[54]

Zia had made his intentions quite clear in an interview with Gavin Young of the *Observer*, London, on 1 October 1978. He said, 'If the Supreme Court says, "Acquit him", I will acquit him. If it says, "Hang the blighter", I will hang him.'[55]

Several persons also advised Zia that if he let Bhutto loose, his own days would be numbered. According to Roedad Khan, on one occasion, Zia told him, 'Roedad Sahib, it is his neck or mine.'[56] Wali Khan conveyed to Zia on 12 December 1977, 'Bhutto is a viper,' adding, 'He will bite you hard if you do not crush his head.' A little later he told Zia, 'There are two corpses and a solitary grave. If the Bhutto body is not buried first, you may be the one to lead the way.'[57]

Bhutto was hanged on 4 April 1979. However, according to Mushahid Hussain, since then, like Macbeth, Zia seemed to have been spooked by 'Banquo's ghost'. Zia had visited the Pakistan consulate general in New York in October 1980 during his visit to the US to address the UN General Assembly. In the consulate library, he casually opened a book and a photograph of Bhutto stared Zia in the face. Impulsively, Zia threw the book and shouted, 'Don't you have better books,' and irritably walked out of the library.[58]

The difference between Bhutto and Zia was described thus by an observer: 'Bhutto "took the decency out of politics"; humiliated and harassed his opponents; and very often even his own recalcitrant supporters became victims of his vindictiveness. On the other hand, Zia's unfailing courtesy, the now famous "double handshake and triple embrace", his broad smile and (perhaps a put on) self-effacing humility seldom failed to impress his visitors and won over many of his erstwhile opponents.'[59]

Zia's Coup

On the morning of 25 June 1977, Bhutto had called a meeting of the army chief, the corps commanders and some of his close cabinet colleagues. It was during this meeting that Gen. Tikka Khan came up with the suggestion that Zia would quote frequently. Tikka said, 'Sir, I say we should just knock out five to six thousand of their men ... that will cool them off.' According to Zia, it was then that the idea of getting rid of the Bhutto government came to his mind as he felt that it was bent upon bloodshed.[60]

On the intervening night of 4–5 July 1977, Zia launched Operation Fairplay, the code name for the coup. Bhutto and his ministers were arrested and martial law was imposed. Zia became the chief martial law administrator—CMLA—an acronym that would soon be lampooned as Cancel My Last Address, in view of Zia frequently going back on his promise to hold elections.[61] The 1973 Constitution was suspended, not abrogated, a tactic to avoid being charged for high treason, the punishment for which was the death penalty or life imprisonment. By about 3 a.m., all the relevant political leaders had been arrested. Thereafter, Zia spoke to Bhutto on the telephone and informed him about the developments. Bhutto was told that he would be escorted to Murree at seven in the morning.

Zia used to affectionately call Gen. Faiz Ali Chisti *murshid* (mentor, guide). Before Chisti left to implement 'Operation Fairplay' Zia uttered these memorable words: '*Murshid mujhe mat marwa dena*' (*Murshid* don't get me killed.)

(Jamsheed Marker, *Cover Point: Impressions of Leadership in Pakistan*, Karachi: OUP, 2016, p. 126.)

After speaking to Bhutto, Zia woke up the chairman of the Joint Chiefs of Staff Committee, Gen. Shariff, and told him: 'Sir, I've done it!' 'Done what?' asked the annoyed Shariff.' 'Removed Bhutto', replied Zia. 'Why are you calling me now?' questioned Shariff. Zia told him that he (Shariff) had experience with Ayub Khan and would be able to advise on the next steps to be taken to put martial law into effect. Shariff banged the phone on him.[62]

Reactions on Bhutto being arrested were revealing. Rao Abdul Rashid, a retired police officer asked, 'Which army has taken over?' Ghulam Mustafa Khar questioned, 'What about Abdul Hafiz Pirzada and Mumtaz Bhutto?' When told they had already been arrested, he took a deep breath and said: 'Thank God, the devils have reached their destiny. I do not mind if you people even kill me now.'[63]

The Los Angeles Times aptly summed up the coup: 'It was not so much the ambitions of the generals as it was the quarrelsome blundering of the politicians that led to this week's restoration of military rule in Pakistan.'[64]

Politics

Zia's political acumen that remained latent throughout most of his career, started surfacing occasionally after he became a major general.[65] After the coup, he came into his own and as a master survivor, demonstrated an amazing ability to manipulate his opponents. A deft tactician and handler of political crises, with 'an instinctive understanding of the political dynamics of the country,' Zia would become Pakistan's longest serving military ruler.[66]

That Zia was unpopular, especially during the Movement for the Restoration of Democracy (MRD) in Sindh, was well known. One example of this was when Zia visited Dadu in Sindh. His motorcade drove through a ghost town with the shops being closed. Several protestors threw stones and waved their fists at him. However, what stole the show was that hundreds of stray dogs were released on the streets with the slogan 'Zia is a dog', reminiscent of the agitation against Ayub. Unfortunately, the local martial law authorities were not amused and shot the poor dogs dead.

To guard against such an embarrassment in the future, it was ordered that all stray dogs in Sindh be killed. However, such was the resentment, that in another town that Zia visited, instead of dogs, dozens of donkeys with the banner marked 'Death to Zia' were used. Mercifully, no donkeys were killed perhaps because, as one observer mused, '... the country had a more urgent need of the animals'—a thinly veiled allusion to the mulish attitude of the populace, notably in Punjab.[67]

Zia used to visit Saudi Arabia regularly for Umrah. On such visits, he would be accompanied by many hangers-on. All of them would fly in the presidential plane at government expense. Since his time, 'such expense-account piety has acquired the status virtually of a constitutional obligation for Pakistani leaders and officials'.

(Iqbal Akhund, *Trial and Error: The Advent and Eclipse of Benazir Bhutto*, Karachi: OUP, 2000, p. 88.)

***

Zia loved poking fun at the foreign service. During envoys' conference, he would make remarks like a few envoys were 'talking encyclopedias', never short of words and ever eager to inflict their opinions on others. Some others spoke at length to justify their 'brief comments'. Yet others visibly suffered from 'localitis' in their assessment of events. ...

Zia actively participated in the postings and transfers of ambassadors and senior diplomats. On such occasions, he would poke fun by asking, 'Which Mafia group does this individual belong to?' or, 'Doesn't he love to serve Pakistan from a distance?'

(K.M. Arif, *Khaki Shadows: Pakistan 1947-1997*, Karachi: OUP, 2001, pp. 416–17.)

Elections were held in 1985 on a party-less basis, i.e., all the candidates had to contest as independents. Normal electioneering and use of loudspeakers was banned. Following the elections, the newly elected members met on 23 March 1985 to 'elect' a leader of the House. The non-party elections escalated corruption to new heights. According to Imran Khan, unaffiliated candidates had to be enticed into the king's party through bribery. This created a 'culture of corruption and sowing the seeds for much trouble to come'.[68]

Zia had decided to nominate Muhammad Khan Junejo for the job on the recommendations of Pir Pagara. While announcing Junejo's nomination as the candidate for the prime ministership Zia said, 'I have decided on Muhammad Khan Junejo, who is a fine gentleman and, despite being a Sindhi, is such a good man that he has married only once.'[69] Another reason for his selection was his low profile, so much so that Junejo was described in the *Nation* of Lahore as someone who had the 'extraordinary capacity to be inconspicuous in the most conspicuous situation'.[70] It would not be long, however, before Junejo would start asserting himself, much to Zia's discomfort.

Zia met Junejo at President's House and congratulated him on his election to the National Assembly. He then revealed: 'I have decided to nominate you as the prime minister of Pakistan.' The revelation did not surprise Junejo since Pir Pagara had already told him. Thus, instead of expressing gratitude, he asked, 'Mr President, when do you plan to lift the martial law?' Zia was taken aback at this lack of civility but retained his composure and replied calmly: 'Martial law is now in your support. It will help you to settle down in your right appointment. I will lift it whenever you are in control of the situation.' The relationship between the president and his nominated prime minister thus started on an icy note, writes K.M. Arif.[71]

After becoming prime minister, Junejo was eager to review the Inter-Services Pakistan Day parade held on 23 March each year together with the president. He also wanted to arrive at the parade ground riding in the imperial-style, horse-drawn carriage in the company of Zia. During discussion, he told Zia that Prime Minister Bhutto had done so before. Zia, however, countered that 'Two wrongs don't make a right' and that the president reviewed the parade as the supreme commander of the armed forces. Junejo was shown a videotape of the Indian Republic Day parade to understand the position of the Indian prime minister on such an occasion. Junejo then proposed that if the president reviewed the parade on 23 March, the prime minister should be the chief guest at the flag-hoisting ceremony on 14 August, Independence Day. The deal was struck.

(K.M. Arif, *Working with Zia: Pakistan's Power Politics, 1977-88*, Karanchi: OUP, 1995, p. 237.)

The 1988 annual budget during the prime ministership of Junejo had to be withdrawn due to a hue and cry over the huge defence allocations. Junejo had to declare several cost-cutting measures that included replacing the cars of officers with fuel-efficient smaller cars. In response to a question if such measures would also apply to army officers, Junejo good-humouredly said, 'We shall squeeze the generals too into the Suzuki' (a small car like the Indian Maruti). This upset the army officers who called it 'General bashing' by the civilian government.[72]

Zia announced elections for November 1988 largely to hamper Benazir's ability to campaign. The intelligence agencies had informed him that Benazir was expecting a baby in November and Zia had anticipated she would not be able to campaign. 'But for once she had outwitted him. Knowing his spies would obtain her medical records, she had managed to have them swapped and [she] was actually due in September.'[73]

Besides Zia, there were two others who as a troika governed Pakistan: Gen. Arif and Ghulam Ishaq Khan. The common saying was that the talkative Zia always said 'yes', the taciturn Arif said nothing and the austere Ishaq always said 'no'. As a result, they achieved 'a perfect balance on every issue, so that Pakistan stood still while the world moved on'.[74]

Despite being the astute politician that he was, Zia met his match in President Zail Singh of India. In March 1983 Zia visited

India for the Non-Aligned summit. During his call on Zail Singh, he waxed eloquent on peace with India even though Pakistan was assisting terrorists in Indian Punjab. Zail Singh listened to the general for a while and then in chaste Punjabi told Zia that it cannot be that a woman '*Akh vi maare, tay ghund vi kaddae*' (cannot wink provocatively, and cover her face at the same time). Though everyone laughed, the president was able to convey that Pakistan's two-faced policy of assisting the terrorists and expressing a desire for friendship could not go hand in hand.[75]

East Pakistan had broken away in 1971 to become Bangladesh largely due to the attitude of the West Pakistan elite. Despite this, there has been very little change in the attitude of the Punjabi elite towards the smaller provinces in the rump Pakistan.

Abida Hussain narrates a significant incident in this regard.

Once the governor of Punjab during Zia's time, Gen. Jilani Khan, admonished her about a bizarre situation outside her Lahore residence. He said that there were two police jeeps there, one to escort her husband's ministerial vehicle, and the other to follow an opposition leader, Wali Khan, who was staying at her residence.

Abida Hussain replied: 'I do not understand what you wish to say. General Fakhar (her husband) and I live with my mother and Wali Khan is her honoured guest. He and his wife always stay with us when they visit Lahore, and it is good of him to ignore the fact that Fakhar is in the cabinet of a military government which he opposes, in principle, as a diehard democrat.'

Ghulam Jilani Khan persisted and in a stern voice said: 'Look here, Begum Abida, I have served in the Frontier, even in Sindh and Balochistan. They are nothing—these *chotte subay wallas* (these folk of the smaller provinces). Punjab is Pakistan, never forget that.' He banged his fist on the table.

> Abida could not believe what she had just heard. She retorted: 'Pakistan is Balochistan and Frontier and Sindh and Punjab. And nobody should forget that, General, not after what we did to East Pakistan.'
>
> (Syeda Abida Hussain, *Power Failure: The Political Odyssey of a Pakistani Woman*, Karachi: OUP, 2015, pp. 208–09.)

Islamization

Zia is best remembered for his Islamization measures that decisively distorted the remnants of Jinnah's Pakistan. Such has been the force of his accomplishments that they survive till date and it does seem unlikely that they would be replaced.

The key measures that he took included establishment of a Federal Shariat Court that would strike down laws repugnant to Islam; state assumption of power to collect zakat and ushr; barring Ahmadis from calling their prayer houses as mosques, from possessing and reading the Quran or using the Muslim ways of greeting one another; amending the penal code to provide for punishment for desecration of the Holy Quran and for punishing blasphemy with death or life imprisonment (later on, the shariat court made death for blasphemy mandatory); making the Objectives Resolution—so far the preamble to the constitution—a substantive part of it; subjecting parliamentarians to disqualification on the basis of a religious criterion and distorting the education system by giving it an ideological context.[76]

It was not long before 'Islamization moved inevitably towards Sunnification'. This was to the detriment of the Shias and sharpened the sectarian divide in the country. It also affected the rights of the minorities. Polarizing the country on sectarian lines was especially unfortunate given that several Shias had been very prominent in the Pakistan Movement—the Agha Khan, the raja of Mahmudabad, M.A. Ispahani and above all Jinnah himself who had Ismaili roots before becoming a Shia. As far as the minorities were concerned, as Farzana Sheikh notes, 'The sweeping changes associated with Zia's Islamist brand of politics in the 1980s left little doubt that Zia himself associated the strengthening of Pakistan's Muslim identity with the steady erosion of the rights of its dwindling non-Muslims.'[77]

There was an interesting conversation between the communist president of Afghanistan, Nur Mohammad Taraki, and the deeply religious Zia on 9 September 1978 in Kabul:

Taraki: The (communist) revolution has given land to eleven million people.

Zia: As Muslims, we believe that all land belongs to Almighty Allah and man is His custodian on earth.

Taraki: All land belongs to the tiller.

Zia: Human being must fear God.

Taraki: God is aadil[just]. We don't have to fear a just God.

Zia: People have certain obligations towards God and human beings.

Taraki: To serve the people is to serve God.

(K.M. Arif, *Working with Zia*, Karachi: OUP, 1995, p. 308.)

***

Zia was keen on two schemes—to permanently fix Pakistan's Independence Day to 27 Ramzan instead of 14 August and to modify the national flag of Pakistan with Arabic inscriptions. However, he was unable to implement either of them.

(Faiz Ali Chishti, *Betrayals of Another Kind*, Delhi: Tricolour Books, 1989, p. 107.)

The United States

Zia had no illusions about Pakistan's relations with the US. Some of his famous comments in this regard were: 'Being friends with America is like living on the banks of a great river. Every four years it changes course, and leaves you either flooded or high and dry.'[78] On another occasion he described it as 'a handshake, not an embrace'.[79] Zia frankly told Secretary of State George Shultz in December 1982 that the US and Pakistan formed 'a union of unequals' and 'were incompatible' in terms of culture, geography and national power.[80]

In November 1979, some flatterers suggested to Zia that he should undertake a measure that would attract public attention. One option could be if Gen. Zia started going to his office on a bicycle and, also visit Rawalpindi in a like manner. So, on 17 November 1979 Zia cycled to his office, a mere 500 yards from his residence. The event received a lot of publicity. Encouraged, Zia decided to enlarge his bicycle odyssey by visiting Rawalpindi on 21 November.[81]

It just so happened that on 21 November a group of religious zealots seized the Holy Kaaba in Mecca. Under the circumstances, Zia was advised against going to Rawalpindi that day on a bicycle. However, Zia decided to persist with the unannounced programme. During the cycle trek the entire security apparatus was devoted to his protection. He spoke at several spontaneous gatherings and even distributed several hundred bags of atta (wheat flour) and quilts among the poor. At Waris Khan Chowk, when asked about the Kaaba siege, Zia let slip that according to some international transmissions, the Americans had instigated the attack. On hearing this, the people raised slogans like, 'Down with America', 'Islam Zindabad', 'Death to America', and slogans in favour of Zia. Thereafter, the crowd surged towards the US embassy in Islamabad.[82]

The student wing of the Jamaat-i-Islami had also concluded that somehow the US was involved in the events at Mecca. It mobilized students at the Quaid-i-Azam University in Islamabad and they marched to the US embassy and laid siege to it. The mob climbed the walls, destroyed everything in sight and then set fire to the building. Two Americans and two Pakistani employees of the embassy died in the process. Strangely, US officials were unable to contact anyone in Pakistan government who could control the situation since they were all, ostensibly, focused on Zia and his bicycle. Even though the army barracks were hardly a thirty-minutes' drive from the embassy, the troops took about four hours to rescue the embassy staff. They arrived around 4 p.m. by which time the rampage had continued for hours.[83]

In April 1988, Richard Armitage and Richard Murphy, assistant secretaries from the US Defense and State Departments, respectively, met Zia in Islamabad. The first session related to the nuclear issue. The Americans expressed grave concerns about Pakistan's activities. Zia, however, gave his assurances about its peaceful nature. They were not convinced and believed that Zia was lying. During the second session that pertained to the scenario in Afghanistan after the Geneva accord, Zia argued strongly for continuation of the arms supply. The Americans were stunned because the Geneva accord banned induction of additional arms into Afghanistan. Zia's response was that the US should supply the arms and leave the rest to him, proclaiming that Islam permitted him to lie for a good cause. The American officials concluded that on both occasions Zia 'lied to us for a good cause'.[84]

Zia had rejected the $400-million assistance offered by President Carter after the Soviet invasion of Afghanistan saying it was 'peanuts'. This peanuts comment soon entered the glossary of political journalism. A poem by Felicia Lamport became famous in the US media:

Is far too absurd to discuss
You people must be nuts
To offer such peanuts
As 400 million to us.
Though peanuts may do
For your Washington crew,
Your stinginess ought to abash you.
If you want us to spar
With the USSR
You'd better come up with a cashew.

(K.M. Arif, *Working with Zia: Pakistan's Power Politics, 1977-88*, Karachi: OUP, 1995, p. 335.)

General Vernon Walters, President Reagan's special envoy, met Zia three times to pressurize him on the nuclear issue. Each time, Zia assured the envoy that Pakistan would 'never embarrass' the Regan administration on this issue. He would then add the clincher in his unique style: 'We can hardly make a bicycle; how can we think of making a bomb.'[85]

Having overthrown an elected government there were a lot of misgivings in the US about his visit to Washington DC in December 1982. Prior to the visit, several senators advised Reagan to pressurize Zia on democracy in Pakistan. After the visit, the senators asked Reagan whether he had discussed restoration of democracy in Pakistan with Zia. Regan replied: 'He is no dictator. He was a nice guy. He was the only foreign leader I have seen visiting the White House, who even shook hands with the marine guards, with the waiters and with practically everyone in sight. If he was so good to people, he can't be all that bad.'[86]

Zia used to meet foreign leaders alone for one-on-one talks. Thus, neither his staff nor the foreign office knew what was discussed or agreed. There were no authenticated minutes of Zia's meetings with several leaders like King Khalid and King Fahd of Saudi Arabia, the Shah of Iran, President Daoud of Afghanistan, Prime Minister J. Callaghan of the United Kingdom, Gen. Zia-ur-Rahman of Bangladesh, etc.

(Faiz Ali Chishti, *Betrayals of Another Kind*, Delhi: Tricolour Books, 1989, p. 108.

Zia's Death

On 14 August 1988 Zia died in a mysterious plane crash after visiting the army firing range at Tamewali, near Bahawalpur. During the trials, troops in a US M1 Abrams tank missed all ten of their targets.[87] The aircraft had been in the air for less than ten minutes when it literally dropped out of the sky. Without a word or distress signal from the crew, it crashed into the desert. Much of the aircraft and those on board were burnt beyond recognition before rescue teams reached the scene. In its wars, Pakistan had lost only one general. In Zia's plane crash, however, Pakistan lost two full generals, one lieutenant general, three major generals and five brigadiers.[88]

7

Benazir Bhutto: Paradise Lost

Early Life and Personality

BENAZIR BHUTTO, THE ELDEST CHILD of Zulfikar Ali Bhutto and Begum Nusrat Ispahani, was born on 21 June 1953 in Karachi. She completed her O-levels from the Jesus and Mary Convent, in Murree. From 1969 to 1973, she studied for an undergraduate degree (bachelor of arts with a major in governance) at Radcliffe College, Harvard University. Later, she would call her time at Harvard 'four of the happiest years of my life'. She then studied for a second undergraduate degree, in philosophy, politics and economics, at Lady Margaret Hall, University of Oxford. Thereafter, she attended St Catherine's College, Oxford. She was elected president of the Oxford Union Debating Society, the first Asian woman to hold that post. She was also president of the Oxford Majlis Asian Society.

In her bid to become president of the Oxford Union, Benazir, according to Imran Khan, would have an open house every Sunday in Lady Margret Hall. She would serve cheese and snacks all afternoon.[1]

According to Shyam Bhatia who was their contemporary in Oxford, Benazir and Imran Khan were friendly but as grown-ups they rarely shared the same wavelength. Jemima Khan, Imran Khan's former wife, described Benazir as a 'kleptocrat in a Hermes headscarf'. According to her, Benazir's two terms as prime minister were conspicuous by 'incompetence, extra-judicial killings and brazen looting'.[2]

While she was at Oxford, Benazir tried to get the university to award her father an honorary degree. However, the proposal met with much opposition from a section of the students due to Bhutto's involvement in the Pakistan Army crackdown and atrocities in Bangladesh that the university finally rejected the proposal.

It was Bhutto who put his finger on one of Benazir's prominent personality traits when he wrote from his death cell to her: 'In the winter of 1957, when you were four years old, we were sitting on the terrace of Al-Murtaza. It was a fine morning. I had a double-barrel gun in my hand. One barrel was 22 and the other 480. Without thought, I shot a wild parrot. When the parrot fell to the ground near the terrace you cried your eyes out. You had it buried in your presence. You cried and cried. You refused to have your meals. A dead parrot in the winter of 1957 in Larkana made a little girl weep in sorrow. Twenty-one years later, that little girl has grown into a young lady with nerves of steel to valorously confront the terror of the longest night of tyranny. Truly, you have proved beyond doubt that the blood of warriors runs in your veins.'[3]

Those who worked closely with her like Iqbal Akhund, security adviser in her first term, also highlighted courage to be Benazir's most remarkable quality. 'Combative and scrappy, she seemed to be at her best when she was alone and fighting with her back to the wall – a courage that was physical as well as moral.'[4]

The Benazir who came into power was a very different figure from the one remembered by her Oxford contemporaries.

According to William Dalrymple, writing after her assassination, 'English friends who knew her at Oxford remember a bubbly babe who drove to lectures in a yellow MG ...'[5] The politician Benazir, who embraced the rough and tumble of Pakistani politics, was well known in Islamabad for chairing twelve-hour cabinet meetings and for surviving on four hours' sleep. This was the Benazir who continued to campaign even after a suicide bomber attacked her convoy the day she returned to Pakistan in October 2007. This was the Benazir who did not heed the threats to her life in order to continue fighting. 'This other Benazir Bhutto, was fearless, sometimes heroically so, and as hard as nails.'[6]

It was not courage and toughness alone that Benazir was known for. Like her father, she was arrogant to the core. Mumtaz Bhutto, Benazir's uncle and founding member of the PPP, whom Benazir had expelled from the party in 1985, claimed: 'Benazir wants everyone in the Movement for the Restoration of Democracy [MRD—a movement launched by the combined opposition parties against Zia] to believe they are breathing because of the PPP and everyone in the PPP to believe they owe their political existence to her.'[7]

William Dalrymple also noted that there was 'something much more majestic, even imperial' when she became prime minister. The way she walked and talked 'in a deliberately measured and regal manner and frequently used the royal "we".' When she found that the sun was not shining in quite the way she wanted it to during the interview, she told Dalrymple, 'The sun is in the wrong direction'.[8]

A third element in her personality was loyalty, something that Benazir prized above everything else. According to Christina Lamb, 'She had increasingly surrounded herself by sycophants. Insisting to the end, "I'm the only people's leader" she had distanced herself from the people by constructing around her house in Karachi towering twenty-foot steel reinforced concrete walls mounted with machine-gun turrets, the structure resembling a Foreign Legion fort.'[9]

Had Benazir evolved by the time she was returning to Pakistan in October 2007? While addressing the Middle East Institute in September 2007 she was asked how she could possibly remain her own woman in a coalition with Musharraf? Benazir replied, 'I would like to remain my own person.' She described how she was 'very much my own person' in her first term, but then 'decided to be co-opted' in her second term to return to power. 'But I think on the third term around, being over fifty now, I would like to be my own person, even if it means not lasting very long. Because even when you try to last long by making the compromises – compromises that you think will help you stay in power – you still don't stay long anyway.' Wendy Chamberlin, director of the Institute was struck by this humble and honest response and felt that it might actually be the start of something, an unexpected evolution.[10]

Benazir had a strong belief in fate or destiny. For her, Zia's death was an accident—divine retribution being meted out by the hand of God, rather than any sabotage. 'It may be superstition', she said, 'but I believe it. Look how all those involved [in Bhutto's hanging] came to a bad end – Tara Masih [Bhutto's hangman] dies of cancer, a swarm of bees attacked the funeral of Maulvi Mushtaq [the Lahore chief justice who had sentenced Bhutto to death], another judge died of a heart attack!'[11]

Benazir's sartorial style evolved from wearing sweatshirts and jeans in college and not covering her hair to wearing the traditional salwar-kameez and covering her hair when she became a contender for her father's political legacy, the leadership of the PPP and later of Pakistan itself.[12] When she returned to Pakistan from the UK, she took extra care to clothe herself fully and clasp her hands tightly to avoid inadvertently extending them for a handshake.[13]

Benzair was fond of mimicking political leaders.[14] She inherited this skill from Bhutto who was also excellent at mimicking professors and friends.[15]

Bhutto and Bhutto

Many people have commented on how Benazir's blind spot was her father. Mary Anne Weaver, for example, writes: 'Benazir remembered only one side of her father.' In her selective memory, there was no place for his acknowledged acts of brutality and the rigged 1977 elections. All she remembered was, 'the genius without flaws; the populist reformer and spellbinding orator, who restored national pride after the humiliating defeat by the Indian army in 1971; the man who returned Pakistan to – and gave it its longest period of – civilian rule.' Coupled with these selective memories was her obsession with absolute loyalty to her father's legacy. No criticism of Bhutto was allowed.[16]

Bhutto started grooming Benazir to be his political heir and encouraged her from a very young age to understand international affairs. He read her stories of Napoleon when she was only six years old from the thousands of first edition volumes he had; at eight he introduced her to Zhou Enlai; at ten, when he was foreign minister, he woke her up at night when President John F. Kennedy was assassinated. At that time, she was travelling with him in the foreign minister's private railway carriage in the autumn of 1963. 'This is no time to sleep,' he said urgently. 'There has been a great tragedy. The young President of the United States has been shot.' Though Benazir had only heard vaguely of the US president, Bhutto ensured she stayed by his side as he received the latest news about Kennedy. Bhutto had met Kennedy several times at the White House and admired his liberal social views.[17]

In 1969 when she was sixteen, Bhutto secured her admission to Radcliffe, courtesy the US State Department and packed her off there despite her own misgivings. By her own account, Benazir was initially lonely, shy and detested the cold weather. What kept her going was the first anonymity of her life. By the second term, things improved; she adopted American ways and dress, 'became addicted to peppermint-stick ice cream and rock concerts, memorized lengthy passages of Kate Millett's *Sexual Politics* and marched against the war in Vietnam.'[18]

Prior to her leaving for Harvard University in 1969, Bhutto took Benazir to the family graveyard at Garhi Khuda Baksh and told her, 'You are going far away to America. You will see many things and travel to places you've never heard of. But remember, whatever happens to you, you will ultimately return here. Your place is here. Your roots are here. The dust and mud and heat of Larkana are in your bones. And it is here that you will be buried.'[19]

During the last stages of the 1971 Indo-Pak war, Bhutto taught her a crucial lesson in diplomacy—the importance of deception. At the UN, he told her to interrupt his meetings in the Pierre Hotel that he was having with the Americans or the Soviets or the Chinese by announcing imaginary phone calls from one or the other delegations not in the room. 'If the Soviets are here, tell me the Chinese are calling. If the Americans are here, tell me that the Russians are on the line or the Indians. And don't tell anyone who really is here. One of the fundamental lessons of diplomacy is to create doubt: never lay all your cards on the table.' This, he said, would keep his adversaries guessing about his next moves.[20]

Bhutto took her to Simla for the summit with Indira Gandhi after the 1971 war. There she met Indira Gandhi. The similarity between the two was obvious. Benazir writes that she was both unnerved and intrigued by Indira Gandhi whom she described as a woman of 'silk and steel': with 'a cold aloofness' about her. 'She kept staring at me', Benazir writes. 'Was she seeing herself in me? She was so small and frail. Where did that famed ruthlessness come from?' After mentioning that Indira's father was dead, she asked, 'Was she lonely?'[21]

During one of Bhutto's state visits to the US, Benazir was sitting next to Henry Kissinger at a formal White House dinner. The conversation was about elitism at Harvard. The next night Kissinger met Bhutto at another dinner and said: 'Mr Prime Minister, your daughter is even more intimidating than you are.' Bhutto was thrilled, taking the quip as a compliment. Benazir who was bewildered wrote, 'I am still not sure.'[22]

Towards the end of her life, did Benazir start having doubts about her father's political philosophy? In the house of Lashari Raisani in Quetta, on 16 December 2007, just eleven days before her assassination, she looked at a photograph of Bhutto on the wall and said, 'My father would say, keep going, keep fighting, but it's more complicated than just that, than one battle after another. You have to find a way to stop the fighting.[23] Was her compromise with Musharraf a way to stop the fighting?

Given the kind of influence that Bhutto had on her, several of his pithy sayings would have had a deep impact on her. Some of the significant ones were:

'These days shall pass. What is important is that we pass them with honour.'

(Iqbal Akhund, *Trial and Error: The Advent and Eclipse of Benazir Bhutto*, Karachi: OUP, 2000, p. 317.)

***

'Consistency is a virtue of small minds.'

Quoted in interview with Oriana Fallaci, *L'Europeo*, April 1972, cited in Christina Lamb, *Waiting for Allah: Pakistan's Struggle for Democracy*, p. 55.

'Never resist a military coup. The Generals want us dead. We must give them no pretext to justify our murders.'

(Benazir Bhutto, *Daughter of the East*, London: Hamish Hamilton, 1988, p. 82.)

***

'Armies do not take over power to relinquish it. Nor do Generals commit high treason to hold elections and restore democratic constitutions.'

(Ibid., p. 84.)

The 1977 Elections

An early glimpse of Benazir's arrogance and how she would treat the opposition was apparent in her views about the Pakistan National Alliance (PNA) in the 1977 elections. She wrote that she never doubted the election results. 'The PNA leaders were not great men or even fine men. Most were much older than my father and had had their time. They hadn't had the benefit of my father's education, not his extensive experience in government and international diplomacy. In Pakistan, my father was in fact unique … Many of those opposing my father were small, provincial men whose myopic views had failed Pakistan in the past and would do so again in the future.'[24]

Such sentiments could hardly be characteristic of a person who believed in democratic values let alone have imbibed them. Clearly, Benazir was in her father's mould—an autocrat. However, unlike her father she never had the majority to implement her authoritarian views. Despite this, after the 1988 election results were announced, Benazir made the cover of *Time* magazine, something her father did not.[25]

Like Bhutto, Benazir was also convinced of the dubious role played by the Americans in sustaining the PNA agitation. As evidence, she cited that Pakistan's intelligence agencies had noted recurrent meetings between American diplomats and members of the PNA: 'People had fistfuls of American dollars and were leaving their jobs to demonstrate for the PNA that paid them better;' private transporters struck work in Karachi but transported people to PNA demonstrations. She wrote that in 1958 the US had trained the Pakistan Army in the art of immobilizing a government through strikes. These secret manoeuvres were called 'Operation Wheel Jam'. Ironically the PNA's nationwide strike was also called Operation Wheel Jam.[26]

Entry into Politics

The one handicap that Benazir began with in politics was that she was never formally trained in indigenous languages—Urdu and Sindhi. English was her strong suit but hardly suited to the mass politics of Pakistan. She spoke well extempore, 'but when reading out a prepared text, she tended to sound like a schoolmistress taking a class in adult literacy'.[27] However, the fact that she was Bhutto's daughter, young and dynamic, was enough for her to be cheered whenever she spoke in her strange mixture of Urdu and Sindhi.

It was also not an easy entry into politics. Zia was determined to make it as difficult for her as possible. He put Benazir in solitary confinement for five months from March till August 1981 in Sukkur jail where temperatures often reached 120 degrees F. Her cell was like a giant metal cage that was lit with a bare ceiling bulb that was switched off at seven every evening. Her most difficult moment in prison was 'The day that a jail official told me' – falsely – 'that I was to be tried inside the jail, by a special military tribunal, and sentenced to death. I was stunned – I couldn't believe that they'd do it, though one side of me said they would. A few hours later, someone left a bottle of poison inside my cell.'[28]

Later, Benazir would unhesitatingly say that what sustained her during those years was 'Anger'.[29]

In April 1986, Benazir returned to Pakistan after two years of self-imposed exile. Wherever she went, she got a huge reception and became a symbol for the revival of democracy in Pakistan. At one memorable meeting in Peshawar she declared: 'There is fear in the heart of the usurper. The time has come for the usurper to run away.' The crowd echoed: '*Za, za,* Zia!, Zia *za*!' (Go, go Zia, Zia go.)[30]

1988 Elections

As soon as Zia announced parliamentary elections, Lt Gen. Hamid Gul, the DG ISI, who had called Benazir and her mother Nusrat Bhutto 'gangsters in bangles',[31] went to work to stymie Benazir. He succeeded in creating an anti-Bhutto alliance of Islamists and conservative politicians that included Nawaz Sharif, called the Islami Jamhoori Ittehad (IJI or Islamic Democratic Alliance—IDA).

A vicious propaganda campaign was launched to denounce Benazir's Western background. Thousands of leaflets were air-dropped that depicted Benazir dancing in a Paris nightclub and her mother, in a Western evening dress, dancing with President Ford. This was touted as evidence of their 'anti-Islamic' behaviour. Media was selectively briefed that she would ship babies to Paris, let Americans into Pakistan's nuclear plant,[32] 'roll back' the nuclear programme; prevent a mujahideen victory in Afghanistan and stop plans for jihad in Kashmir in its tracks. The ISI was clearly preparing for jihad in Kashmir, notes Husain Haqqani.[33]

Despite all that the ISI could throw at her, Benazir came out ahead in the elections. As the leader of the largest single party in the National Assembly, it was her right to form the government. The president, Ghulam Ishaq Khan dithered and procrastinated. It was only after a nudge from the US ambassador Robert Oakley who called on the president and clarified that the US believed that Benazir should be sworn in that eventually got him to do so.[34] She was sworn in on 2 December 1988 as the first woman prime minister in the Muslim world. In an interview with Shuja Nawaz, Oakley confirmed that there were negotiations about whether she would be allowed to take office. A 'gentleman's/gentlewoman's understanding was reached that she wouldn't get involved in the nuclear programme, army promotions and assignments or Afghanistan. These things were left to the president and the chief of the army staff.'[35]

The key elements of the 'deal' that were worked out were:[36]

- Retention of President Ghulam Ishaq Khan;
- Continuation of foreign minister, Sahibzada Yakub Khan;
- Pursuit of an economic policy devoted to free enterprise;
- No interference in internal army matters such as postings, transfers, promotions and retirements.

Benazir was given two names, one each for foreign minister and finance minister. She accepted Yakub Khan for the former but declined Mahboobul Haq as finance minister since he had opposed Bhutto. Then the principal secretary to the prime minister V.A. Jaffrey, an economist, was invited for lunch by the US ambassador Robert Oakley. While the lunch was focused on economic matters, Jaffrey got a call from the prime minister's office informing him that he was to be sworn in as adviser on economic affairs. At the swearing in, since Benazir did not recognize Jaffery, she asked those assembled, 'Which one of you is Mr Jaffrey.' Jaffrey stood up so that the she could at least recognize the person whom she had just nominated as her adviser on economic affairs![37]

Though Benazir became prime minister, the provincial government of the all-important province of Punjab was a different matter. Here, the ISI under Lt Gen. Hamid Gul ensured that the IJI, led by Nawaz Sharif, formed the government. He is on record as having said, 'Although we could not take Jalalabad,[38] we managed to save the Punjab.'[39]

In Power

Apart from having a very narrow political space in which to govern due to the 'deal' to come into power, Benazir, who came to be referred to as 'Alice in Blunderland'[40] by some of her own ministers, was also constrained by other handicaps. The first was that the jiyalas (PPP workers who had sacrificed for the party under martial law) now looked forward for rewards—employment, plots and permits. It was a no-win situation because there weren't too many rewards to begin with.[41]

Benazir's ministers joked that it was the only cabinet in the world where every member's bio-data would include prison records.

(Christina Lamb, *Waiting for Allah: Pakistan's Struggle for Democracy*, New Delhi: Viking, Penguin Books India, first published 1991, p. 41.)

Second, the restoration of democracy after the long years of Zia's martial law and her being the first ever elected woman prime minister of an Islamic nation released a volcano of expectations. But even with the enormous political and administrative power at her disposal, 'she did not know what to do with it'. In the event, Benazir could achieve very little. Women, especially those who looked forward to liberation from the repressive hudood laws of Zia, were disappointed.[42]

Third, during her first term, her authority over the military was insignificant. Even when she asked for the ISI files on her brother Mir Murtaza, the agency refused give them to her.[43] She was also weakened because, according to her adviser, Naseerullah Babar, her contacts with the army were limited. The army chief, Gen. Aslam Beg did brief her on military matters but he restricted her contacts with the corps commanders and senior officers. Babar urged her to visit the army cantonments but due to her multiple problems with the president (who sat on files), the army chief (who played a duplicitous role) and Nawaz Sharif (acting independently in Punjab) she was unable to do so.[44]

Benazir and President Ghulam Ishaq Khan, whom she would soon refer to as 'Ghulam the Grim', began awkwardly. After

> swearing her in and congratulating her, he turned to leave saying, 'It's prayer time.' Benazir asked if she could join him for prayers. He, however, said, the mosque was for men only, adding as an afterthought, that she could watch …
>
> Later, when accompanied by Maj. Gen. Babar, she went to his chambers, he told her casually that a hijacked Russian aircraft was heading towards Pakistan. This disconcerted Benazir since she had just been sworn in! Babar, however, reacted saying loud enough for the president to hear, 'We'll block all the airfields,' which was precisely what was done. The president would continue to test Benazir as would the army chief.
>
> (Mary Anne Weaver, *Pakistan: In the Shadow of Jihad and Afghanistan*, New Delhi; Vining, Penguin, 2003, pp. 192, 204.)

Fourth, her fight with the opposition and especially with the Punjab chief minister, Nawaz Sharif, was bitter. Relations with Nawaz were so bad that when she visited Lahore as prime minister, he did not think it fit to go to the airport to receive her.[45] He also denied her permission to hold a rally at the Minar-e-Pakistan in Lahore.

Consequently, for Benazir, the priority was survival and this preoccupation made her lose momentum quickly. Bogged down in distributing favours and fending off attacks, policy initiatives got neglected.[46]

One telling example of how the PPP parliamentarians were intimidated was during the no-confidence motion filed by the opposition against Benazir's government in November 1989. When the proceedings began, Khurshid Cheema from Sialkot was produced in parliament by the opposition alliance. However, crying '*bachao, bachao*' (save me, save me) he darted from the opposition benches to the treasury benches and alleged that the opposition had threatened him with dire consequences if he did not vote against the government. Like him, government MNAs (Members of National Assembly) were picked up in Punjab government cars and taken to rest houses in a hill station where they were well looked after to vote against the PPP.[47]

At one of her cabinet meetings, the ministers found before each seat a copy of Dale Carnegie's book *How to Win Friends and Influence People*. This was Benazir's way of telling them that they needed to improve their personal skills.

(Iqbal Akhund, *Trial and Error: The Advent and Eclipse of Benazir Bhutto*, Karachi: OUP, 2000, p. 315.)

***

A major discomfiture for Benazir was that the same publisher had published her autobiography *Daughter of the East* and Salman Rushdie's *Satanic Verses*. She was greatly embarrassed by the demand of the agitators protesting Rushdie's book that all books by that publisher, irrespective of the subject and author, should be banned in Pakistan.

(Ibid., p. 60.)

Did Benazir know about Pakistan's nuclear weapons programme and if so, how much? Some believed that she was not trusted enough by the establishment and so was not in the know; others suspected that she had chosen to distance herself from it. It was the American ambassador to Pakistan and the director of the CIA that briefed her about the programme. Despite this briefing, Benazir stated in the US Congress, to loud applause, that Pakistan neither possessed nor intended to assemble a nuclear bomb. Till that moment she was hugely popular in Washington. However, after this obviously false assertion, US attitudes began to change.[48]

> Curiously, even though Benazir and her father had been victims of martial law, or perhaps because of it, Benazir retained the outward symbols of militarism. Bhutto had started the practice of including a military secretary and ADCs in his staff and she continued the same. For example, as Iqbal Akhund notes, 'at the flag-hoisting ceremony on Independence Day, with trumpeters sounding off, Benazir came down the steps of parliament flanked by two strapping guardsmen in all their finery.' He lamented: 'Such militaristic displays were incongruous in a democracy and hardly appropriate for a civilian government restored after much tribulation and travail. But we love this sort of thing and it pleased the army to be on show.'
>
> (Ibid., p. 117.)

As per the Islamabad Act No. LIX of 1975, under the head 'Salary, Allowances and Privileges of the Prime Minister', a prime minister was allowed one duty-free car (per tenure) which did not exceed Rs 400,000. On becoming prime minister for the second time, Benazir ordered a Mercedes S 600L for herself (in addition to the Mercedes 500 she had obtained in her first term). The car makers were thrilled and they promptly printed Benazir's picture in its brochure of the car, with the caption: 'Beauty for a beautiful lady: A Mercedes for a prime minister'. Gohar Ayub Khan notes aptly: 'And all this was coming from a prime minister who so eagerly claimed to sympathize with the poor.' She was eventually forced to return both cars to the government due to opposition protests. This saved her the blushes of charges being framed against her. Benazir retaliated by requisitioning all the Mercedes cars and even a sports car that Nawaz Sharif had purchased as prime minister by using state money for his personal use.[49]

Benazir's first government was dismissed on 6 August 1990. On that day, the chief of protocol had an appointment with her at 2 p.m. However, at that time he got an urgent call from his wife informing him that a close family friend wanted to borrow one of his sherwanis for the interim prime minister (Ghulam Mustafa Jatoi) for his swearing in ceremony at 5 p.m. that day. Jatoi had left his own in Karachi and there was no time to bring it from there. The chief of protocol was shocked and when he informed her, he realized that Benazir was totally unaware of the president's moves to dismiss her.[50]

Till the moment troops surrounded her secretariat, Benazir did not believe that she could be dismissed. Arif Nizami, the editor of the *Nation* had written an exclusive story forecasting her dismissal. He told Christina Lamb that on 6 August morning Tariq Rahim, the parliamentary affairs minister, asked him the source of his story, accusing him of publishing inputs handed out by the military intelligence. At the same time, Benazir deputed her close aide Happy Minwalla, to see the US ambassador and the president. The latter informed him he was not about to do anything 'extra-ordinary'. Reassured that the dismissal story was false, Benazir continued to formulate her speech for the World Children's Summit that she would be co-chairing with Britain's Princess Diana.[51]

The decision to dismiss Benazir had been taken at a corps commanders' meeting held on 21 July 1990.[52] This decision was conveyed to the president if he did not do so himself.[53] While delivering a lecture at the National University of Science and Technology in Rawalpindi, Abdul Qadeer Khan, the nuclear scientist, narrated that he had on several occasions asked army chief Gen. Beg to get rid of Benazir, as she was hindering the further development of Pakistan's nuclear programme.[54]

There were warning signals. On a visit to Libya in July 1990, President Muammar Gaddafi of Libya had warned Benazir that the next two weeks were highly fateful for her tenure as prime minister. Benazir, however, chose to ignore the warning due to her self-assurance and arrogance about her strong position.[55]

Margaret Thatcher, then the leader of the opposition in the House of Commons, once invited Benazir to tea when she was at Oxford. Thatcher was returning her father's hospitality. Curiously, despite differences in age, the two women became good friends. The friendship would blossom when they were both prime ministers and they consulted each other frequently on their secure telephones on political strategy and common foes. On one occasion, the two met for tea at the Dorchester Hotel at a time when the power struggle between President Ghulam Ishaq Khan and prime minister Nawaz Sharif was getting out of hand during his first term. Benazir, after briefing Lady Thatcher, asked for her advice.

'Side with neither of them,' Lady Thatcher advised. 'They will both use you and dump you. Let them fight it out and bleed each other.' And that is exactly what they did.[56]

The two times that Benazir became prime minister were quite different from each other. In 1988 she was untested but was seen as a crusader who came to power after a long and intense struggle against military dictatorship. In her second stint, Benazir was seen as a crafty politician who, after her earlier experience, was determined to be on the right side of the Pakistan Army and the Americans.[57]

However, like her first term, Benazir's second term also became increasingly disappointing. The impression gained ground that it was beyond her to tackle Pakistan's problems. Matters were made worse by the perception that she and her husband Asif Zardari were hopelessly corrupt. Consequently, even some of her closest advisers and ministers, those who had stayed with her through thick and thin, began to move away. Many observed that she had 'returned to power changed: there was a new vindictiveness, based on her obsession with having been removed from power in the past. There was also impertinence, bordering on arrogance, that only she could rule, and a turning away from the liberal politics she had long embraced.'[58] Her failing was her conceit: her belief that her intellect was superior to others. Hence she began to cut herself off from the realities surrounding her.

There was a marked change of style in Benazir's first televised national address after becoming prime minister for the second time. Bhutto's photograph was conspicuous by its absence from the telecast. During her first term, Bhutto's photograph, together with that of Jinnah, used to be an inevitable part of the background set-up.[59]

After he had won the presidential elections, Farooq Leghari, Benazir's hand-picked party loyalist, said at a dinner:'After the swearing-in ceremony tomorrow, I would like to address the nation.'Benazir's reaction floored all those present. She told Farooq Leghari that this was not necessary, adding, 'In any case we want to play down the presidency.' There was a stunned silence. Those present were highly embarrassed. Many felt that this did not augur well for the government and the portents did not look promising.[60] On 5 November 1996, Farooq Leghari would dismiss Benazir on much the same charges as had Ghulam Ishaq Khan.

To protest a selective process of accountability that Nawaz in his second term as prime minister had launched against her and her family, Benazir declared in February 1999 that she was going into exile in Dubai. In what would be her last appearance in the National Assembly, she described the government of Nawaz Sharif as one of 'ganjas' or bald men. In this list, she included Nawaz, Shahbaz, ministers Sartaj Aziz, Mushahid Hussain, Khalid Anwar, Siddiq Kanju, Majeed Malik, Shujaat Hussain, Nisar Ali and Sheikh Rashid, all of whom she alleged wore wigs. What brought the house down was her pronunciation of 'ganja' that was as unusual as it was hilarious.[61]

One of Benazir's most embarrassing moments was when Senator Jesse Helms, chairman of the Senate Foreign Relations Committee, introduced her mistakenly as 'the distinguished prime minister of India'. Helms said he had just completed 'a delightful hour-and-a-half conversation' with Benazir talking mostly about India.[62]

Benazir used to recount with great merriment a story about Shaukat Aziz, prime minister under Musharraf. 'Shaukat Aziz tells everyone that "there is no woman I can't pick up in two weeks". But when he tried his charms on Condi Rice, she just stared him down. She withered him.'

(Ron Suskind, *The Way of the World: A Story of Truth and Hope in an Age of Extremism*, New York: HarperCollins, 2008, p. 210.)

Asif Zardari

It was a bee sting that brought Benazir and Asif Zardari together. A bee had stung Benazir in Windsor Park. Consequently, her hand was swollen and she was in pain by the evening when the Zardaris arrived at their flat. Seeing her condition, Asif arranged for a doctor and a car and insisted on taking her to a hospital. This charmed Benazir immensely for, as she revealed, 'For once, I was not the one in charge.'[63] At that time, Zardari's family was of modest means, with limited holdings and a run-down movie theatre in Karachi. 'Zardari's only experience of higher education was a stint at a commercial college in London.'[64]

In Benazir's own words, 'An arranged marriage was the price in personal choice I had to pay for the political path my life had taken.' Due to her high profile, the possibility of her meeting a man in the normal course, getting to know him and marrying him was remote. She realized that in the male chauvinistic society that Pakistan was, being single would work against her. She was aware that even the most discreet of relationships would give rise to loose talk and rumour-mongering. The one concession she made to modernity was that she told her mother not to pay dowry.[65]

For her wedding in 1987 in Karachi, Benazir had invited the diplomatic community. For the Western ambassadors in Islamabad especially, the invitation posed a dilemma. The Afghan war was one that necessitated their being sensitive to how Zia would react. After a closed-door meeting in Islamabad the issue was resolved diplomatically: the invitation was accepted but instead of the ambassadors the consuls general in Karachi were deputed to attend.[66]

Unlike Benazir's formal personality, Zardari was more affable. He would have a grin even when he was being tried in special courts in Karachi. He would show visitors marks of torture on his tongue while remaining in control of the situation and even turning it in his favour. 'He exuded an energy and affability that earned him the title "a friend of friends".' He once told a visiting lady journalist, 'Where have you been all this time? How come it's taken you all this time to discover my good looks?'[67]

However, while Zardari could get away with his flirtations, his obsession with taking kickbacks from businessmen earned him the nickname, 'Mr Ten Percent', during Benazir's first term as prime minister. The moniker has stuck and was further amplified to 'A to Z', using his first and last initials.[68]

Abida Hussain, a politician from Punjab and later Pakistan's ambassador to the US, writes in her book that once in Dubai, in September 2005, Benazir asked her if her husband had ever been unfaithful. Abida confessed that she had her moments of suspicion, but there was nothing serious. At this, Benazir with deep sadness mentioned that perhaps she had not been as lucky. She, however, loved Asif deeply and so forgave him even when he hurt her.[69]

Nusrat Bhutto

The one major disagreement Benazir had with her mother Nusrat Bhutto was about who was Bhutto's political heir. Nusrat Bhutto did not agree that it was Benazir. According to her, 'He didn't choose Benazir – I did. I was to have been my husband's political heir. But because I was ill, I told the party that I would like Benazir to stand in my stead, so they coined the phrase "co-chairman," which we both still are.'[70]

Murtaza Bhutto, her brother, also disputed Benazir's assertion of being Bhutto's heir. He claimed that it was he who had been chosen as the political heir of their father. As proof, Murtaza mentioned that he had been asked to manage their father's Larkana constituency during the 1977 elections and not Benazir. Some of Bhutto's supporters agreed saying that Bhutto would rather 'his daughter was spared the rough and tumble of politics, preferring that she join Pakistan's Foreign Service'.[71]

In his last letter to Benazir from his death cell, Bhutto had written, 'I am fifty years old and you are exactly half my age. By the time you reach my age, you must accomplish twice as much as I have achieved for the people. Mir Ghulam Murtaza, my son and heir, is not with me. Nor are Shah Nawaz and Sanam-Seema. This message has to be shared with them as a part of my heritage.'[72] Reference to Murtaza as his heir must have been uncomfortable for Benazir.

However, Benazir vigorously disputed Murtaza being Bhutto's heir. She claimed that her father had always wanted her to enter politics.

Once Murtaza returned to Pakistan in 1993, his mother, Nusrat Bhutto, helped him organize his election campaign for the Sindh provincial assembly. He contested over twenty seats in an attempt to prove a point about his popularity. In the event, he could win only from one constituency. Benazir, however, was furious at her mother's role in helping Murtaza. She reacted by removing her as co-chair of the PPP. Her mother responded by saying of Benazir, 'I had no idea I had nourished a viper in my breast.'[73]

During a debate on Kashmir in the National Assembly, a legislator, Mian Mohammad Zaman, stated that India thought that Kashmir is her '*Atut Ang*' (inseparable part). At this, Nusrat Bhutto, who had been arguing with him earlier, protested on a point of order, 'Mr Speaker, he just said "*Mai tang tor doonga*"' (I will break your legs) and insisted that he should take back his words,[74] much to the amusement of the members.

Army

As prime minister, Benazir's attitude towards the armed forces was cautious. At one time, when she was asked whether her government would try to reduce the defence budget, she said matter-of-factly: 'Not unless we want the army to take over again.'[75] On another occasion, in an interview to *The Daily Express* of London when asked about the possibility of a military coup, Benazir said, 'Ultimately it depends on the commitment of the armed forces to democracy. If they are committed they will not intervene. If they are not, they do not need any pretext – they will simply make any.'[76] Then again, in the wake of the strikes organized by the Mohajir Qaumi Movement (MQM) in Karachi on 7 and 13 February 1990 that were accompanied by widespread destruction, army chief Aslam Beg told her that the corps commanders favoured intervention. Benazir responded: 'Go ahead and do what you please, I can't stop you. But you should realize what the consequences would be.'[77]

Benazir told Indian journalist Shyam Bhatia that while the credit for the nuclear programme went to her father, she was the mother of the missile programme. She had done more for Pakistan than all the military chiefs of Pakistan combined.[78] During her visit to North Korea at the end of 1993 she had bought an overcoat with the 'deepest possible pockets'. The reason? She was carrying on her person CDs containing critical nuclear data about uranium enrichment that the North Koreans wanted. It was handed over on arrival at Pyongyang. On the return flight, she brought back missile information on CDs from North Korea. In fact, the appreciative North Koreans presented the disassembled parts of the Nodong missile for her to carry back for the Pakistani scientists to study it safely in their own laboratories.[79] That's how Pakistan's missile programme was kick-started.

Kashmir

During the unrest that began in Jammu and Kashmir (J&K) in 1989, Benazir was in the forefront of inciting the people of Kashmir against the then governor of J&K, Jagmohan. In 1990, she was seen on TV making outrageous cutting gestures with her right hand striking the open palm of her left, as she shouted, 'Jag-jag, mo-mo, han-han.'[80]

In a rare appreciation of Zia, Benazir once said in response to a question: 'Zia did one right thing. He started the whole policy of proxy war by supporting the separatist movements in Punjab and Kashmir as way of getting back at India.' She added, 'It should be clear also that Pakistan never forgot the humiliating loss of Bangladesh at the hands of India.'[81]

Pakistan observes 5 February as a national holiday to express solidarity with the people of Kashmir. On 4 February 1990, Benazir's government had called for an all-party conference on Kashmir to establish a non-partisan, 'national' position on the issue. This was done so that the opposition could not outmanoeuvre her on the Kashmir issue. Realizing that Benazir had stolen a march, Nawaz Sharif, as Punjab CM, who had attended the 4 February meeting, gave a call for a strike on 5 February. This was done even though international affairs did not fall within the purview of a provincial government. Benazir then pre-empted Nawaz's call by declaring a public holiday on 5 February, the day of the strike.[82]

What neither Benazir nor Nawaz realized then or even later was that the Solidarity Day coincided with the 1984 brutal murder of the Birmingham-based Indian diplomat Ravindra Mhatre by Kashmiri terrorists. Symbolically at least, Pakistan's support of terrorism and terrorist activities in Kashmir begins from this date.

Benazir's Return to Pakistan

Benazir's return to Pakistan in October 2007 was the result of a deal that had been brokered by the US through 2006–07. Benazir and her representatives started lobbying the US State Department from the spring of 2006 about her possible return to Pakistan after seven years of self-imposed exile. At that time, there were very few takers. By spring 2007, the situation had changed. Musharraf's sacking of the chief justice of the Supreme Court had led to countrywide demonstrations. According to Condoleezza Rice, 'the US state department came to believe that Musharraf was on borrowed time', though this view was not shared by others within the administration.[83]

It was then the US started to look at Benazir as an instrument to support a beleaguered Musharraf by 'forging an alliance between the two strongest political forces in the country: Musharraf and Benazir'. It was difficult but a power-sharing arrangement between them 'would shift the weight of politics towards the moderates and undermine the Islamists, as well as Nawaz Sharif who, more than any other prominent figure in Pakistani politics, was suspected of maintaining close ties to the militants'.[84]

Richard Boucher, the assistant secretary of South and Central Asian affairs, was the key person for the US mediation effort. He shuttled back and forth between the two leaders and their top advisers. He narrowed their differences enough for a face-to-face meeting that took place in July 2007 in the UAE. The discussions, however, were inconclusive.[85]

The situation turned dramatic when on 8 August 2007, US Ambassador to Pakistan Anne Patterson made an urgent telephone call and informed Condoleezza Rice that Musharraf was considering imposing an emergency. At 2 a.m., Condoleezza spoke to Musharraf for fifteen minutes and talked him out of the move saying that 'you will have no credibility, and I don't see how you can run for president after you've imposed a state of emergency'.[86]

According to Rice, by early October, there were four outstanding issues: Musharraf's uniform—when would he shed it, (before or after the elections); Benazir's immunity from corruption cases; Benazir becoming prime minister for a third term despite a constitutional term limit of two terms; and finally, Musharraf's support for her return to Pakistan before the elections.[87]

Rice says she put 'those questions to Musharraf in a phone call on 3 October at 4.47 p.m. At 5.47 p.m. I got back to Bhutto with his response. At 6.18 p.m. I talked to Musharraf again. At 6.53 p.m. I called Bhutto. That continued every half hour until 11.28 p.m., with nine more calls back and forth.' Through this phone diplomacy, a tentative deal was worked out that was 'not firm but detailed enough that Benazir could be permitted to return to Pakistan to stand in the parliamentary elections that would be held by mid-January'.[88]

Interestingly, as part of the deal, Benazir had worked out an arrangement with Musharraf to empty out her and Zardari's Swiss bank accounts. Prior to her return to Pakistan—which would be fraught with danger—she told her son Bilawal about the family's secret bank accounts. Unknown to her, the US National Security Agency (NSA) had been tapping her phone conversations.[89]

What had complicated the deal were rumours that Musharraf planned to take off his uniform only after the presidential elections had taken place. Benazir told Rice that she was sceptical that Musharraf would implement his promise. She told Rice, 'I'm taking this as a US guarantee that he will'. The deal was announced on 4 October 2007. Musharraf won the presidential elections on 6 October and Benazir returned to Pakistan on 18 October. Her return was met with an assassination attempt in Karachi that she narrowly escaped.[90] A day after the assassination attempt, Musharraf called Benazir and said, 'I'm not the enemy, Bibi.'[91]

However, there were further problems. Musharraf had again decided to impose an emergency because of an anticipated Supreme Court decision against him for contesting elections in uniform. He feared that he could be tried for treason. This time Rice was unable to convince him not to do so. She told President Bush, 'He's done,' but Bush felt otherwise, 'He's got the army with him.' Bush was emphatic. 'I don't want anyone pulling the rug out from under him. The US is not going to be in a position of trying to bring him down.' The vice-president chipped in saying, 'Musharraf was essential to the war on terror.'[92] Rice felt that the US had gone public in support of democracy in Pakistan and Musharraf had demolished any chance of a peaceful transfer of power.

Imposition of emergency wrecked the American plan for a power-sharing agreement between Benazir and Musharraf. Condoleezza called Bhutto to 'reconsider but she was firm'. Benazir announced that she would no longer deal with Musharraf, setting up a confrontation in the January elections. Benazir told her close supporters, 'My success and his failure are now the same thing. There is no middle ground.'[93]

Benazir's Assassination

Did Benzair have a premonition about her impending fate? According to Heraldo Munoz, who headed the UN investigation into the assassination, during a flight to Aspen, Colorado, when she was travelling with US ambassador Zalmay Khalilzad and his wife, just prior to her return to Pakistan, a flight attendant offered

Benazir some freshly baked cookies. She declined as it would adversely impact her weight. However, she called the attendant back and said, 'Oh what's the difference, I'll be dead in a few months anyway.'[94]

Benazir was concerned about her security. She met several important US senators like Senator John Kerry to request assistance in this regard. Musharraf had assured the State Department about Benazir's security. However, aware of how things worked in Washington, Benazir reiterated that Musharraf would listen only to the White House and 'Vice President Cheney should be the one to call him to hold him responsible for her security.'[95]

Though she was reassured—and even said: 'I can't help but feel confident. This is the capital of the world. And if they're behind me, everything should work out. It really should'—there were uncomfortable signs. In a conversation with Musharraf from the office of Congressman Tom Lantos, Benazir wanted to confirm that US officials had 'conversations with you that make it clear that my safety is your responsibility'. 'Yes, some have called,' Musharraf said, and then laughed. 'The Americans can call all they want … You should understand something. Your security is based on the state of our relationship.'[96]

Even prior to her return to Pakistan in April 1986 under Zia-ul-Haq, Benazir had received many threats and inputs about possible plots to kill her. Twenty-one years later, in 2007, another dictator, Musharraf and his government also conveyed dire warnings to Benazir about threats to her life. She, however, received them with reservations because she felt Musharraf was using those threats to scare her to restrict her campaigning. She understood the risks but her concern about a rigged election motivated her to undertake an active campaign. This involved heightened public exposure with attendant risks.[97]

After she returned to Pakistan and in the wake of the 18 October incident, Benazir realized that the US vice-president was not going to intercede with Musharraf regarding her security. This upset her a lot. In Quetta in early December 2007 she told her followers, 'The vice president needs to make a call that I know from talking to diplomats he's not made. He needs to call Musharraf and say, "You hold the cards. If something happens to her, we will hold you responsible." Why can't he make that call?' Realizing that she had miscalculated American support, she told her supporters, 'I took a gamble on democracy, and all I asked of the US is that they cover my bet,' adding, 'Is that too much to ask? But what I am beginning to think is that they've made their choice. That's why Cheney's not calling. They decided to go with their favourite dictator rather than this most cherished American ideal. Why would anyone do something like that?'[98]

Her election speeches thus became very aggressive about Musharraf and her benefactor, the US. For example, while addressing a rally in Quetta in November 2007 Benazir said, 'Every dictator has to date been supported by the US. All we have got under Musharraf are dead bodies in Karachi and warlords in Afghanistan.' This embarrassed the US hugely. Not surprisingly, Anne Patterson, the US ambassador, privately conveyed to Benazir to tone down her rhetoric.[99]

What Benzair did not assess correctly was that the moves to broker a deal between her and Musharraf and reinstate her in Pakistan was, in fact, launched and led by Rice and the State Department. Vice-President Cheney's position was 'don't mess with this'. According to one of his advisers, 'Our feeling was that arranging this marriage can only backfire on us. Bhutto is complicated and unpredictable. It's best to just support Musharraf, give him whatever he wants or needs to stay in power.'[100]

In the intervening night of 26 and 27 December 2007, ISI chief Maj. Gen. Nadeem Taj met Benazir in her house around 1.30 a.m. when her security adviser Rehman Malik was also present. Taj warned her about a possible terrorist attack against her at Liaquat Bagh, Rawalpindi, later that day. As if to reinforce the warning he disclosed that intelligence officers from Saudi Arabia and the UAE had also conveyed credible information about a possible attack. Such information coincided with the intelligence that the ISI had, including about three separate Pakistani Taliban cells that were supposedly planning to attack her. Benazir, however, did not take these reports as credible. She told the DG ISI that it appeared that the government and the ISI did not want her 'to do politics'. She reiterated her demand that she should have proper protection. She, nevertheless, agreed to minimize her exposure at the rally, though she did not do so.[101]

Later, on 27 December 2007, just as Benazir had finished addressing a huge rally in Liaquat Bagh, Rawalpindi, she was assassinated. It was the same venue where Pakistan's first prime minister Liaquat Ali Khan was assassinated in 1951. Benazir's tragedy was that despite her own party forming a government in 2008 in which her husband was the president, there was neither an aggressive investigation, nor an aggressive prosecution. Though she herself had identified key suspects, they were not investigated. As has been well put, 'Ambition for the living trumped grief over the fallen,'[102] and that 'the controversy surrounding her assassination will endure as much as her memory'.[103]

At the time of writing, it does look that the assassination of Benazir will join the already long list of unresolved political assassinations in Pakistan.

8

Nawaz Sharif: The Comeback Kid

Early Life

NAWAZ SHARIF WAS BORN ON 25 December 1949 and brought up in Lahore. Unlike Benazir who grew up in the Sindhi feudal tradition coupled with a Western education, Nawaz's exposure was urban and Pakistani. He studied in Government College, Lahore, where his performance was apparently lacklustre. Anecdotal evidence suggests that his participation in class and his ability to reply to questions was rather limited.[1]

Following his graduation, he was inducted into the family business. Given his lack of accomplishments, he was asked to do public relations for the company. As a backup plan his father Mian Muhammad Sharif arranged with Pakistani actor Saeed Khan Rangeela to get Nawaz into the movies, a dream of his. Unfortunately, after a few days, Saeed Khan Rangeela sent him back, expressing regrets to Mian Sharif that Nawaz was unsuitable for acting and the movie industry. A desperate Mian Sharif then hired cricket coaches to train his son. Unfortunately, Nawaz's physical fitness was not up to it. Anecdotal evidence suggests that by midday on his first day at training, Nawaz Sharif threw the bat down and left the stadium saying, 'This is too tough for me.'[2]

It is believed that at some stage Nawaz wanted to become a police officer, much against the wishes of Mian Sharif. However, the fond father got the Punjab governor, Gen. Jilani Khan,[3] to appoint him as a civil defence sector commander. There he got the opportunity to look and act like a police officer.

Both Nawaz and his younger brother Shahbaz were interested in politics. During the agitation launched by the Pakistan National Alliance (PNA) against Bhutto in 1977, Nawaz formally entered politics by joining Asghar Khan's Tehrik-i-Istiqlal party.[4]

However, fate had other ideas. Gen. Jilani Khan was building his private house in Lahore, the responsibility of which was given to a retired friend and colleague, Maj. Niazi. Niazi sought the help of an overeager Mian Sharif, especially for building an iron fence around the house. For Mian Sharif, a shrewd businessman, this was too good an investment opportunity to pass up. He used it as leverage with Jilani to get several favours for his son.[5]

According to Hassan Abbas, during the construction, the governor often ran into Shahbaz Sharif, Mian Sharif's second son at the site. Shahbaz was bright and impressed the governor. When Gen. Zia decided to induct civilians into provincial cabinets, Mian Sharif, by now well known to the governor for his personal service requested a position for his son. A few days later, Mian Sharif was informed that Shahbaz would be the finance minister in the Punjab cabinet. This was not what Mian Sharif had wanted since Shahbaz was required to run the family business. Without him, it was feared that the business would suffer tremendously. So Mian Sharif went back to the governor and explained the misunderstanding that it was his other son, Nawaz Sharif, the PR man, he wanted to be given a job. Jilani was generous enough to accept this and so Nawaz Sharif was transformed from a PR man of a small steel mill into the finance minister of the largest province of Pakistan. Later he would become chief minister of the province.[6]

Apart from Gen. Jilani, other factors were also working in Nawaz's favour. After the execution of Bhutto, Gen. Zia was keen to build an alternative leadership to the PPP in each of the provinces, especially in Punjab. This was in anticipation of the inevitable return of Benazir to Pakistan who would need to be countered politically. Initially, Zia had considered grooming Abida Hussain, a politician from south Punjab and later Pakistan's ambassador to the US and her husband Fakhar Imam as the power couple to take on Benazir. According to Abida Hussain, Siddique Salik, a close Zia aide and one who died with him in the plane crash in 1988, told her that Zia was dissuaded from doing so by his director, military intelligence, Gen. Hamid Gul. Gul underlined that while they had the requisite background, education and training, they were Shias. If they were groomed, it would upset the Saudis. Hence, Zia shelved the idea. Later, Gen. Jilani persuaded him to choose Nawaz Sharif instead and groom him for leadership.[7] Nawaz had the added advantage of having a grouse against the Bhuttos for nationalizing their iron foundry in the 1970s.

Later on, Jilani would regret his decision to recommend Nawaz Sharif to Gen. Zia. He told A. Cowasjee, a noted business tycoon and columnist, 'Someone had to be found to neutralize Benazir Bhutto and the PPP, and we thought a businessman, uncorrupted by politics, might do better, might help enrich the country and the people. That he enriched himself and his family is unforgivable.'[8]

The stars clearly favoured the Sharifs: Gen. Zia returned the iron foundry that Bhutto had nationalized; and Nawaz was invented as a leader to counter the influence of Benazir. In return, he was permitted to build a business empire by misusing his position first as Punjab's finance minister, later as the chief minister of Punjab and finally as prime minister.

Though a failed actor, Nawaz carried his penchant for the movies into politics. When Nawaz was chief minister of Punjab,

> Nawab Akbar Bugti, the then chief minister of Balochistan, had organized a meeting of the combined opposition parties in Quetta. Prior to the meeting, Nawaz left the room to make an urgent phone call from Bugti's office. Bugti informed the gathering that the chief minister of Punjab was using the telephone sitting in the office of the Balochistan chief minister for the first time in Pakistan's history. Nawaz took a long time to return, so Abida Hussain was sent to call him. When she went to the CM's room, Bugti's PA told her that Nawaz was singing on the phone. She asked the PA to knock hard on the door. Soon enough Nawaz returned to the meeting.
>
> (Syeda Abida Hussain, *Power Failure: The Political Odyssey of a Pakistani Woman*, Karachi: OUP, 2015, pp. 337–38.)

Nawaz Sharif's favourite singer was Mohammad Rafi, the legendary Indian playback singer. He liked classical ragas like Bhairavi and Darbari. A big fan of Hindi films, his chosen actors were Dilip Kumar, Waheeda Rehman and Madhubala.[9]

Personality

According to Shuja Nawaz, 'Sharif represented a new breed of businessmen-cum-politician, with a strong conservative bent, ideally suited to reflect the needs of the growing urban population of Punjab and to undermine the support of both the left and the right, including the Islamic parties.'[10]

When Nawaz started off in politics, he was considered 'a polite, well-mannered young man who smiled easily and was difficult to dislike. Sumptuous repasts exerted the greatest pull on him, and even those very partial to him could not help but comment on the amazing brevity of his attention span.'[11] People noticed that he rarely followed discussions attentively but if the subject was of interest to him, especially if it involved a personal financial angle, he could be quick and decisive. At these moments, he would suddenly interject forcefully, for which he seemed to have come prepared.[12]

Later, Nawaz would develop into a more complex personality and even those who had known him for decades would not be able to understand him fully. In 2009, Sartaj Aziz, a close aide of Nawaz, wrote that he was 'very impulsive by nature and therefore thrived on dramatic moves rather than well-considered decisions'. Sartaj attributed this to Nawaz's strong belief in the importance of his personal power, a belief that was based in his public popularity. Not surprisingly, he adopted 'a system of personalized decision-making, without adequate consultations or participation of his cabinet colleagues, parliament or other relevant bodies'. It was this need to consolidate his personal power base rather than the institutions that were the mainstays of a viable democratic system, which eventually led to his dramatic downfall.[13] This analysis was as true of his first dismissal as of his second and third.

According to Gen. Musharraf, 'Though he [Nawaz] was a city boy his mental make-up was largely feudal – he mistook dissent for disloyalty.'[14] Musharraf also called Nawaz Sharif a 'closet Taliban'. Former ISI officer Khalid Khwaja supported Musharraf's assertion. He said he was present when Nawaz met Osama bin Laden on six different occasions. 'I should know,' Khwaja told the *Guardian*. 'I arranged those meetings.'[15]

Christina Lamb notes that chubby and petulant Sharif told her once that he fancied himself as a Mughal king. She, however, felt that with his balding head and short stature his resemblance was more like a little Buddha. She wrote 'Sharif had none of the charisma of Bhutto, and, a wooden speaker, was uneasy on a platform or with journalists'[16]

Nawaz Sharif's fondness for food is legendary. Christina Lamb notes that 'equipped with the chief minister's helicopter and Cessna plane, he could cover far more ground sustained by the whole chickens he would devour for breakfast'.[17] Visuals showing him consuming burgers on London's Oxford Street just prior to his heart surgery in 2016 would be a permanent testimony to his culinary tastes.

> In the March 1985 elections, Nawaz won seats for both the National Assembly and the Punjab assembly. Seeing him in the visitors' gallery in the National Assembly he was asked if he was going to take over as chief minister of Punjab. In response, he gave a strange glance, full of meaning and mystery, but did not answer the question. According to Sartaj Aziz, in later years, this glance became characteristic of him, appearing whenever he could not give a straight reply yet could not fully conceal his inner reactions or conflicts. On this occasion, it was clear that he had not received a nod from the real masters so he was sitting in the National Assembly as a visitor.
>
> (Sartaj Aziz, *Between Dreams and Realities: Some Milestones in Pakistan's History*, Karachi: OUP, 2009, pp. 89–90.)
>
> ***
>
> Imran Khan who first met Nawaz at a cricket club in the late 1970s felt he 'seemed a regular guy with little drive or ambition, more interested in cricket than politics. His real dream would have been to be captain of the Pakistani cricket team. He just loved the glamour of the sport.'
>
> (Imran Khan, *Pakistan: A Personal History*, London: Transworld Publishers, 2011, pp. 130–31.)

Imran Khan writes about an incident that goes to heart of Nawaz's personality and illustrates his mindset. There was a warm-up match against the West Indies at the Gaddafi stadium in Lahore in the run up to the cricket World Cup in October 1987. Imran Khan was captaining Pakistan. Just before the match the secretary of the cricket board Shahid Rafi told Imran that the chief minister of Punjab, Nawaz Sharif, would captain the team that day. Imran was surprised but thought that Nawaz would be the non-playing captain, wanting to see the match from the dressing room. However, Imran was stunned to see Nawaz walk out for the toss with Viv Richards, the West Indian captain. Nawaz was dressed in cricket whites. He won the toss and elected to bat. In the dressing room, Nawaz started putting on his pads. No one in the team could believe that he was going to partner Mudassar Nazar in opening the innings against one of the greatest fast-bowling attacks in cricket history. While Mudassar was well-protected with batting pads, thigh pad, chest pad, arm guard, helmet and reinforced batting gloves, Nawaz simply had his batting pads, a floppy hat—and a smile!

An unprotected Nawaz Sharif, without any experience of playing at this level of cricket, walked out against the blistering pace attack by the West Indies, the kind of which had not been seen before or since. There was a certain risk of grave injury if a short-pitched ball was aimed at his body because Nawaz would not have the reflexes to defend himself. Imran quickly inquired if there was an ambulance ready.

The first ball—by a 6-ft-6-inch West Indian fast bowler—went into the gloves of the wicketkeeper before Sharif could even lift his bat. Luckily for Sharif, the second ball shattered his stumps before he could move.[18]

The incident, according to Imran Khan, reflected Sharif's penchant for circumventing the whole process of working his way up the ladder and instead wanting to start at the top. He became finance minister without being a politician and got power without having to earn it the hard way. It was his loyalty and subservience to Zia, rather than experience or merit, that enabled him to vault into politics and progress speedily from finance minister in 1981 to chief minister in 1985 and later prime minister.[19]

Nawaz suffered in comparison with Benazir. As the American journalist Kim Barker put it, Benazir was 'smooth, a master performer, charisma personified, always in control. Sharif seemed more like a baffled everyman, nondescript and beige.'[20]

Nawaz seemed to have developed a crush on Kim Barker offering to find her a boyfriend. Later he suggested Asif Zardari and when she turned that down, he offered himself to be her friend. When she rebuffed him, he 'admitted that he was not as tall as she would like, not as fit as she would like, that he was fat and he was old. But he would still like to be her friend.' He even claimed that he would only become prime minister again if she were his secretary. He offered to buy her an iPhone with a new number since phones in Pakistan were tapped. She declined to accept it. Unfortunately for Nawaz, she saw him as 'just another sad case, a recycled has-been who squandered his country's adulation and hope, who thought hitting on a foreign journalist was a smart move'.

Nawaz had even confided to her after the Mumbai attacks that the attackers were from Pakistan. He also told her about the lone surviving terrorist belonging to Faridkot, in Okara district.

(Kim Barker, *The Taliban Shuffle: Strange Days in Afghanistan and Pakistan*, New York: Anchor Books, 2012, pp. 228, 233–34, 251, 252–53.)

***

On 11 September 1989, the Muslim League held a public meeting at Mochi Gate, Lahore, where the speakers used thinly disguised sexual innuendoes that marked a new low in politics. Prominent editor Mazhar Ali Khan noted that by denigrating Benazir, the speakers showed their disrespect for all women and womanhood. Worse was when Nawaz, the chief minister of Punjab, publicly advised his parliamentarians to sing the war song '*Jang khaid nahin hondi zananian di*' (war is not a game for women) in the National Assembly. Mazhar Ali lamented, 'There was an uncouthness about the speakers' behaviour that has shocked all decent people of Lahore.'

(Mazhar Ali Khan, *Pakistan: The Barren Years: The Viewpoint, Editorials and Columns of Mazhar Ali Khan, 1975-1992*, Karachi: OUP, 1998, pp. 447–48.)

Business Interests

Prior to the entry of Nawaz into politics, the line between business and politics in Pakistan was pretty well established. While feudal elements dominated the power structure and used the power of the state to increase their landholdings, the outright misuse of the financial resources of the state reached its peak under Nawaz. As Ayaz Amir puts it, '... the first interest of this dynasty was always the building up of their business empire. Politics and power were means to that end.'[21]

Mian Sharif and his six brothers founded the Ittefaq foundry in 1939. This was nationalized under Bhutto's government. Thereafter, Mian Sharif went to the UAE where he set up a steel re-rolling mill. When Zia came to power, he returned the Ittefaq foundry to the Sharifs, while Nawaz was appointed finance minister in the Punjab cabinet. At that time, the Ittefaq group had little more than the foundry and a textile mill. The entire family's earnings were few million rupees. In 1981–82, according to Ittefaq Industries report, the turnover had been Rs 337 million. By 1986–87 it was at least Rs 2,500 million.[22]

Starting with only a seventh-share in a family-owned steel foundry, the Sharif family's business fortunes prospered at an electrifying speed and it soon became one of the wealthiest in

> the country. As *Dawn*'s weekly columnist Ardeshir Cowasjee commented, had Nawaz not been firstly the finance minister of Punjab, then its chief minister, and finally prime minister, the Sharif family would have been unable to borrow even five per cent of what they did borrow by misusing his powers. He also issued orders that specifically benefited his family business.'
>
> Ardeshir Cowasjee, 'End of Story', *Dawn*, 3 January 1999, http://www.oocities.org/collegepark/library/9803/cowasjee/cowas_end_story.html (accessed on 3 December 2017).

With the acquisition of political power in the 1980s, new industrial units were set up speedily: Ittefaq Sugar Mills in 1982, Brothers Steel in 1983, Brothers Textile Mills in 1986, Ittefaq Textile units 2 and 3 in 1987, Khalid Siraj Textile Mills in 1988. Work was also started on Brothers Sugar Mills and Ramzan Sugar Mills. These were the last projects set up under the banner of Ittefaq. After Nawaz Sharif became prime minister in 1990, his father Mian Sharif began to establish projects separately from his other brothers. This would eventually lead to a family split.[23]

All these mills were financed through loans from the government. Zia-ul-Haq approved Nawaz's loan requests as also his loan write-off requests. Not surprisingly, the first Public Accounts Committee of the PPP government found that the two top loan defaulters, whose loans had been written off were Choudhury brothers, Rs 22 billion, and Mian Sharif Rs 21 billion. These are still on record in the PAC Report of 1989.[24]

By the time of Zia-ul-Haq's fatal plane crash in 1988, Mian Muhammad Sharif's family was earning a net profit of US $3 million, up from a few million rupees in 1981. By the end of the decade their net assets were worth nearly US $350 million according to their own admission.[25]

The business grew exponentially after Nawaz Sharif became the prime minister. At that time, the group changed the modalities of its operations—project loans were taken from the foreign banks and only working capital was taken from the nationalized commercial banks. The project financing from foreign banks was ostensibly secured against the foreign currency deposits, many of which were held in benami accounts, as claimed by the then interior minister Naseerullah Babar at a press conference. In 1992, PPP leader Salman Taseer released an account of Nawaz Sharif's financial dealings alleging that the family had taken loans of up to Rs 12 billion, which were never paid back.

> In the 1990s, the house of Ittefaq split up with 119 offsprings, siblings and spouses of the seven founding brothers battling in courts for the division of the assets of the Ittefaq group. According to an agreement reached in the Lahore High Court by members of the family sometime in 1996, the house of Ittefaq was split into two groups. The first comprised the families of Mian Muhammad Sharif, Mohammad Shafi, Barkat Ali, Yousaf Aziz and Idrees Bashir while the second group comprised of the families of Meraj Din and Siraj Din. Members of the Ittefaq group are currently operating in three groups, namely, Sharif Group, Ittefaq Group and Haseeb Waqas Group.
>
> (Shahid-ur-Rahman, 'Who owns Pakistan', p. 137.)

Two representative examples will suffice about the modalities of how Nawaz used political power for profit making. The first was privatization. As chief minister of Punjab, Nawaz presided over the liquidation/privatization of several units of Punjab Industrial and Development Corporation (PIDC) like Pasrur Sugar Mills, Samundri Sugar, Rahwali Sugar, Paras Textile, Harappa Textile Mills and Ghazi Textile Mills Ltd. How and on what prices these units were sold were unknown but according to 'company review' in the *Dawn* in May 1991, Pasrur Sugar Mills was sold to United

Sugar Mills of United Group for a 'token price of Re one only'. Samundri Sugar Mills was sold to Monoos and Rahwali Sugar to a Muslim League politician, Sheikh Mansoor, following single-line advertisement in newspapers under the caption, 'Bids invited for Rahwali Sugar Mills'.[26]

This kind of privatization continued when Sharif became prime minister. Thus, within a month of being sworn in as prime minister for the first time on 6 November 1990, bids were invited for the privatization of Muslim Commercial Bank (MCB) on 15 December 1990. Its privatization to the Mansha Group and others was announced on 9 January 1991, within two months of his assuming power. Even though there were two higher bids, including from the original owner Adamjee, the third bidder—Mansha Group—was declared winner.

The second example is of manipulating customs duties to favour the Ittefaq Group. In 1991–92 when Nawaz was the prime minister, the customs duty on shredded and bundled scrap was reduced from Rs 1,500 to Rs 500 per tonne but the custom duty on ship-breaking was reduced from Rs 1,500 per tonne to Rs 1,000 only. This difference in customs duty inflicted a death blow to the ship-breaking industry but yielded Rs 1,024 million to Ittefaq foundry.[27]

When Nawaz was dismissed on 18 April 1993, the Dissolution Order listed 'the lack of transparency in the process of privatization and in the disposal of public/government properties' as one of the grounds for dismissal. Although the Nawaz government was restored by the Supreme Court, three judges found its privatization to be faulty and in conflict with the provisions of the constitution. A fourth judge, Justice Sajjad Ali Shah, who had dissented from the main judgment restoring Nawaz's government, found corruption in privatization as a valid ground for dismissal of the government.[28]

Given Nawaz's track record of using public office as a means of getting rich, a newspaper even claimed that 'all four Pakistani dictators put together have made less corrupt-money than Nawaz Sharif'.[29]

Nawaz Sharif's extravagant home and gardens in Raiwind, near Lahore, have been the subject of much controversy largely due to the public money spent on it. Kim Barker called it Nawaz Land, 'given the amusement-park feel and the fact that his name and picture were on everything, from hospital to billboards'. She added that his face, '... amiable, slightly podgy, topped with hair plugs, stared at her like the Cheshire cat.' The grounds themselves were 'a cross between a golf course and a zoo, with several football fields of manicured grass and wild animals in cages, leading up to a miniature palace that looked slightly like a wedding cake ...'[30]

Style of Governance

Nawaz was prime minister thrice—from November 1990 to July 1993, from February 1997 to October 1999 and from May 2014 to July 2017. All three terms were ended prematurely—once each by the president, the army chief and the judiciary respectively.

Nawaz is associated with two expressions in Pakistan's political lexicon. One is 'lifafa (envelope) journalism' and the other is 'changa-manga politics'. The former refers to the practice of buying off journalists with cash while politicians were bribed with plots of government-owned land.[31] This was meant to ensure that journalists did not publish stories of the Sharifs bullying banks into giving them multimillion-rupee loans.

'Changa-manga politics' came to the fore in 1988 when Nawaz paid off and then literally hijacked a group of independent provincial legislators to an isolated rest house in the forest of Changa Manga outside Lahore. Here they were lavishly entertained till it was time to vote for Nawaz's government. This was done to ensure that the PPP could not make them a counter-offer to form the government in Punjab. By this tactic, Nawaz outmanoeuvred Benazir in Punjab and cornered the decisive vote of the independent members to form the government.[32]

A noticeable feature of Nawaz's governance style has been his dictatorial attitude. This was quite evident in his second tenure when he had an absolute majority in the National Assembly. He started off with clipping the powers of the president to dismiss an elected prime minister by repealing the infamous eighth amendment to the constitution. He then dismissed a navy chief on corruption charges and even sent the army chief packing for talking about a national security council. He then got rid of the chief justice and the president. In addition, Benazir, the leader of the opposition, had been disqualified from holding public office for seven years. All this had placed Nawaz in a position that perhaps no other prime minister enjoyed in Pakistan's history. However, instead of using these opportunities to provide good governance, his rule turned into a despotic government, which did not accept the rule of law and institutional limits on the use of power.[33]

Despite having got rid of every other significant centre of power, Nawaz's hunger for amassing more power had not been satiated. In August 1998, he introduced the fifteenth constitutional amendment in the National Assembly. In the garb of enforcing Islamic rule in Pakistan, the bill in effect represented a bid to grab unrestricted power with the directives of the government in this sphere being put beyond the jurisdiction of courts and judicial review.[34] It would have given Nawaz dictatorial powers as the 'amir-ul-momineen' or leader of the faithful.

The bill, with minor changes, was passed in the Lower House on 9 October 1998. But Nawaz was just a little short of the numbers in the Senate. Despite mobilizing the clergy to threaten the senators, the bill could not pass. Before he could get a majority in the Senate in March 2000, Musharraf booted him out in a coup.

In his long political career, Nawaz has not hesitated to use force to achieve his objectives. A classic example is of the meeting the

Muslim League Central Executive held in an Islamabad hotel to elect office-bearers of the party in 1988. As Muhammad Khan Junejo tried to get himself re-elected president, Sharif's men stormed the meeting, ensuring that Junejo could not do so.[35] According to Khaled Ahmed 'the meeting declined into an orgy of eating. Nawaz's Punjabi followers fell on the food, ate from the donga (serving dishes), threw the bones on the floor, and wiped their 'shorba' (gravy)-covered hands on the curtains. After they left the hotel shouting victory, the dining hall looked like a wasteland.'[36]

Little less than a decade later, in 1997, Nawaz, his party leaders and workers physically attacked the Supreme Court of Pakistan, forcing the chief justice to flee from the court. Nawaz sanctioned such an extreme measure because the chief justice had the temerity to start contempt proceedings against him. As will be noted later in this chapter, something similar is being attempted against the judiciary in the Panama papers case.

Despite his best efforts, Nawaz was not able to get any traction with the Western media. For example, in 1997 Nawaz addressed the UN General Assembly and spoke about Kashmir and a no-war pact with India. His bilateral meetings were high-profile ones. Though his speech and meetings were covered extensively in the Pakistani media there was no mention in the American press. Nawaz was quite dismayed at this. Mushahid Hussain, the information minister suggested that the prime minister should address the journalists in person to get good coverage. Hence, a press conference was arranged at the Roosevelt Hotel in New York that was attended by many correspondents but only three of them were non-Pakistanis. Once again, there was no reporting about the press conference in any US paper or TV channel.[37]

Christina Lamb writes about an incident when she had returned to her hotel after covering a rally in Sharif's Lahore constituency. The crowds were disappointing and she left. Later, Nawaz requested her to return because 'it [the rally] was now much bigger'. Reluctantly Lamb went back and far more people had indeed appeared. However, she could not help imagining Sharif's men desperately rounding up innocent residents to appear before a Western journalist.[38]

Nawaz Sharif was infamous for his 'monarchical-style' and his habit of ruling through verbal orders. There was no proper body of advisers and he used 'publicity' 'as substitute for policy'. His immediate successor after his dismissal in 1993, Moeen Qureshi, the interim prime minister, admitted that the 'Government was being used as an instrument of political patronage' and 'being run as a feudal estate rather than as a representative government'.[39]

His monarchical style was reflected in his propensity to wander around the country and hold open courts, sometimes televised live, where people could personally approach him and get justice. One example of this was his handling of the public meeting of the Faisalabad Development Authority on 10 March 1997. Three officers 'appeared to be party to the purchase of defective water meters and to have misappropriated large sums of government funds'. In a fit of righteous wrath, Sharif 'ordered their arrest and they were, in fact, handcuffed by the police and taken into custody in his presence'.[40]

As a Punjabi, Nawaz had the advantage of not seeing himself as an 'outsider', a feeling that persisted about Junejo and Benazir.[41] Nawaz had championed the cause of Punjab vis-à-vis other provinces. '*Jaag Punjabi Jaag, teri pagri nu lagi aag*' (wake up Punjabis, wake up, your turban, i.e., pride, has caught fire, is being destroyed) was a slogan used by Nawaz's party frequently in elections. On one occasion, during a meeting at the home of Shujaat Hussain, Nawaz asked, 'What do we get out of ousting Benazir and replacing her with Jatoi? They are both Sindhis after all.'[42] His kitchen cabinet too was comprised almost entirely of Punjabis. He liked to surround himself with people who stuck with him whether there was any need for them or not.

All through his three terms, Nawaz has run the country with a coterie of family members and confidants. The cabinet system of governance had been given a go-by. According to a report, the federal cabinet, which was supposed to meet at least fifty-two times in a year, only managed to meet six times during 2016. Likewise, the Punjab cabinet under Nawaz's brother Shahbaz met for a total of three times in 2016. The report blamed consistent lack of institutionalized decision making as the main cause of the poor performance of the federal and provincial governments in 2016. The Supreme Court in August 2016 struck down Rule 16 (2) of the Rules of Business of the Federal Government, 1973, that gave the prime minister the discretionary power to bypass the federal cabinet. It reminded the prime minister that his decisions had no legal value unless taken in the cabinet meeting.[43]

Though Nawaz liked to equate his survival with that of democracy, his record as a parliamentarian has been quite dismal. By mostly remaining absent from their sittings, he has shown his disregard for the National Assembly and the Senate. During his years in the opposition, 1993–96, Nawaz hardly attended the National Assembly, perhaps fearful that the PPP would raise issues concerning his private dealings and business interests. He started attending the assembly more frequently in 1996 when Benazir ran into trouble.[44]

In the first parliamentary year of his third term, Nawaz attended the National Assembly for merely seven days. It was when the government appeared to be in danger due to Imran Khan's dharnas in 2014 that he started appearing regularly in assembly sessions. Once parliament (Majlis-e-Shura) stood with him and bailed him out, his attendance dropped again. In 2016, he attended only 10 per cent of the total sittings of the National Assembly and his brother the chief minister of Punjab only attended 8 per cent of the total provincial assembly sittings. As per a report released by the Free and Fair Elections Network (FAFEN), out of 289 sittings conducted in thirty-two sessions between June 2013 and May 2016, Nawaz was present a total of thirty-nine times: a paltry 13.5 per cent attendance.[45]

In 2015–16, Nawaz Sharif attended the Senate only once out of the 103 sittings of the House. This was in violation of Rule 61(2A) that had been amended by the senators in 2014 to make it mandatory for the prime minister to attend the zero hour of the Senate at least once a week.[46]

Worse, the PPP proposed an amendment to the National Assembly's rules making it mandatory for the prime minister to attend parliament every Wednesday and answer questions. However, the treasury benches categorically rejected the move on the grounds that the prime minister had to 'deal with many other administrative issues'.[47]

Nawaz's disregard for the opposition was in evidence when in May 2017 he compared his political rivals to terrorists. Addressing a gathering in Sukkur he said the agenda of terrorists was to create disruption, chaos, law and order situation and to push Pakistan back to the dark ages. 'A similar objective was being pursued by those who stage sit-ins, cause agitation and hinder country's march ahead.'[48] Thus, for Nawaz, holding protests and asking him to step down due to the Panama Papers controversy was just as bad as the bloodshed and violence enacted by terrorists. The fact that the democratic opposition was well within its constitutional rights to demand accountability was not relevant to Nawaz.

Nuclear Tests

Though Pakistan conducted its nuclear tests in 1998, as early as 1991, during Nawaz's first term, President Ghulam Ishaq Khan briefed Abida Hussain who was going to the US as ambassador on the issue. He told her that she needed to keep the Americans engaged in dialogue on the nuclear issue for about eighteen months. This was the time required for Pakistan to the take its nuclear programme to the level of deterrence.[49]

The nuclear tests are indicative of Nawaz's decision-making process. After India's nuclear tests in May 1998, an emergency meeting of the cabinet was called to consider Pakistan's response. Nawaz Sharif informed the cabinet that the army chief was non-committal and said it was up to the cabinet. Gohar Ayub Khan strongly advocated that Pakistan should do likewise. Most colleagues agreed with him. Abida Hussain suggested a review after six months. In the interim, they should enjoy the world heaping blame on India. Nisar Ali, Mushahid Hussain and Sartaj Aziz supported her point of view.[50] In a subsequent meeting, Nawaz announced he was not in favour of testing but quickly retracted when he found he was isolated.[51]

Two factors seemed to have tilted the balance in favour of testing: cynicism about the American promises and the reassurance of the Saudi government to go ahead. By taking the Saudis into confidence Nawaz played on the Saudi ego and developed a very special relationship with Prince Abdullah. An additional factor was Nawaz's belief that Pakistan's nuclear status would attract more funding from Islamic countries than that promised by the Americans.[52]

Pakistan successfully conducted five nuclear tests on 28 May 1998. Nawaz was present at the test site in Chaghai as were the majority of the ministers who had opposed the test, making victory signs. On the other hand, those who had supported the tests were left behind in Islamabad.[53]

Buoyed by the tests, Nawaz visited Kuwait and addressed the Pakistani community there. The diaspora praised the tests but disapproved the freezing of their foreign currency accounts. As was his wont, without consulting the finance minister, Sartaj Aziz, Nawaz announced the withdrawal of the freeze. This shocked Sartaj Aziz who anxiously began to stop the news from spreading. Fortunately for him, the news did not travel far. The freeze remained in place.[54]

This was not the only example of his penchant for impetuous decisions without proper consultations. He almost agreed to join a mutual defence pact with a Gulf state that provided for the two countries to come to each other's assistance in the case of a conflict. Nawaz was unaware that there were three or four islands in dispute between this Gulf state and Iran. Had Pakistan signed the defence agreement, it would have led to hostility with Iran. When briefed, Nawaz asked, 'Which islands are these, and where are they?'[55] He was once again going to take a decision without knowing the facts of the case.

> The policy of playing a duplicitous role in Afghanistan did not begin with Musharraf. Pakistan had recognized the Taliban government in May 1997. However, they did not want to sever their links to the erstwhile mujahideen government. Hence, Nawaz had a message sent to the chief minister of NWFP to contact the president of the former government, Prof. Rabbani, and bring him and his colleagues to Islamabad. Arrangements were even made to send a plane to Mazar-i-Sharif to fetch them. However, the Taliban got wind of the plan and sent a stern message that they would shoot down the Pakistani plane if it flew over their territory. Later, the Taliban complained through a private source that 'the Pakistanis were neither good friends nor good foes and that we were trying to straddle both positions simultaneously'.
>
> (Gohar Ayub Khan, *Glimpses into the Corridors of Power*, Karachi: OUP, 2007, pp. 289–90.)

Nawaz and the Army

Nawaz had begun his political career, courtesy the help and encouragement of the martial law administration in 1981. Not surprisingly, initially he avoided any opposition to the role of the army in Pakistan's politics. When the military forged the Islamic Democratic Alliance (IDA) in the run-up to the 1988 elections, he was its ardent supporter and became its head. Hamid Gul, director general, Inter-Services Intelligence (ISI) and Maj. Gen. Asad Durrani (the then director general military intelligence [DGMI]) often remarked with delight that Nawaz Sharif was a product of their agency, their pride and symbol.[56] According to an affidavit filed in the Supreme Court by Gen. Durrani, Nawaz Sharif, among other politicians, received 3.5 million rupees from them in the run-up to the 1990 elections.[57]

Nawaz remained the army's protégé for quite some time. After Zia's death in August 1988, Nawaz was quite unsure about his own future role. He, together with the chief minister of NWFP Gen. Fazle Haq, went to see the army chief Gen. Aslam Beg and implored him to impose the martial law.[58] For three years after Zia's death, Nawaz would go to his grave and pay tribute to his political mentor.[59]

Later, however, after taking over as prime minister, Nawaz started distancing himself from the army leading to an eventual deterioration of relations. This was when Nawaz felt that he had developed his own mass base and no longer needed the army's support. This feeling would soon lead to Nawaz discovering his democratic credentials and asserting civil authority vis-à-vis the military.[60]

Gohar Ayub Khan notes that in the 1993–96 period, the ISI had bugged specific rooms and tables in a leading hotel of Islamabad as also Nawaz Sharif's rooms in Murree. After that Nawaz would visit spy shops in London and pick up counter-bugging equipment.

(Ibid., p. 256.)

Nawaz Sharif has had the distinction of appointing five army chiefs in his three tenures as prime minister. The distinction is, however, dubious, since his relations with each of them have been far from happy.

He appointed Asif Nawaz Janjua as the army chief in 1991, but relations with him were tense till the general died in harness. Waheed Kakar was appointed in 1993. He together with President Ghulam Ishaq Khan booted Nawaz out; Pervez Musharraf was appointed the chief by Nawaz in 1998 who deposed him in a coup. Raheel Sharif whom Nawaz had appointed in 2013 whittled down Nawaz's stature in proportion to the increase in his own. His last appointment has been Qamar Javed Bajwa and though no breakdown in relations have been reported at the time of writing, undercurrents were obvious.

When there was tension between Nawaz and the then army chief Gen. Janjua, someone close to the prime minister announced that they would make a 'Gul Hassan'[61] out of him. One of the MNAs (Member of the National Assembly) reported this to the army chief. Thereafter, Gen. Asif used to bring an additional escort when he came from Rawalpindi to Islamabad.[62]

The Sharifs tried hard to win over the army chiefs. One of the tactics used was to develop personal relationships. For example, Mian Sharif (Abba-ji) sat down his two sons before the new army chief Asif Nawaz and told him in Punjabi, their common language: 'These two are your younger brothers. If they misbehave, just tell me and I shall fix them!'[63] Abba-ji would enact a similar drama with Musharraf in 1999.

The other tactic of winning over generals was gifting them new BMW cars. Hence the corps commanders came to be known as 'Crore Commanders'.[64] One day, Shahbaz Sharif visited Gen. Asif Nawaz Janjua and presented him the keys to a BMW, saying: 'Abba-ji has sent as a gift for you.'[65] Gen. Janjua refused with thanks. Later, as he prepared to leave after a meeting with Nawaz in Murree, the prime minister accompanied him to his car, surrounded by colleagues and asked, 'What car are you using?' 'A Toyota Crown,' replied Gen. Janjua, pointing to the old model he had used for his visit. 'This car does not befit you,' said Sharif in Punjabi and signalled to a colleague who trotted off and drove back a new BMW sedan. Sharif presented the keys to the BMW to Gen. Janjua saying: 'This is the car that you deserve.' Gen. Janjua was momentarily frozen by Nawaz's audacity. Recovering, he returned the keys to the PM saying, 'Thank you very much, Sir! I am happy with what I have'.[66]

Nawaz's views on the ISI were revealed in the series of interviews he gave to journalist Sohail Warraich that was later published as a book. According to Nawaz, the ISI did nothing apart from politics. Instead of its true role, the agency was focused on making and breaking political parties, manipulating elections, changing the loyalties of politicians by blackmailing MNAs. He averred that without curtailing the role of the ISI, no government could progress and the political system would not be stable. He suggested that there should be no serving officer in the ISI and that if the army chief wanted to be a super prime minister, he should be elected.[67]

Kargil 1999

The US had been watching the growing Kargil crisis in 1999 with concern. Given the potential for escalation, the US was keen that Pakistan withdraw its forces back, behind the Line of Control (LOC) immediately. The US sent several messages in this regard to Pakistan and India; it went public calling upon Pakistan to respect the LOC; President Clinton called leaders of both the countries in mid-June and sent letters to each pressing for a Pakistani withdrawal and Indian restraint.[68]

Faced with Pakistan's growing isolation, Nawaz became alarmed. On 2 and 3 July 1999, he spoke to President Clinton and appealed for immediate American intervention to stop the fighting and to resolve the Kashmir issue. Clinton maintained a consistent position: he could help only if Pakistan first withdrew to the LOC, not otherwise. Sharif said he was coming and would be there on the 4 July. Thus, even prior to the Clinton–Sharif summit of 4 July 1999, Clinton had fixed the bar: a clear commitment on withdrawal from the LOC.

Interestingly, Nawaz took his wife and children with him for the trip. The US assessed this as his apprehension of returning home if the summit failed or that he had been asked by the military to leave.

Sharif's commercial PIA flight was diverted from JFK, New York, to Dulles Airport, Washington DC. The Americans had asked the Saudi ambassador to the US, Prince Bandar bin Sultan, to meet Nawaz on arrival to assess his state of mind and 'weigh in forcefully' with him. After meeting Nawaz at the airport, the Saudi ambassador told Bruce Riedel that the prime minister was 'distraught, deeply worried about the direction the crisis was going towards disaster, but equally worried about his own hold on power and the threat from his military chiefs who were pressing for a tough stand'.

If what Bandar bin Sultan reported was correct, clearly Nawaz was being economical with the truth when he asserted later (see chapter on Musharraf) that Musharraf asked him to extricate the army from Kargil when he met him at the airport prior to his departure for Washington.

According to Bruce Riedel, before the summit meeting, the American side took two important decisions. One was of not letting Nawaz be alone with the president. This was to ensure that he could not later claim commitments that had not been made by Clinton. Basically, Nawaz was not trusted and it was apprehended that he may twist any conversation in his favour. Second, nothing of import should be said when Foreign Secretary Shamshad Ahmad was in earshot since he was known to be very close to the ISI.

As the US had anticipated, during the delegation-level talks and later in his meeting with Clinton, Nawaz asked several times to be left alone with the president. On each such occasion, Clinton refused saying he wanted a record of the discussions.

The key point Nawaz emphasized was 'a deal that would allow Pakistan to withdraw with some saving of face'. Without this, 'the fundamentalists in Pakistan would move against him and this meeting would be his last with Clinton'. He had even requested China 'to press India to agree to a fixed timetable for talks to resolve Kashmir. According to Riedel, 'Sharif's brief was confused and vague on many details but he seemed a man possessed with fear of war.'

Clinton, however, was very direct that there were no options except withdrawal to the LOC, or Pakistan would face isolation and would 'fight a wider and dangerous war with India without American sympathy'. He also made clear that 'there could be no quid pro quo, no hint that America was rewarding Pakistan for its aggression, nor for threatening its nuclear arsenal at India. If the United States appeared to be acting under a nuclear threat its ability to restrain othersfrom threatening use of their nuclear forces would be forever undermined.' According to Riedel, Clinton also told Sharif that he had warned him on 2 July not to come to Washington unless he was ready to withdraw without any precondition or quid pro quo. Clinton also accused him of setting up the US to fail but he would not let that happen. His ominous words were, 'Pakistan is messing with nuclear war.'

Finally, Nawaz agreed to the draft statement prepared by the US side. The key sentence read 'the Prime Minister has agreed to take concrete and immediate steps for the restoration of the LOC'. The statement also called for a ceasefire once the withdrawal was completed and restoration of the Lahore process. Clinton told Sharif that this language meant a Pakistani withdrawal. Reluctantly, the prime minister said yes. Nawaz asked for an additional sentence: 'The President would take personal interest to encourage an expeditious resumption and intensification of the bilateral efforts (i.e., Lahore) once the sanctity of the LOC had been fully restored.' The US side agreed to this.

As the US delegation was exiting from Blair House, Sharif's foreign secretary Ahmad, made a last-minute effort to reopen the text. He approached Sandy Berger with a list of alterations in the text. Sandy dismissed him with a curt 'your boss says it is ok as is'.

Subsequently, after the Pakistani withdrawal and ceasefire, Clinton asked Sharif to send someone trusted to discuss the follow-up on his 'personal commitment' to the Lahore process. It was only in September that Nawaz sent his brother Shahbaz Sharif, the chief minister of Punjab. However, instead of discussing Kashmir, Shahbaz only wanted to discuss how the US could help Nawaz stay in power. 'He all but said that they knew a military coup was coming,' notes Riedel.

Panama Papers

What have come to be called the 'Panama Papers' are over eleven million documents of a Panamanian law firm Mossack Fonseca that were leaked by the International Consortium of Investigative Journalists (ICIJ) on 3 April 2016. These documents detailed financial information of more than 200,000 offshore entities containing personal financial information about individuals and public officials who had used shell companies for their wealth. The children of Prime Minister Nawaz Sharif and their properties in London were named in the papers, together with Russia's Vladimir Putin, the king of Saudi Arabia, Iceland's prime minister and Britain's David Cameron.

The 'Panama Papers' are perhaps the greatest challenge that Nawaz Sharif has had to face in his over three decades in politics. The reason is that for the past thirty years Nawaz's proclivity has been to use the electoral verdict as an excuse to indulge in corruption on a massive scale. That he could do so for so long was due to his ability to short-circuit the judicial process and 'manage' the judiciary to ensure favourable decisions for himself and his family. For the first time in his career, he is now faced with the blindness of the law like other mortals; his transgressions are facing judicial scrutiny without his being able to manipulate the due process. This is something he has not been able to come to terms with.

> Nawaz's own approach to corruption was evident during a speech at an inauguration function in May 2017. He said, 'There is so much corruption in the country that if we get involved in probing them all our time will be consumed in the investigations and we will not be able to deliver. There are so many scandals and frauds that they cannot even be listed.
>
> (PM's observations on corruption, *Dawn*, 8 May 2017, https://www.dawn.com/news/1331657/pms-observations-on-corruption [accessed on 9 September 2017]).

Two issues have damaged Nawaz's case. First, no one else in the world named in the Panama Papers has questioned their veracity or said they were fabricated or called it an 'international conspiracy'. Second, it has been the failure of Nawaz and his family to provide the money trail that leads to suspicions about the legality of the source of funds. The critical questions that Nawaz has not been able to answer satisfactorily are: when were the London flats bought; with what money were they bought; and whether the money used was declared in election declarations and income tax returns.

At the nub of the charges against Nawaz are the four flats—16, 16A, 17 and 17A at Avenfield House, Park Lane, London, purchased by two offshore companies Nielsen Holdings Limited and Nescoll Limited in June 1993 and July 1996. It has been difficult for the Sharifs to deny the ownership of the flats in view of the March 1999 decision of the High Court of Justice, Queen's Bench Division, in the Hudabiya Paper Mills loan default case ordering the Sharif family to pay $32 million as debt owed to Al-Taufiq Company. As per the judgment, the Sharif's acquired a loan for Hudabiya on 15 February 1995 by pledging the London properties. The 2013 general elections nomination forms filed by Nawaz Sharif show 'Hudabiya Paper Mills' as one of his companies. The question being asked is what was the source of legitimate funds from which this debt was paid and whether it is a fact that a sum of £7 million was raised against the apartments from the Deutsche Bank in Switzerland.[69]

In the mid-1990s the FIA had carried out an investigation giving details of the London apartments and foreign bank accounts said to be worth $70million. The report had also disclosed the family's offshore accounts. The report was widely published in foreign newspapers. Nawaz termed the report as 'malicious' and threatened to sue the papers. When he became the prime minister for the second time in February 1997, the FIA investigation was terminated on grounds of being politically motivated.[70]

Another complicating factor for Nawaz is the confessional statement of former finance minister Ishaq Dar, made on 25 April 2000 before the district magistrate, Lahore, and regarded as being irrevocable. This was the time when Dar had turned approver against Sharif who had been ousted in a coup by Gen. Pervez Musharraf. Dar had admitted that he had been handling money matters of the Sharif family. He revealed that Mian Nawaz Sharif and Mian Shahbaz Sharif were involved in money laundering worth at least $14.886 million. He also confessed that he and some other associates had opened fake foreign currency accounts in different international banks and the entire amount in these banks had finally landed in the accounts of Hudabiya Paper Mills Limited.

In April 2017, the apex court ruled by a 3:2 decision that there was insufficient evidence to remove him. However, it ordered the formation of a Joint Investigation Team (JIT) to further investigate the matter. The JIT report submitted to the Supreme Court bench was highly damaging to the Sharifs.

Though the charges were yet to be proved in a court of law at the time of writing, the JIT report came to the following conclusions:[71]

- The PM and his family has assets beyond known sources of income;
- No document could be produced that showed the money trail for the purchase of the London properties and the businesses of the PM's sons;
- The trust deed of the four flats in Park Lane was false. Maryam Nawaz was found to be the beneficial owner of the London flats;
- Sharif-owned enterprises were mostly 'loss-making' and did not explain the family's wealth;
- The Dubai customs reported that no scrap machinery was transported from Dubai to Jeddah in 2001–02 as claimed. Thus, documents produced by the Sharifs regarding the sale of 25 per cent of the mill's shares were 'unauthentic, unverified, fake and fabricated';
- The alleged transaction of twelve million dirhams in UAE that were supposed to have been invested in the Qatari royal family's business had never taken place; the Qatari prince Hamad bin Jassim bin Jaber al Thani's letter produced to show a money trail was thus a piece of fiction, a 'myth';
- New offshore companies chaired by Sharif were discovered;
- Recommended that the National Accountability Bureau (NAB) file references against Nawaz and his children.

The JIT also noted that the assets of Nawaz's sons, Hussain Nawaz and Hassan Nawaz, showed a big surge the early 1990s and then again in 1997–98, without any declared source of income. This was the time when Nawaz Sharif was in power. The conclusion would appear to be that the surge in assets was through 'irregular means' with the sons acting as a 'proxy' to build the family's assets.[72]

What emerged during the JIT investigations, through the Jebel Ali Free Zone Authority (Jafza), was that Nawaz not only served as the head of Capital FZE but also drew a salary of 10,000 dirhams (about Rs 286,000 at today's rates) from 7 August 2006 to 20 April 2014. According to UAE's labour laws, all employees have to receive a salary through a bank account under the Wage Protection System, 'failing which the firm can be blacklisted and shut down'. Nawaz had not disclosed that he was the chairman of Capital FZE before running for prime minister.[73]

On 28 July 2017, Nawaz Sharif was disqualified under Section 99(1)(f) of the Representation of the People Act, (ROPA) and Article 62(1)(f) of the constitution as a member of the National Assembly by a three-judge bench consisting of Justice Ejaz Afzal, Justice Azmat Saeed and Justice Ijazul Ahsan for non-declaration of his 'receivable' [salary] from Capital FZE in the nomination papers. The other two judges of the bench—Justice Asif Saeed Khosa and Justice Gulzar Ahmed—had already disqualified Sharif on 20 April due to discrepancies in his and his children's statements. In the final verdict of 28 July, the five-judge bench had also ordered the NAB to file corruption and money laundering references against the Sharifs and Ishaq Dar. The Supreme Court also nominated Justice Ijazul Ahsan as the monitoring judge to oversee the filing of references and the trial in the accountability court.

Consequently, NAB has filed four references against the Sharif family about the London properties, the establishment of sixteen companies, including Flagship Investment Ltd in the UK and Azizia Steel Mills and Hill Metal Establishment in Jeddah. The former premier and his sons have been named in all three references, while his daughter Maryam and son-in-law Capt. Safdar have been named in the Avenfield reference.[74]

The reaction of the Sharif family and the PMLN was on expected lines. The ministers rejected the JIT report as 'trash'; Maryam tweeted 'JIT report rejected',[75] the JIT was also called a 'joke, comedy circus' that was working in the name of accountability of the Sharif family but its process had nothing to do with accountability. His son-in-law went even further and said Panama case was a conspiracy not against Prime Minister Nawaz Sharif but the 'two-nation theory and the ideology of Pakistan'.[76]

Nawaz has also exhausted the judicial process with the Supreme Court dismissing all his review petitions in September 2017.[77] This, according to experts, would leave Nawaz with no other option but to appear before the court.

Another blow to Nawaz has been the Supreme Court's ruling that has disqualified him from heading the Pakistan Muslim League (Nawaz) (PMLN). Despite being disqualified as prime minister, Nawaz had managed to retake the party leadership through the controversial Elections Act 2017. This amended the requirements necessary for the top party leadership to possess. However, the Supreme Court ruled in February 2018 that any person disqualified for being elected was ineligible to lead a party. So, he was removed again from the post of party president.

Seen in a larger context, the Panama Papers go beyond issues of tax evasion and money; they are a graphic portrayal of the malaise that is plaguing Pakistan: the political system has evolved in a manner that allows the powerful to loot the country with impunity.

At the time of writing, Nawaz's political career is clearly at stake. If proved guilty, Nawaz and his family can face up to several years in jail, heavy fines and freezing of property. For him, the fight is about saving himself and his legacy, his family fortune accumulated over thirty years in politics, including three tenures as prime minister and passing on his political legacy to his daughter. Will he be successful?

As Shahzad Chaudhry has aptly put it: 'Rather than bring [his] experience to govern better and to carve a favourable policy towards the state and its people he [Nawaz] got frivolously engaged with institutions at the altar of exaggerated egotism. In the bargain, he lost his political capital instead of putting it to more productive use. This has been his singular failure in his third tenure when he should have been at his sagacious best.'[78]

Nawaz and his brother Shahbaz are by far the longest-serving duo in Pakistani politics. Nawaz has been around since 1981 when a dictator made him the finance minister of Punjab. He has been dismissed by a president, toppled in a coup, sent into exile and removed by the judiciary. Twice, he has bounced back. Despite this luck, the tragedy of Nawaz Sharif is that neither has he learnt from past blunders nor has he demonstrated the intellectual capacity to handle the big problems facing Pakistan. With over three-and-a half decades in politics, Nawaz must be considered a part of the problem rather than a solution.

9

Pervez Musharraf: Shoot and Scoot

Early Life and Personality

MUSHARRAF WAS BORN IN DELHI on 11 August 1943 into an educated middle-class family. Musharraf's father Syed Musharrafuddin, a graduate of Aligarh Muslim University, worked in the Foreign Office as an accountant. His mother, Zarrin, was a graduate from Delhi's Indraprastha College and had a master's degree from Lucknow University in English literature. The family migrated to Pakistan in 1947 supposedly on the last train out of Delhi for Karachi.[1]

Soon, Musharraf along with his parents travelled to Turkey owing to his father's deputation in Ankara(1949–56), where he learned to speak fluent Turkish. Throughout his career Turkey would hold a fascination for him: he opted for Turkey to do his mid-career training course, though the alternative was the United States; he chose a Turkish newspaper to give his first foreign interview after the coup; he listed Mustafa Kamal Ataturk as the 'most admired person' on his official profile. During a visit to the

Turkish military academy in Istanbul he admitted that he wanted to fight as a volunteer during Turkey's 1974 invasion of Cyprus. He told the audience: 'I have such motivation that I am ready to fight with Turkish forces if Turkey requires volunteers.'[2]

By his own admission, he was 'an ill-disciplined young man – quarrelsome, irresponsible and careless'.[3] In mid-1965, despite the gathering clouds of war with India, he 'granted' himself six days' leave after it was refused by his commanding officer. Court-martial proceedings were initiated against him but the outbreak of the 1965 war saved him. In his career, he was regarded as 'an exceptional leader' but also a 'bluntly outspoken, ill-disciplined officer. He was given a number of punishments for fighting, insubordination and lack of discipline.' Yet providence saved him more than once. He narrowly missed being Zia's military secretary. Had he been so appointed, he would have been with Zia on the C-130 that crashed in Bahawalpur.[4]

Others described Musharraf as 'a chameleon: a man who can be anything'.[5] 'He had a certain wild streak in him and critics pointed out to his rakish attitude that often got him into trouble and accounted for some of the written and spoken critiques of his personal behaviour.'[6] One of his commanding officers described him as 'a cipher'. He was described by nearly everyone as 'voluble and impetuous', a soldier who took risks too bold, too ill-considered.[7] Abida Hussain writes that he was reputed to be 'a hot-headed commando, prone to knee-jerk reactions, and capable of irresponsible conduct'.[8]

Benazir met Musharraf early in her first term as prime minister during the visit of a Turkish delegation. Musharraf, then a brigadier, was the official translator. Benazir described him as 'very bright and smart' and quite a 'jolly officer'.[9]

Army Career

Musharraf joined the Pakistan Army as a young cadet in 1961 and was commissioned as an officer in 1964 in the artillery. He took part in both the 1965 and 1971 wars against India. Later, he joined the Special Services Group (SSG commandos). Musharraf always took pride in being a commando and in later years he would frequently wear the SSG uniform. He also commanded a newly raised SSG base at Khapalu in the Siachen area. Musharraf was deputed to the United Kingdom twice for military training. He was posted as director general of military operations (DGMO) in the early 1990s before becoming a lieutenant general in 1995, when he commanded a strike corps of the army.

Musharraf came into prominence in May 1988, when the Shias, who were in a majority in Gilgit, rose in revolt against the Sunni-dominated administration. Zia put the SSG group commanded by Musharraf in charge of suppressing the revolt. Musharraf resorted to a policy of bringing in Punjabis and Pakhtuns from outside and settling them in Gilgit and Baltistan to reduce the Kashmiri Shias to a minority in their traditional land. Such a policy is continuing till today.

In its issue of April 1990, *The Herald*, the monthly journal of the Dawn group of publications of Karachi, wrote that in May 1988, sectarian tensions flared up into full-scale carnage due to invasion of Gilgit by thousands of non-resident armed tribesmen. They were not stopped. They indulged in arson and looting, destroying crops and houses around Gilgit town. The number of dead and injured was put in the hundreds. 'But numbers alone tell nothing of the savagery of the invading hordes and the chilling impact it has left on these peaceful valleys.'[10]

Musharraf was the third senior-most lieutenant general for consideration as army chief after Nawaz dismissed Gen. Karamat. Musharraf claimed that this was due to manipulation by the former army chief, Gen. Waheed Kakar, who wanted to promote Lt Gen. Ali Kuli Khan. Had this not happened, Musharraf claims he would have been the senior-most lieutenant general while Ali Kuli would have retired before the promotion of the next chief was considered. Two other factors were against Musharraf becoming army chief. Gen. Jehangir Karamat, the army chief who had succeeded Gen. Kakar, appointed Ali Kuli to the prized position of chief of general staff (CGS), indicating his preference for the next chief. Second, the president of Pakistan, Farooq Leghari, the supreme commander, was a college classmate of Ali Kuli.[11]

However, Nawaz Sharif surprised everyone by appointing Gen. Musharraf as the COAS on 8 October 1998. In so doing, Musharraf had superseded Lt Gen. Ali Kuli Khan and Lt Gen. Khalid Nawaz, the Quartermaster General. Several reasons were speculated upon for Nawaz's choice that included Musharraf keeping Nawaz Sharif informed about criticism of the government during the corps commanders' conferences. Another was Nawaz's feeling that Musharraf, being a Mohajir, would not be able to command the loyalty of the Punjabi-dominated army.

Sharif would later tell Shuja Nawaz that Musharraf's confidential reports stated he was not fit for the appointment of chief of army staff. Even the 'agencies' had indicated that he was not 'suitable' for the post since he was 'quick in taking action and could be easily roused. ...Takes actions without deep thought.'[12] With hindsight, Nawaz admitted that he acted in 'haste' and was given 'wrong advice' that made him ignore Ali Kuli Khan. He attributed this to Lt Gen. (Retd) Iftikhar Ahmed Khan, the defence secretary, and his brother and the prime minister's close aide, Chaudhury Nisar Ali Khan, who had personal issues with Ali Kuli Khan.[13]

Musharraf writes that as a corps commander, he was automatically part of the army's highest decision-making body—the corps commanders' conference. Thus he became aware of how opposition politicians instigated the army chief against the sitting government. During the frequent periods of animosity between the president and the prime minister, the army chief would be drawn into the fray to act as conciliator. His conclusion was: 'In the absence of institutional checks and balances over government leaders, the only recourse to those out of power was the commander of the army.'[14]

Kargil

Even before he dislodged Nawaz Sharif as prime minister, Musharraf had become infamous for launching the Kargil intrusions against India in early 1999. Prior to its actual implementation, the operation had been considered at least twice earlier and rejected on both occasions.

The first occasion was during the tenure of Zia. After the presentation, Zia's conversation with the DGMO, as narrated by a senior army officer to Hassan Abbas, went somewhat as follows:

Zia: When we take Kargil, what do you expect the Indians to do? ... I mean, don't you think they will try and recapture it?

DGMO: Yes, sir, but we think that the position is impregnable and we can hold it against far superior forces.

Zia: Now that's very good, but in that case, don't you think the Indians will go for a limited offensive elsewhere along the line of control, take some of our territory, and use it as a bargaining chip?

DGMO: Yes, sir, this is possible, but ...

Zia: And if they are beaten back there also, don't you think they will attack across the international frontier, which may lead to a full-scale war?

DGMO: That's possible, sir.

Zia: So, in other words, you have prepared a plan to lead us into a full-scale war with India![15]

This scathing observation by Zia-ul-Haq led to the proposal being shelved for the first time. The second time the operation was mooted was under the Benazir government. Benazir remembered a presentation made during her second term at the Joint Staff Headquarters chaired by Air Chief Marshal Farooq Feroze Khan. She had subjected the then DGMO, Pervez Musharraf, to a series of questions that also contested his political claim that by taking Srinagar, Pakistan would have won. She opposed the idea on the 'concrete grounds that it was not a political reality to think that you could go into Srinagar and put a flag ... because there were other international treaties and UN resolutions that could also be brought into force and a particular power situation in the world.'[16]

Musharraf's recollection of that briefing, however, was expectedly different. 'In that presentation I told her that the time window for the resolution of Kashmir dispute is short. Because, with the passage of time, the India–Pakistan equation, military equation and economic equation is going against us ... she minded that a lot.'[17] Interestingly, Bhutto had used much the same argument with Ayub. (See chapter 3.2, Ayub: A Bridge Too Far.)

Thus, the common grounds for rejecting the plan on both occasions was the same—that it would lead to a full-scale war with India, something that Pakistan was not prepared for.

The third time, the planners were successful since it was Musharraf who was in charge. Apart from Musharraf himself, the key advocates were Lt Gen. Mohammad Aziz Khan, CGS, a Kashmiri, Lt Gen. Mahmood Ahmad, the commander of X Corps, in whose area of operations Kargil lay and Maj. Gen. Javed Hassan, force commander northern areas, (FCNA) who would implement the operation. The last named, as a lieutenant colonel, had carried out a study of India titled 'India: A Study in Profile' and concluded that India was a weak state and needed only a push to disintegrate while the 'Hindu' had no stomach for a fight.[18] A naturally reckless Musharraf was greatly influenced by the zeal of these three generals.

What Musharraf sought to achieve by the Kargil intrusions was to threaten the main Indian supply route, National Highway 1A, linking Srinagar to Leh via Dras and Kargil. This was in retaliation for India interdicting the Neelam Valley Road in Pakistan-occupied Kashmir (POK). The whole plan hinged on two critical assumptions: India would not be able to replenish supplies quickly to launch a counter-attack even though Pakistan had no information on Indian reserve stocks in Leh and beyond;[19] India would not or could not respond in enough strength to dislodge the

Pakistanis. Both the assumptions would be proved wrong due to the ferocity of the Indian response. The 1965 infiltrations had also been based on assumptions that proved to be wholly incorrect.

According to Shuja Nawaz, there was a larger 'Kashmir operation, the details of which have not been revealed so far. An interesting aspect of the larger operation was the intention to use fighters from Afghanistan. Mullah Mohammad Rabbani, the Taliban president of Afghanistan at that time, was asked by Pakistan if he could provide 20,000–30,000 "volunteers" for the Kashmir jihad. He startled the Pakistanis by offering 500,000.'[20]

The moot question in the whole Kargil fiasco was whether Nawaz was briefed about the operations and if he gave the go-ahead. In his book *In the Line of Fire*, Musharraf writes that the army briefed the prime minister in Skardu on 29 January 1999 and in Kel on 5 February 1999 when Pakistan's 'defensive manoeuvre' was explained as a response to developments in Indian Kashmir. Thereafter, Nawaz was also briefed on 12 March at the Inter-Services Intelligence (ISI) headquarters. This included a comprehensive review of the situation inside 'Occupied Jammu and Kashmir' as also along the LOC. Subsequently, the director general of military operations briefed him in detail on 17 May and briefings were also held on 2 June and 22 June.[21]

According to Nawaz, the briefing by the army in Skardu on 29 January 1999 was about tourism while the 5 February meeting in Kel was in the open air. Road projects were discussed. Tourists were also roaming about in the area so there was no way a sensitive issue like Kargil could have been discussed.[22]

Musharraf's assertion has also been sharply contradicted by Sartaj Aziz, the then foreign minister who was present during the 5 February briefing. Aziz writes that the briefing pertained explicitly to the Indian interdiction of the Neelam Valley Road and the successful completion of an alternative road through the Kaghan Valley. There was no mention of the Kargil sector.[23]

In fact, if what Musharraf says is true, and Nawaz had been briefed about the Kargil operation on 5 February 1999, clearly

Nawaz knew about the operation even before the Lahore bus yatra of Prime Minister Vajyapee on 20 February 1999. This would be an astounding act of betrayal and deceit on the part of Nawaz Sharif.

According to Sartaj Aziz, by March 1999, the mujahideen with the assistance of the Northern Light Infantry (NLI) had occupied several heights in the Kargil–Dras sector. It was only then that Gen. Musharraf and his team decided to 'brief' the prime minister on 12–13 March about the operation, and that too only obliquely. On the first day, a report of the Kashmir Study Group was discussed against the backdrop of the ongoing negotiations on Kashmir with India, especially after Prime Minister Vajpayee's visit to Lahore in February. On the second day, the situation inside 'occupied' Kashmir was presented but there was no mention about any operation being launched. What the briefing did was to flag the increased 'mujahideen' activity inside Kashmir, especially in the Kargil–Dras sector and a plan to provide them stinger missiles. Such activity was felt to have a beneficial impact on the Kashmir negotiations since India would be forced to accept the urgency of a solution. Aziz is categorical that no mention was made about the role of the Pakistani army or paramilitary personnel or crossing the LOC to occupy any positions.[24]

Aziz quotes Musharraf stating in the briefing: 'We know the Indians. They will negotiate seriously only under maximum pressure. Besides, we cannot take responsibility for restraining mujahideen activity inside occupied Kashmir. We can, however, postpone the proposal to give stinger missiles to mujahideen if that would create any complication.'[25]

Sharif agreed to go ahead but quite possibly his nod was based on his understanding that regular troops were not involved in the operation and it was only a question of putting pressure on India. Nawaz would have undoubtedly been looking to cash in if the 'mujahideen' succeeded.[26] This is also borne out by the fact that when noted journalist Sohail Warraich asked him directly that if he was so opposed to Kargil why did he not get the Defence Committee of the Cabinet to stop it, Nawaz chose to remain silent.[27]

Sartaj Aziz speculates that one reason why Nawaz was drip-fed information rather than being briefed fully about the actual plan was that Musharraf and three generals had not anticipated the intensity of the Indian response or the danger of a broader conflict.[28]

In an interview to Shuja Nawaz, Lt Gen. Ziauddin, the man whom Nawaz appointed as army chief to replace Musharraf in October 1999, made some interesting revelations that show Nawaz in a poor light. According to him, it was at the 17 May briefing that discussions were held on the Kashmir operations in general and Kargil in particular. He recalled Nawaz saying: 'This is a military operation. All I can stay is that ... there should be no withdrawal, no surrender of any post because that will greatly embarrass us.' He asked if 'we could hold on'. Both Aziz Khan and Mahmud Ahmed affirmed that they could and discounted the possibility of an Indian attack across the international boundary. Hence, in Ziauddin's view, Sharif was fully in the picture from then on, a fact confirmed by Mahmud taking maps to the prime minister's house to brief Nawaz on the developing situation. Nawaz could have halted the operation at the time as posts fell but he left 'everything to the army to decide'.[29]

Sartaj Aziz concedes that as the foreign minister of Pakistan, he was unaware of the operation till the morning of 17 May and neither were his views asked for about its diplomatic ramifications.[30] Hence, Nawaz's assertion—that the army hoodwinked him even after 17 May, when it insisted it were the mujahideen doing all the action, not the Pakistani troops—is not tenable in the light of what his foreign minister had to say.

That the other services had not been consulted and were not on board was revealed by a telling question asked by navy chief Admiral Fasiuddin Bukhari at a Kargil meeting on 13 June. He queried Musharraf: 'Since I have been away, may I ask what are the objectives of this large-scale mobilization? We want to go to war over a few desolate heights that we may have to vacate anyway during the forthcoming winter.'[31] Musharraf's reply is not, however, recorded.

The other moot question about Kargil is whether Musharraf asked Nawaz to speak to and visit President Clinton or was it Nawaz's own initiative. Musharraf claims that in the meeting of the Defence Committee of the Cabinet (DCC) on 2 July, he briefed Nawaz on the exact military situation and 'I told him as far military is concerned, I can assure you we are quite okay.' In response to Nawaz asking 'Should we withdraw or not?' Musharraf says he refused to answer that and said, 'Mr PM, I have told you the military situation and I told you that militarily, we'll stand. Now whether to withdraw or not is a political decision and I'm afraid you will have to take that decision.'[32] According to Musharraf, the DCC meeting was inconclusive and it had been decided to meet again on Monday morning. However, Nawaz summoned him to the airport at night to see him off. He had taken a sudden decision to go to Washington without consulting anyone and 'the decisions taken in Washington were totally his'.[33]

Musharraf also claimed that in 1999, Pakistan's nuclear capability was not yet operational—exploding a bomb did not mean that a nuclear force could be deployed or a bomb could be delivered on a selected target. Thus, 'talks of preparing for nuclear strikes was preposterous'.[34]

Interestingly, neither Nawaz nor Musharraf mention about the 24–25 June 1999 visit of the US Centcom commander Anthony Zinni. He had been directed by the White House to lead a presidential mission to Pakistan to prevail upon Nawaz and Musharraf to withdraw their forces from Kargil. In his meetings, Zinni told them: 'If you don't pull back, you're going to bring war and nuclear annihilation down on your country. That's going to be very bad news for everybody.' According to Zinni, neither Musharraf nor Nawaz argued with this reasoning. He realized, however, that the problem was the national humiliation that the Pakistan leadership would have to bear. Thus, what was needed was 'a face-saving way out of the mess'. A meeting with President Clinton was put on the table. However, Zinni insisted that the meeting would be announced only after a withdrawal of forces. Even though Nawaz was initially disinclined to withdraw before the summit meeting he finally came around and ordered the withdrawal.[35]

In a subsequent interview with Shuja Nawaz, Zinni made the following points: First, he confirmed that Nawaz 'finally came around and he ordered the withdrawal' and a meeting with President Clinton was set up for July. Second, it was Musharraf who encouraged Prime Minister Sharif to hear Zinni out since earlier, Nawaz was unwilling to meet him. Third, in the meeting with Nawaz, Musharraf did not utter a word. Fourth, Zinni recalled stating that he needed evidence of Pakistani preparation to pull back before Clinton would finally agree to a meeting. He told Shuja Nawaz that this happened soon after his return to Washington. US satellites picked up movements indicating that the Pakistanis were getting ready to move back. It was then that he gave the green light to the White House.[36]

Clearly, according to Zinni's version, both in his book and in the interview to Shuja Nawaz, Musharraf was not only aware about the US suggestion for a withdrawal but assisted Zinni in making the argument for it before Sharif. Additionally, he was also aware that the offer of a meeting with Clinton was dependent on agreeing to a withdrawal and Nawaz had, in fact, agreed to such a withdrawal in Musharraf's presence. Musharraf's autobiography and his subsequent claims that he was not aware that Nawaz would agree to a withdrawal were thus a travesty of truth because they suggest that he was not a party to Sharif's plans, which he was.

According to Nawaz's brother, Shahbaz Sharif, he asked Nawaz to meet Gen. Zinni. Initially, Nawaz refused but later agreed to meet him after Musharraf asked him. In the meeting, ceasefire, withdrawal of Pak forces from Kargil, and Nawaz's meeting with President Clinton were discussed. However, Shahbaz holds that prior to this meeting, Musharraf and Zinni had agreed that forces would be withdrawn from Kargil and there would be a ceasefire.[37]

Some, like Gohar Ayub Khan, believe that Nawaz knew about the whole operation. As evidence Ayub cites that the Kargil conflict was discussed in the cabinet on 3 June 1999. Nawaz showed his colleagues a letter received from President Clinton asking for the withdrawal of mujahideen forces from the posts they had occupied. Ch. Nisar Ali, the then minister for petroleum and natural resources, inquired as to who had ordered the Kargil operation. The PM did not reply. Instead, after fidgeting nervously, he read out Clinton's letter. The meeting ended inconclusively. Gohar Ayub Khan contends that 'had PM Nawaz Sharif not been in the loop beforehand, he would have pushed for withdrawal using the cabinet's approval and President Clinton's letter as the basis for his decision'. That's why it remained a mystery why he did not oppose it during the army briefings. The one explanation was that he was hoping that if the operation was successful he would then be able to take credit for it.[38]

In an interview that he gave a Pakistani journalist that was later published as a book, Nawaz gave his version. In it, Nawaz said he was not taken into confidence and when he was briefed, he was told that the army would not be involved, only the mujahideen. However, in the operation, the entire Northern Light Infantry perished: two thousand martyred and hundreds wounded; the death toll was higher than the 1965 and 1971 wars put together. After such heavy losses, when he asked Musharraf about army losses, he said Indians were carrying out carpet-bombing, something they did not anticipate. 'I must tell you that when the Washington pact was concluded, the Indian Army had got Kargil vacated. They were advancing swiftly. It was I who saved our army from dishonor and disgrace.'[39] Nawaz also claimed that Musharraf came to the airport when he was leaving for the US, 'to plead with him to extricate the army from Kargil where the Indians had begun to make progress'. This was quite contrary to what Nawaz told the Saudi ambassador, as noted in the previous chapter, on arrival in Washington DC.[40]

Musharraf claimed that the ceasefire in Kargil was a military triumph. In his words, 'The Kargil conflict emerged out of a tactical manoeuvre of limited dimensions but had significant strategic effects.'[41] However, to others, it was obvious that the Kargil operation lacked proper strategic planning. As a senior air force officer put it '… his (Musharraf's) adventurous assault in Kargil had brought about an all-round embarrassment. Only Bill Clinton's 4th of July intervention could help save us some face. Gen. Musharraf still doesn't agree with this conclusion but there hasn't been a bigger strategic blunder in Pakistan's recent history.'[42] Instead of getting international support, all the major powers, including Pakistan's old ally China, asked Pakistan to revert to the LOC. Pakistan had to comply. In the process, it was made obvious to the world that the so-called 'mujahideen' were being controlled by Pakistan.

Musharraf's tall claims about the Kargil operation contrasted harshly with the autopsies of dead Pakistani soldiers that revealed the presence of grass in their stomachs. This indicated that the Pakistan Army had left their soldiers on their own because of which they ran out of food supplies.[43]

Another consequence of Kargil was, as noted by Bruce Riedel, that the refusal of the US to reward Pakistan for its aggression and the US insistence on withdrawal to the LOC had an immediate and positive impact on the Indo-US relationship. 'Doors opened in New Delhi to Americans that had been shut for years. The Indian elite—including the military—and the Indian public began to shed long-held negative perceptions of the US.'[44]

This was hardly the outcome anyone in Pakistan could have wanted.

The Coup

Following the Kargil intrusions and retreat, relations between Musharraf and Nawaz had become tense. One telling example was on 8 September in the lobby of the Shangri-La Hotel outside Skardu, where Musharraf was showing off a new Italian laser-guided pistol to the information minister, Mushahid Hussain. Just then Nawaz walked into the lobby and asked Musharraf, 'General who are you aiming it at?'[45]

For months after President Bill Clinton's intervention, it was believed that Nawaz would sack Musharraf. But he didn't. Nawaz may have made up his mind to dismiss Musharraf on 13 June, when after the briefing in Lahore he told Sartaj Aziz in the car going to the airport, 'Musharraf has landed us in a terrible mess, but we have to find a way to get out of this impossible situation.' But then Nawaz prevaricated. An immediate dismissal at the end of the Kargil war may not have provoked a reaction from the army since the corps commanders had not been taken into confidence about the Kargil plan.[46]

The delay in dismissing Musharraf was to prove lethal for Nawaz. While Nawaz procrastinated, Musharraf busied himself by visiting military formations, seeking support of his army colleagues for a 'counter coup' in case any action was taken against him. Musharraf told them that they would not allow another humiliation to befall the army like the dismissal of Gen. Karamat.[47]

By October 1999, Musharraf felt that a truce had been reached and they had agreed to move on. Musharraf thought that he had convinced Nawaz to display unity in public instead of making a spectacle of themselves.[48] Two reasons were responsible for this changed attitude.

First, Nawaz had elevated Musharraf to the additional position of chairman, Joint Chiefs of Staff Committee (CJCSC) concurrent with his existing position as army chief. However, what Musharraf omits to mention in his book is that a day after the extension of his tenure as CJCSC was notified, he made a press statement that he 'had not made any deal with the government for this extension. I am also not aware if this decision will give greater stability to the government.'[49] Second, Nawaz had invited Musharraf and his wife to accompany him and his wife to Mecca for a pilgrimage in August 1999. For these reasons, Musharraf did not think Nawaz would exploit his absence abroad to Colombo to sack him as army chief.[50]

> Prior to their departure for Mecca, Nawaz invited the Musharrafs for dinner at his residence in Raiwind that was presided over by his father, known as Abba-ji. After dinner Abba-ji turned to Musharraf and announced: 'You are also my son, and these two sons of mine dare not speak against you. If they do, they will be answerable to me.' Musharraf writes that he was most embarrassed, but put it to this being the way of the old man. In retrospect, Musharraf felt that was all a pretence: the prime minster was lulling Musharraf into a false sense of security, the last act of which was the dinner with Abba-ji. Musharraf was to learn later that Abba-ji had already made up his mind that Nawaz should sack him. He had told some people that he 'did not like the look in my eye'.
>
> (Pervez Musharraf, *In the Line of Fire*: *A Memoir*, New York: Free Press, 2006, pp. 112–13.)

In hindsight, Musharraf would say in his book that there were hints of what was coming, but these hints were overlooked. For example, Mrs Ziauddin, the spouse of the DG ISI, who was appointed to replace Musharraf as army chief, asked another officer's wife about the demeanour of a chief's wife. One of Ziauddin's relatives wanted to know the difference in ranks worn by a full general and a lieutenant general. These signs were not taken to be of any significance. As he wrote, 'I have no compunction about admitting that the army was caught unawares by the prime minister's sudden action of dismissing me and following it up virtually simultaneously with sudden and abrupt changes in the military high command.'[51] This, according to him, was the coup while the army's response was the 'counter-coup'.

In sacking Musharraf and appointing Lt Gen. Ziauddin, DG ISI, as army chief, Nawaz Sharif revealed how little he knew about the internal dynamics of the army. All the key officers—the commander of the 111 Brigade, Brig. Salahuddin Satti; the CGS Lt Gen. Aziz Khan; commander of the X Corps, Rawalpindi, Lt Gen. Mahmood Ahmed; DGMO, Lt Gen. Shahid Aziz; as well as corps commanders of Lahore and Karachi were all known to Musharraf well. Only the DG ISI, Lt Gen. Ziauddin, was close to Nawaz Sharif—but did not command troops.[52]

An interesting sidelight from the air force perspective is provided by Air Vice Marshal Shahzad Chaudhry who was with the air force chief when the coup took place. The latter asked the CGS Gen. Aziz, 'Who is running the government? Why should I not be listening to the prime minister?' On being told that change was under process, he informed him, 'Whatever you guys are doing, it better be quick for I will not listen to someone in the army till the air is cleared on whether the prime minister is still the PM'. This was not liked by those involved in the coup.

He further writes that a PAF VVIP plane that was on its way to Karachi for routine maintenance was diverted to Nawabshah where Musharraf's plane was being diverted. The PAF was, however, unsure if Musharraf would be flown as a prisoner or as a chief executive. Despite the successful coup, Musharraf refused to fly the aircraft as the chief executive and even refused to fly it for several months till his confidence with the air force was re-established. It was apparent that the Kargil episode had created serious divisions among the service chiefs on how they perceived it and its results.[53]

Pakistan in 1999

Musharraf's description of the conditions of the country was not very different from how Generals Ayub, Yahya and Zia described the conditions when they took over in 1958, 1969 and 1977 respectively. Would any army chief taking over today describe the conditions any differently?

In his address to the nation on 17 October 1999, Musharraf said, 'Fifty-two years ago, we started with a beacon of hope and today that beacon is no more and we stand in darkness. There is despondency and hopelessness surrounding us with no light visible anywhere around. The slide down has been gradual but has rapidly accelerated in the last many years.' He added that the economy had crumbled, their credibility lost, state institutions demolished and provincial disharmony had harmed the federation. 'In sum, we have lost our honour, our dignity, our respect in the comity of nations. Is this the democracy our Quaid-e-Azam had envisaged? Is this the way to enter the new millennium?'[54]

Following the coup, Nawaz Sharif was arrested, imprisoned and charged with hijacking. In July 2000, he was sentenced to life in prison. However, before the corruption and money-laundering cases could be finalized, Musharraf was pressurized to release him.

On behalf of Saudi Arabia, Saad Hariri, the son of Lebanon's prime minister Rafiq Hariri, conveyed that continuation of better Pak–Saudi relations depended on Musharraf's decision on the Saudi request to release Nawaz and his family members. The US also chipped in by encouraging the Saudis to press Musharraf hard for Sharif's freedom.[55] Finally, Musharraf negotiated a deal with the Saudis: Nawaz and his family members would be allowed to go into exile on condition that he and his brother quit politics for a certain time.[56] In December 2000 Sharif was exiled to Saudi Arabia.

Politics

Musharraf's style of governance was simple. He told the media: 'I do not believe in power sharing. … I believe in unity of command. There has to be only one authority for good government.'[57]

Musharraf tried hard to survive in the complex politics of Pakistan. At one stage, he had about eighty federal ministers, most were political bribes for support. Soon his government became indistinguishable from the 'lost decade' of the 1990s when Benazir and Nawaz had successively run the country aground.[58]

At one time, Musharraf considered co-opting Imran Khan to bolster his government, to give him 'the strength to take on the crooked politicians'. Imran was, however, shocked when Musharraf gave him the names of the politicians in his 'coalition of reform'. Some of them, writes Imran, 'were the epitome of corruption in the country'. Imran, accordingly declined to join Musharraf as it would deprive him of all credibility, given that anti-corruption was his key platform. Musharraf warned him that he would lose if he did not join.[59]

Musharraf's last gamble was the National Reconciliation Ordinance (NRO). This power-sharing agreement, brokered by the US State Department would allow him to run for re-election as president and enable Benazir Bhutto to return to Pakistan, contest elections and become prime minister. As a quid pro quo, Imran Khan notes, 'more than 8,000 bureaucrats, government officials, bankers and politicians charged with corruption offences between 1986 and 1999 were given an amnesty, including Benazir and Zardari.' These persons were suspected of illegally depriving Pakistan of Rs 1,060 billion, of which Benazir and Zardari accounted for Rs 140 billion. The NRO also negated thousands of criminal cases like murder suspected to have been committed by the Mohajir Qaumi Movement (MQM) in Karachi.[60]

One of his knee-jerk reactions that Musharraf would not be able to live down was what he said in his interview with the *Washington Post* on 13 September 2005 regarding Mukhtran Mai, a rape survivor. Musharraf said, 'You must understand the environment in Pakistan. This [rape] has become a moneymaking concern. A lot of people say if you want to go abroad and get a visa for Canada or citizenship and be a millionaire, get yourself raped.'[61]

In his memoir, Musharraf claimed, with some pride, that he had transferred over seven hundred al-Qaeda suspects to the US. Quite possibly, in his enthusiasm to prove his loyalty to the Americans, Musharraf did not realize or if he realized, chose to ignore constitutional provisions. As per Article 4A of the constitution, any person on Pakistani soil cannot be given over to another authority unless he is taken to a court of law and provided with a chance to prove his innocence. Musharraf had thus brazenly violated the constitution.[62]

This is how Mullah Zaeef, the Taliban government's ambassador to Pakistan describes in his book, *My Life with the Taliban*, how he was seized by the Pakistanis and handed over to the Americans:

> They ripped the black cloth from my face and for the first time I could see where I was. Pakistani and American soldiers stood around me, ... The Pakistani soldiers were all staring as the Americans hit me and tore the remaining clothes off from my body. Eventually I was completely naked, and the Pakistani soldiers – the defenders of the Holy Quran – shamelessly watched me with smiles on their faces, saluting this disgraceful action of the Americans. They held a handover ceremony with the Americans right in front of my eyes. That moment is written in my memory like a stain on my soul. Even if Pakistan was not able to stand up to the godless Americans, I would at least have expected them to insist that treatment like this would never take place under their eyes or on their own sovereign territory.[63]

On 27 December 2007, just as Benazir had finished addressing a huge rally in Liaquat Bagh, Rawalpindi, she was assassinated. While the conspiracy to kill Benazir has not been investigated fully, Musharraf cannot escape political and moral responsibility since it happened on his watch. At a minimum, he failed to provide her the security she so urgently and repeatedly requested. Moreover, he was not doing her a favour. As a former prime minister, she was entitled to receive foolproof security, especially against the backdrop of the failed assassination attempt on 18 October 2017, the day she returned to Pakistan.

What compounds Musharraf's responsibility was that an interior ministry letter, dated 22 October 2007, had instructed all provincial governments to provide stringent VVIP-level security to Shaukat Aziz and Ch. Shujaat Hussain as former prime ministers. Annexure to the letter listed the specific protective measures to be taken by the provincial authorities. It was indeed discriminatory and unjustifiable that this directive for ex-PMs Aziz and Hussain did not include a similar clear instruction for the protection of Benazir who had been attacked in Karachi just four days earlier.[64]

In August 2008, Musharraf was forced to accept the writing on the wall. The politicians ganged up against him. With Zardari and Nawaz joining hands and preparing to impeach him for illegally suspending the constitution and for misconduct, he had few options left. He had resigned as the army chief on 28 November 2007. His voice trembling and a tear in his eye, on 18 August 2008, Musharraf went on national television and announced his resignation and following in the footsteps of Nawaz and Benazir, sought sanctuary in London.

After his departure for London, Musharraf was indicted in five cases: the detention of judges (including Chief Justice Iftikhar Choudhury) in 2007, the Red Mosque operation in Islamabad, the death of Benazir, the death of Akbar Bugti and imposition of emergency declared illegal by the Supreme Court on 31 July 2009. Even with these cases against him, Musharraf returned to Pakistan to contest the May 2013 elections. However, his nomination papers were rejected in four constituencies. He was arrested on 21 April 2013, put under house arrest and judicial proceedings initiated. In January 2014, the Supreme Court disposed of the review petition filed by Musharraf against the 31 July 2009 verdict denouncing the 3 November 2007 proclamation of emergency. Therefore, he was to be tried for treason.[65] It took the 'establishment' several deft manoeuvres to have him leave the country again. At the time of writing, Musharraf is safely ensconced in London though he keeps threatening to return to Pakistan.

Notes

Introduction

1. Rafia Zakaria, *The Upstairs Wife: An Intimate History of Pakistan*, Boston: Beacon Press, 2015, pp. 52–54.
2. Shaukat Hayat Khan, *The Nation That Lost Its Soul*, Lahore: Jang Publishers, 1995, pp. 182–83, cited in Sherbaz Khan Mazari, *A Journey to Disillusionment*, Karachi: Oxford University Press (henceforth OUP), 1999, p. 216 and p. 152 fn. 45.
3. K.M. Arif, *Working with Zia*, Karachi: OUP, 1995, p. 36.
4. Henry Kissinger, *The White House Years*, first Indian edition, New Delhi: Vikas Publishing House, 1979, p. 862.
5. Arshad Sami Khan, *Three Presidents and an Aide: Life, Power and Politics*, New Delhi: Pentagon Press, 2008, p. 179.
6. Imran Khan, *Pakistan: A Personal History*, London: Transworld Publishers, 2011, p. 40.
7. Interview with Oriana Fallaci, *L'Europeo*, April 1972, cited in Christina Lamb, *Waiting for Allah: Pakistan's Struggle for Democracy*, New Delhi: Viking, Penguin Books India, 1991, p. 48.
8. Roedad Khan, *The British Papers, Documents 1958-1969*, Karachi: OUP, 2002, p. xvii.
9. Stanley Wolpert, *Zulfi Bhutto of Pakistan: His Life and Times*, New York: OUP, 1993, p. 263.
10. Christina Lamb, *Waiting for Allah: Pakistan's Struggle for Democracy*, p. 84.
11. Gohar Ayub Khan, *Glimpses into the Corridors of Power*, Karachi: OUP,

2007, p. 180.

12. Gul Hassan Khan, *Memoirs of Lt. Gen. Gul Hassan Khan*, Karachi: OUP, 1993, p. 401.
13. Mushahid Hussain and Akmal Hussian, *Pakistan: Problems of Governance*, Centre For Policy Research, New Delhi: Konark Publishers Ltd, 1993, pp. 134–35.
14. Ron Suskind, *The Way of the World: A Story of Truth and Hope in an Age of Extremism*, New York: HarperCollins 2008, p. 267.
15. Heraldo Munoz, *Getting Away with Murder: Benazir Bhutto's Assassination and the Politics of Pakistan*, Indian edition, New Delhi: Viva Books Private Ltd, 2014, p. 26.
16. Ayaz Amir, 'Dullness, stagnation and corrupt mediocrity', *The News*, 16 December 2016 https://www.thenews.com.pk/print/172146-Dullness-stagnation-and-corrupt-mediocrity (accessed on 2 December 2017).
17. Christina Lamb, *Waiting for Allah: Pakistan's Struggle for Democracy*, p. 68.
18. Ibid., p. 276.
19. V.T. Joshi, *Pakistan: Zia to Benazir*, New Delhi: Konark Publishers Pvt. Ltd, 1995, p. 85.
20. Pervez Musharraf, *In the Line of Fire: A Memoir*, New York: Free Press, 2006, p. 41.
21. Tom Clancy with Gen. Tony Zinni (Retd) and Tony Koltz, *Battle Ready*, New York: G.P. Putnam's Sons, 2004, p. 347.
22. Ilhan Niaz, *The Culture of Power and Governance of Pakistan 1947-2008*, Karachi: OUP, 2010, p. 89.
23. Ibid., p. ix.
24. Syeda Abida Hussain, *Power Failure: The Political Odyssey of a Pakistani Woman*, Karachi: OUP, 2015, p. 1.
25. Heraldo Munoz, *Getting Away with Murder: Benazir Bhutto's Assassination and the Politics of Pakistan*, p. 75.
26. Iqbal Akhund, *Trial and Error: The Advent and Eclipse of Benazir Bhutto*, Karachi: OUP, 2000, p. 77.
27. Imran Khan, *Pakistan: A Personal History*, p. 133.
28. Ibid., pp. 133–34.
29. See chapter on Nawaz Sharif for details.
30. Marvi Sirmed, 'Pakistan's democracy: a sham and a farce', *Daily Times*, 12 March 2017, http://dailytimes.com.pk/opinion/12-Mar-17/pakistans-democracy-a-sham-and-a-farce (accessed on 10 March 2018).
31. Editorial, *Dawn*, 21 June 2001, cited in Ahmed Rashid, *Descent into Chaos*, London: Allen Lane, Penguin Books, 2008, p. 52.

1: End of the Raj: The Last Hurrah

1. Mountbatten Papers, File No. 207, cited in Latif Ahmed Sherwani, *The Partition of India and Mountbatten*, Karachi: D & Y Printers, 1986, p. 15.
2. Mountbatten Papers, File No. 62, cited in ibid., pp. 94–95.
3. Mountbatten Papers, File No. 212, cited in ibid., p. 97.
4. Wali Khan, *Facts are Facts*, Peshawar: Bacha Khan Trust, 2006, pp. 158, 160–61.
5. Latif Ahmed Sherwani, *The Partition of India and Mountbatten*, p. 98.
6. Wali Khan, *Facts are Facts*, p. 208.
7. Ibid., p. 209.
8. Brian Cloughley, *A History of the Pakistan Army—Wars and Insurrections*, Karachi: OUP, 1999, p. 6.
9. Trevor Royale, *The Last Days of the Raj*, London: Michael Joseph, 1989, pp. 216 and 218.
10. Ibid., p. 218.
11. Ibid.
12. Iqbal Akhund, *Memoirs of a Bystander: A Life in Diplomacy*, Karachi: OUP, 1997, p. 9.
13. Trevor Royle, *The Last Days of the Raj*, p. 218.

2: Muhammad Ali Jinnah: *Quaid-i-Azam*

1. M.J. Akbar, *Tinderbox: The Past and Future of Pakistan*, New Delhi: HarperCollins India, 2011, p. 102.
2. Khaled Ahmed, *Pakistan: Behind the Ideological Mask*, Lahore: Vanguard Books, 2004, p. 22.
3. Fatima Jinnah, '*My Brother*' (unpublished manuscript, preserved in the National Archives of Pakistan at Islamabad). Quaid-e-Azam Academy published the work in 1986 (edited by Sharif al Mujahid); Urdu translation entitled *Mera Bhai*, published in 1987. Cited in Khwaja Razi Haider, *Ruttie Jinnah: The Story, Told and Untold*, Karachi: Pakistan Study Centre, University of Karachi, 2004. This edition, Karachi: OUP, 2010, p. 3, fn. 5.
4. Dinshaw Manockjee worked for the East India Company. French merchants who dealt with him called him 'Le petit Parsi', a nickname that stuck and became his surname. Khwaja Razi Haider, *Ruttie Jinnah: The Story, Told and Untold*, p. 16.
5. Ibid., pp. 24–25, 30.
6. Ibid., p. xvii.
7. Sheela Reddy, *Mr and Mrs Jinnah: The Marriage that Shook India*, Gurgaon; Penguin Random House, 2017, p. 19.

8. Ibid., p. 102.
9. Khwaja Razi Haider, *Ruttie Jinnah*, p. xix.
10. Hector Bolitho, *Jinnah and Pakistan*, London: John Murray Publishers, 1954, reprinted, 1956, p. 75.
11. Aziz Beg, *Jinnah and His Times: A Biography*, Islamabad: Babur & Amer Publications, 1986, p. 308, cited in Khwaja Razi Haider, *Ruttie Jinnah*, p. 75.
12. Kanji Dwarkadas, *Ruttie Jinnah: The Story of a Great Friendship*, Bombay: Popular Prakashan, 1968, pp. 7–8, cited in Khwaja Razi Haider, *Ruttie Jinnah*, p. 109.
13. A.A. Ravoof, *Meet Mr Jinnah*, Lahore: Muhammad Ashraf, 1955, pp. 229–30, cited in Khwaja Razi Haider, *Ruttie Jinnah*, pp.109–10.
14. Ibid., p. 110.
15. Sheela Reddy, *Mr and Mrs Jinnah*, pp.124–25.
16. Ibid., p. 331.
17. Rafia Zakaria, *The Upstairs Wife: An Intimate History of Pakistan*, Boston: Beacon Press, 2015, p. 54.
18. Ibid.
19. Ibid.
20. Sheela Reddy, *Mr and Mrs Jinnah*, p. 358.
21. Rafia Zakaria, *The Upstairs Wife*, pp. 52–54.
22. Sheela Reddy, *Mr and Mrs Jinnah*, p. 362.
23. Ibid., p. 370.
24. Ibid., p. 371.
25. Humayun Mirza, *From Plassey to Pakistan*, Maryland, USA: Timespinner, 1999, third edition, 2013, pp. 148–49.
26. Altaf Gauhar, *Ayub Khan: Pakistan's First Military Ruler*, Karachi: OUP, 1996, p. xxvii.
27. Mazar Ali Khan, *Pakistan: The Barren Years: The Viewpoint, Editorials and Columns of Mazhar Ali Khan 1975–1992*, Karachi: OUP, 1998, p. 18.
28. Mohammad Ayub Khan, *Friends, Not Masters*, London: OUP, 1967, pp. 40–41.
29. Sri Prakasa, *Pakistan: Birth and Early Days*, Meerut: Meenakshi Prakashan, 1965, pp. 83–84.
30. Ibid.
31. Ibid., p. 85.
32. US Ambassador in Karachi to Secretary of State, 22 March 1948, 845F.00/3-2248, cited in M.S. Venkataramani, *The American Role in Pakistan 1947-1958*, New Delhi: Radiant Publishers, 1982, pp. 30–31.
33. The Secretary of State to the American Embassy in Karachi, 3 March 1948, 845F.001/3-348) cited in ibid., p. 31.
34. Rafia Zakaria, *The Upstairs Wife: An Intimate History of Pakistan*, p. 59.

35. Nadeem F Paracha, 'Fatima Jinnah: A sister's sorrow', *Dawn*, 4 May 2014 http://www.dawn.com/news/1103505 (accessed on 14 October 2016).
36. Fatima Jinnah, *My Brother*, edited by Sharif al Mujahid, Karachi: Quaid-i-Azam Academy, 1987, p. 11.
37. Hajra Saeed, 'A Woman of Substance', *The Nation*, 9 July 2008, http://nation.com.pk/columns/09-Jul-2008/a-woman-of-substance (accessed on 11 December 2017).
38. Sheela Reddy, *Mr And Mrs Jinnah*, p. 371.
39. Khaled Ahmed, *Pakistan: Behind the Ideological Mask*, Lahore: Vanguard Books, 2001, p. 15.
40. Nadeem F. Paracha, 'Fatima Jinnah: A sister's sorrow'.
41. Shahid Masood on 'News One' TV programme https://www.youtube.com/watch?v=l4l8y8ztraI&feature=youtu.be,(accessed on 11 December 2017).
42. *Morning News*, 29 October 1958, cited in Lawrence Ziring, *Pakistan in the Twentieth Century: A Political History*, Karachi: OUP, 1997, p. 225.
43. Altaf Gauhar, *Ayub Khan: Pakistan's First Military Ruler*, pp. 174–75.
44. Shahid Masood, https://www.youtube.com/watch?v=l4l8y8ztraI&feature=youtu.be (accessed on 11 December 2017).
45. Lawrence Ziring, *Pakistan in the Twentieth Century: A Political History*, p. 283.
46. Syeda Abida Hussain, *Power Failure: The Political Odyssey of a Pakistani Woman*, Karachi: OUP, 2015, pp. 7–8.
47. Ibid.
48. Rafia Zakaria, *The Upstairs Wife: An Intimate History of Pakistan*, p. 60.
49. Ibid.
50. Shahid Masood, 'News One', https://www.youtube.com/watch?v=l4l8y8ztraI&feature=youtu.be (accessed on 11 December 2017).
51. Herbert Feldman, *From Crisis to Crisis: Pakistan 1962–1969*, London: OUP, 1972, p. 70.
52. Rafia Zakaria, *The Upstairs Wife: An Intimate History of Pakistan*, pp. 58–60.
53. Khaled Ahmed, *Pakistan: Behind the Ideological Mask*, p. 15.
54. *Dawn*, Karachi, 11 November 1979, cited in Ziauddin Ahmed, *Liaquat Ali Khan: Builder of Pakistan*, Karachi: Royal Book Company, 1990, p. 71.
55. Ibid., pp. 70–71.
56. K.K. Aziz, *Rahmat Ali: A Biography*, Lahore: Vanguard, 1987, p. 25, cited in Sherbaz Khan Mazari, *A Journey to Disillusionment*, Karachi: OUP, 1999, p. xxviii.
57. Sherbaz Khan Mazari, *A Journey to Disillusionment*, p. xxviii.
58. Nadeem F. Paracha, 'The map man', *Dawn*, 21 June 2015, https://www.dawn.com/news/1189425 (accessed on 11 December 2017).

59. K.K. Aziz, *Rahmat Ali: A Biography*, p. 25, cited in Sherbaz Khan Mazari, *A Journey to Disillusionment*, p. xxviii.
60. Khaled Ahmed, *Pakistan: Behind the Ideological Mask*, p. 13.
61. Ibid., p. 13.
62. Ibid., p. 20.
63. Ibid., pp. 13–14.
64. See the author's *Pakistan: Courting the Abyss*, New Delhi: HarperCollins India, 2016, pp. 13–14
65. Stanley Wolpert, *Zulfi Bhutto of Pakistan: His Life and Times*, New York: OUP,1993, p. 24.
66. Fatima Jinnah, *My Brother*, edited by Sharif al Mujahid, p. 29.
67. Kunwar Khuldune Shahid, 'Shiaphobia', *The Friday Times*, '4 April 2014.

3.1: Ayub Khan I: Unchartered Waters

1. Altaf Gauhar, *Ayub Khan: Pakistan's First Military Ruler*, Karachi: OUP, 1996, p. xxxiii.
2. Gohar Ayub Khan, *Glimpses into the Corridors of Power*, Karachi: OUP, 2007, p. 8.
3. Humayun Mirza, *From Plassey to Pakistan*, Maryland, USA: Timespinner, 1999, 3rd edition, 2013, p. 289.
4. Ibid., p. 214.
5. Secret telegram dated 17 October 1958 from Ambassador Langley to Secretary of State in Washington DC as a briefing for Secretary of Defence, Neil McElroy's forthcoming visit to Pakistan, cited in Humayun Mirza, *From Plassey To Pakistan*, p. 289.
6. Altaf Gauhar, *Ayub Khan: Pakistan's First Military Ruler*, p. xxxiii
7. Samson Simon Sharaf, 'Pakistan's multi-layered perspectives, Part 4', *The Nation*, 19 March 2016, http://nation.com.pk/19-Mar-2016/pakistan-s-multi-layered-perspectives-part-4 (accessed on 11 December 2017).
8. Public Record Office, Ref: DO 35/8944, cited in Roedad Khan, *The British Papers: Documents 1958-1969*, Karachi: OUP, 2002, p. 47.
9. Shaukat Hayat Khan, *The Nation That Lost Its Soul*, Karachi: Jang Publishers, 1995, pp. 182–83, cited in Sherbaz Khan Mazari, *A Journey to Disillusionment*, Karachi: OUP 1999, p. 152, fn. 45.
10. Altaf Gauhar, *Ayub Khan: Pakistan's First Military Ruler*, p. xxxiv.
11. Nawabzada Sher Ali Pataudi, *The Story of Soldiering and Politics in India and Pakistan*, Lahore: Al Kitab, 2nd edition, 1983, p. 114.
12. Ibid., pp. 113–14.
13. Herbert Feldman, *From Crisis to Crisis: Pakistan 1962–1969*, London: OUP, 1972, p. 275.

14. Ibid., p. 276, fn. 6.
15. Nawabzada Sher Ali Pataudi, *The Story of Soldiering & Politics....*, pp. 116–17.
16. Ibid., pp. 131–32.
17. Ayesha Jalal, *The Struggle for Pakistan: A Muslim Homeland and Global Politics*, Cambridge, Massachusetts: Cambridge University Press, 2014, p. 79.
18. Nawabzada Sher Ali Pataudi, *The Story of Soldiering & Politics...*, p. 125.
19. Humayun Mirza, *From Plassey to Pakistan*, p. 220.
20. Ilhan Niaz, *The Culture of Power & Governance of Pakistan 1947-2008*, Karachi: OUP, 2010, p. 146.
21. 'Eyes Only' telegram, from Ambassador Langley to Secretary of State, John Foster Dulles, dated 4 October 1958, cited in Humayun Mirza, *From Plassey to Pakistan*, p. 217.
22. Ibid., p. 214.
23. Jahan Dad Khan, *Pakistan: Leadership Challenges*, Karachi: OUP, 1999, p, 37.
24. Mohammad Ayub Khan, *Friends, Not Masters*, London: OUP, 1967, p. 246.
25. K.M. Arif, *Khaki Shadows: Pakistan 1947-1997*, Karachi: OUP, 2001, p. 27; Lawrence Ziring, *Pakistan in the Twentieth Century: A Political History*, Karachi: OUP, 1997, pp. 224–25.
26. M. Asghar Khan, *We've Learnt Nothing from History, Pakistan: Politics & Military Power*, Karachi: OUP, 2005, p. 12.
27. Khaled Ahmed, *Pakistan: Behind the Ideological Mask*, Lahore: Vanguard Books, 2004, p. 232.
28. K.M. Arif, *Working with Zia*, Karachi: OUP, 1995, p. 14.
29. Khaled Ahmed, *Pakistan: Behind the Ideological Mask*, p. 232.
30. Humayun Mirza, *From Plassey to Pakistan*, pp. 228, 230.
31. Ibid., pp. 229, 231.
32. Gohar Ayub Khan, *Glimpses into the Corridors of Power*, p. 145.
33. Humayun Mirza, *From Plassey to Pakistan*, p. 231.
34. Jamsheed Marker, *Cover Point: Impressions of Leadership in Pakistan*, Karachi: OUP, 2016, p. 48.
35. Humayun Mirza, *From Plassey to Pakistan*, pp. 231.
36. Ibid., p. 232.
37. Ibid., pp. 232–34.
38. Ibid., p. 233.
39. Ibid.
40. Mohammad Ayub Khan, *Friends, Not Masters*, p.39.
41. Ibid., pp. 40–41.
42. Note from Minister Bhutto to President Ayub Khan, in *White Paper: The performance of the Bhutto Regime*, Vol. I, *Mr Z.A. Bhutto, His Family*

and Associates, Islamabad: Government of Pakistan, 1979, pp. 2–3, cited in Stanley Wolpert, *Zulfi Bhutto of Pakistan: His Life and Times*, New York: OUP, 1993, p. 60.

43. Humayun Mirza, *From Plassey to Pakistan*, p. 245.
44. Mushahid Hussain and Akmal Hussain, *Pakistan: Problems of Governance*, Centre For Policy Research, New Delhi: Konark Publishers Ltd, 1993, p. 123.
45. Samuel P. Huntington, *Political Order in Changing Societies*, Cambridge, Massachusetts: Yale University Press, 1967, pp. 250–51, cited in Altaf Gauhar, *Ayub Khan: Pakistan's First Military Ruler*, p. 302.
46. Fazalul Qader Choudhry, *Urdu Digest*, Lahore, June 1969, cited in Herbert Feldman, *From Crisis to Crisis: Pakistan 1962-1969*, p. 279.
47. G.W. Choudhury, *The Last Days of United Pakistan*, Bloomington: Indiana University Press, 1974, p. 13.
48. According to Sherbaz Khan Mazari it was Pir Muhammad Ali Rashidi who told Ayub that he should commence a hereditary reign as the first Badshah of Pakistan. Sherbaz Khan Mazari, *A Journey to Disillusionment*, p. 153, fn. 58. However, according to Ayesha Jalal, it was Khizar Hayat Khan Tiwana who suggested that the best assurance for stability might be for Pakistan to become a monarchy so that succession could remain in Ayub's family. Ayesha Jalal, *The Struggle for Pakistan*, Cambridge, Massachusetts: Cambridge University Press, 2014, p. 107.
49. Z.A. Bhutto, *If I am Assassinated*, New Delhi: Vikas Publishing House, 1979, cited in Tariq Ali, *The Duel: Pakistan on the Flight Path of American Power*, New York: Scribner, 2008, p. 69.
50. V.T. Joshi, *Pakistan: Zia To Benazir*, New Delhi: Konark Publishers Pvt. Ltd, 1995, p. 36.
51. Arshad Sami Khan, *Three Presidents and an Aide: Life, Power and Politics*, New Delhi: Pentagon Press, 2008, pp. 23–24.
52. Altaf Gauhar, *Ayub Khan: Pakistan's First Military Ruler*, p. 189.
53. Tariq Ali, *The Duel: Pakistan On the Flight Path of American Power*, p. 65.
54. Ayaz Amir, 'Sharifovs in Wonderland', *The News*, 10 May 2016, http://www.thenews.com.pk/print/118762-Sharifovs-in-Wonderland, (accessed on 9 September 2017).
55. Tariq Ali, *The Duel*, p. 65.
56. Altaf Gauhar, *Ayub Khan: Pakistan's First Military Ruler*, p. 346.
57. Paul M.Mcgarr, *The Cold War in South Asia: Britain, the United States and the Indian Subcontinent, 1945-1965*, first published in 2013; first South Asia edition, Delhi: Cambridge University Press, 2016, p. 81.
58. Morrice James, *Pakistan Chronicle*, London: Hurst, 1992, p. 110, cited in Paul M.Mcgarr, *The Cold War in South Asia: Britain, the United States and the Indian Subcontinent, 1945-1965*.

59. Tariq Ali, *The Duel*, p. 58.
60. Record of interview between Ismay and Jinnah, India Office Records (IOR), *Mountbatten Papers*, MSS EUR F200/191, Top Secret, 9 April 1947, p. 646; Z.H. Zaidi (ed.), *Jinnah Papers, First Series*, Volume I, Part II, National Archives of Pakistan, 1993, cited in Shuja Nawaz, *Crossed Swords: Pakistan, Its Army and the Wars Within*, Karachi: OUP, 2008, p. 93.
61. Ahmed Faruqui, *Musharraf's Pakistan, Bush's America & the Middle East*, Lahore: Vanguard Books, 2008, p. 105.
62. Mushahid Hussain and Akmal Hussain, *Pakistan: Problems of Governance*, p. 30.
63. Ahmed Faruqui, *Musharraf's Pakistan, Bush's America & the Middle East*, p. 105.
64. Ian Talbot, *Pakistan: A Modern History*, New Delhi: OUP, 1998, p. 172.
65. 'Foreign Relations of the United States, 1955-57', US Government Printing Office, Washington DC, p. 447, cited in Mushahid Hussain and Akmal Hussain, *Pakistan: Problems of Governance*, p. 114.
66. Governor General Ghulam Mohammad quoted in Ayesha Jalal, *The State of Martial Rule*, p. 128, cited in Farzana Shaikh, *Making Sense of Pakistan*, London: C Hurst & Co, 2009, p. 195.
67. Ghulam Mohammad quoted in Dennis Kux, *The United States and Pakistan, 1947–200: Disenchanted Allies*, London: OUP, 2001, p. 60.
68. C.L. Sulzberger, *A Postscript with a Chinese Accent*, MacMillan, 1974, cited in Mushahid Hussain and Akmal Hussian, *Pakistan: Problems of Governance*, p. 35.
69. Dilip Mukerjee, *Zulfiqar Ali Bhutto: Quest for Power*, New Delhi: Vikas Publishing House, 1972, p. 41.
70. Gul Hassan Khan, *Memoirs of Lt Gen. Gul Hassan Khan*, Karachi: OUP, 1993, p. 366.
71. Dilip Mukerjee, *Zulfiqar Ali Bhutto: Quest for Power*, p. 61.
72. Gohar Ayub, *Glimpses into the Corridors of Power*, p. 114.
73. G.W. Choudhury, *The Last Days of United Pakistan*, pp. 39–40.
74. Ibid., p. 40.
75. Arshad Sami Khan, *Three Presidents and an Aide*, p. 49.
76. Jahan Dad Khan, *Pakistan: Leadership Challenges*, Karachi: OUP, 1999, p. 65.
77. Altaf Gauhar, *Ayub Khan: Pakistan's First Military Ruler*, 1996, p. xlvii.
78. Cited in Roedad Khan, *Pakistan: A Dream Gone Sour*, Karachi: OUP, 1997, pp. 168–69.
79. K.M. Arif, *Khaki Shadows: Pakistan 1947-1997*, Karachi: OUP, 2001, p. 102.
80. Ayub's last broadcast on 25 March 1969, *Dawn*, 26 March 1969, cited in G.W. Choudhury, *The Last Days of United Pakistan*, p. 41.

81. G.W. Choudhury, *The Last Days of United Pakistan*, p. 47.
82. Arshad Sami Khan, *Three Presidents and an Aide*, pp. 7–9.
83. Ibid.
84. Ibid., pp. 107–08.
85. Herbert Feldman, *From Crisis to Crisis: Pakistan 1962-1969*, p. 299.
86. Arshad Sami Khan, *Three Presidents and an Aide*, pp. 15–16.
87. Ibid., p. 17.
88. Mary Anne Weaver, *Pakistan: In the Shadow of Jihad and Afghanistan*, New Delhi: Viking, Penguin Books India, 2003, pp. 54–55.
89. Jahan Dad Khan, *Pakistan: Leadership Challenges*, p. 67.
90. Gohar Ayub Khan, *Glimpses into the Corridors of Power*, p. 122.
91. Jamsheed Marker, *Cover Point: Impressions of Leadership in Pakistan*, Karachi: OUP, 2016, p. 70.

3.2: Ayub Khan II: 1965—A Bridge Too Far

1. Cited in Lawrence Ziring, *Pakistan in the Twentieth Century: A Political History*, Karachi: OUP, 1997, p. 281.
2. Brian Cloughley, *A History of the Pakistan Army: Wars and Insurrections*, Karachi: OUP, 1999, p. 64.
3. Sir Morrice James, *Pakistan Chronicle*, New York: St Martin's, 1993, p. 128, cited in Hassan Abbas, *Pakistan's Drift into Extremism*, New Delhi: Pentagon Press, 2005. Reprinted 2007, p. 44.
4. Jahan Dad Khan, *Pakistan: Leadership Challenges*, Karachi: OUP 1999, p. 52.
5. Z. A. Bhutto, *Foreign Policy of Pakistan*, Karachi: Pakistan Institute of Foreign Affairs 1964, cited in Lawrence Ziring, *Pakistan in the Twentieth Century: A Political History*, p. 279.
6. Dilip Mukerjee, *Zulfiqar Ali Bhutto: Quest for Power*, Delhi: Vikas Publishing House, 1972, p. 48.
7. Brian Cloughley, *A History of the Pakistan Army: Wars and Insurrections*, 1999, p. 61.
8. A.R. Siddiqi, *The Military in Pakistan: Image and Reality*, Lahore: Vanguard Books Ltd, 1996, p. 85.
9. Gul Hassan Khan, *Memoirs of Lt Gen. Gul Hassan Khan*, Karachi: OUP, 1993, p. 179.
10. F.S. Ajiazuddin (ed.), *The White House & Pakistan, Secret Declassified Documents, 1969-74*, Selected and Edited, Oxford: OUP, 2002, p. 41.
11. Salman Taseer, *Bhutto: A Political Biography*, Delhi: Vikas Publishing House, 1980, pp. 59–60.
12. Ibid., p. 59.
13. Dilip Mukerjee, *Zulfiqar Ali Bhutto: Quest for Power*, Delhi: Vikas Publishing House, 1972, p. 46.

14. Gul Hassan, *Memoirs of Lt Gen. Gul Hassan Khan*, Karachi: OUP, 1993, p. 116.
15. Altaf Gauhar, Foreword in M. Asghar Khan, *The First Round: Indo-Pakistan War 1965*, London: Islamic Information Services Ltd, 1979, Indian edition, Delhi: Vikas Publishing House, 1979, p. x.
16. Altaf Gauhar, *Ayub Khan: Pakistan's First Military Ruler*, Karachi: OUP, 1996, p. 210.
17. K.M. Arif, *Khaki Shadows: Pakistan 1947-1997*, Karachi: OUP, 2001, pp. 47–48.
18. Ibid., p. 48.
19. Mohammed Musa, *My Version: India and Pakistan War 1965*, Lahore: Wajidalis, 1983, pp. 2 and 4, cited in K.M Arif, *Khaki Shadows: Pakistan 1947-1997*, p. 48.
20. K.M. Arif, *Khaki Shadows: Pakistan 1947-1997*, p. 48.
21. Altaf Gauhar, *Ayub Khan: Pakistan's First Military Ruler*, p. 211.
22. Gul Hassan Khan, *Memoirs of Lt Gen. Gul Hassan Khan*, pp. 223–24.
23. Altaf Gauhar, *Ayub Khan: Pakistan's First Military Ruler*, p. 211.
24. K.M. Arif, *Khaki Shadows: Pakistan 1947-1997*, p. 46.
25. Ibid.
26. Gul Hassan Khan, *Memoirs of Lt Gen. Gul Hassan Khan*, p. 226.
27. Ibid., p. 90.
28. Jahan Dad Khan, *Pakistan: Leadership Challenges*, Karachi: OUP 1999, p. 52.
29. Mohammad Ayub Khan, *Friends, Not Masters*, London: OUP, 1967, pp. 122, 124.
30. Herbert Feldman, *From Crisis to Crisis: Pakistan 1962-1969*, London: OUP, 1972, p. 141, fn. 5.
31. K.M. Arif, *Khaki Shadows: Pakistan 1947-1997*, p. 49.
32. Iqbal Akhund, *Memoirs of a Bystander: A Life in Diplomacy*, Karachi: OUP: 1997, pp. 88–90.
33. K.M. Arif, *Khaki Shadows: Pakistan 1947-1997*, p. 49.
34. Lawrence Ziring, *Pakistan in the Twentieth Century: A Political History*, p. 288; Altaf Gauhar, Foreword, in M. Asghar Khan, *The First Round: Indo-Pakistan War 1965, p. xii.*
35. M. Asghar Khan, *The First Round: Indo-Pakistan War 1965*, p. 76.
36. Altaf Gauhar, Foreword, in M. Asghar Khan, *The First Round: Indo-Pakistan War 1965*, p. xii.
37. Altaf Gauhar, *Ayub Khan: Pakistan's First Military Ruler*, p. 217.
38. K.M. Arif, *Khaki Shadows: Pakistan 1947-1997*, pp. 51–52.
39. Annexure G to GHQ letter no. 4050/5/MO-1 dated 29 August, 1965. Directive from President Ayub Khan to Gen. Mohammad Musa, C-in-C. Pakistan Army, cited in Stanley Wolpert, *Zulfi Bhutto of Pakistan: His Life and Times*, New York: OUP, 1993, p. 90.
40. K.M. Arif, *Khaki Shadows: Pakistan 1947-1997*, pp. 51–52.

41. Stanley Wolpert, *Zulfi Bhutto of Pakistan: His Life and Times*, pp. 89–90.
42. Altaf Gauhar, *Ayub Khan: Pakistan's First Military Ruler*, p. 216.
43. Ishtiaq Ahmed, *The Pakistan Military in Politics – Origins, Evolution, Consequences*, New Delhi: Amaryllis, 2013, p. 130.
44. K.M. Arif, *Khaki Shadows: Pakistan 1947-1997*, pp. 56–57; Iqbal Akhund, *Memoirs of a Bystander: A Life in Diplomacy*, pp. 90–92.
45. Altaf Gauhar, *Ayub Khan: Pakistan's First Military Ruler*, p. 219.
46. Hassan Abbas, *Pakistan's Drift into Extremism*, p. 48.
47. Altaf Gauhar, *Ayub Khan: Pakistan's First Military Ruler*, p. 220.
48. Ishtiaq Ahmed, *The Pakistan Military in Politics: Origins, Evolution, Consequences*, New Delhi: Amaryllis, 2013, p. 137.
49. Arshad Sami Khan, *Three Presidents and an Aide: Life, Power and Politics*, New Delhi: Pentagon Press, 2008, p. 74.
50. Altaf Gauhar, *Ayub Khan: Pakistan's First Military Ruler*, pp. 223–24.
51. Herbert Feldman, *From Crisis to Crisis: Pakistan 1962-1969*, pp. 141–42.
52. Altaf Gauhar, Foreword, in M. Asghar Khan, *The First Round: Indo-Pakistan War 1965*, pp. xvi–xvii.
53. Lawrence Ziring, *Pakistan in the Twentieth Century: A Political History*, p. 294.
54. Ibid.
55. Z.A. Bhutto, 'Response to Zia', White Paper, pp. 88–89, held in Bhutto Family Library Archives (BFLA), cited in Stanley Wolpert, *Zulfi Bhutto of Pakistan: His Life and Times*, p. 91.
56. Iqbal Akhund, *Memoirs of a Bystander: A Life in Diplomacy*, p. 96; Altaf Gauhar, *Ayub Khan: Pakistan's First Military Ruler*, pp. 223–24.
57. Arshad Sami Khan, *Three Presidents and an Aide: Life, Power and Politics*, p. 69.
58. Iqbal Akhund, *Memoirs of a Bystander: A Life in Diplomacy*, p. 99; Gohar Ayub Khan, *Glimpses into the Corridors of Power*, Karachi: OUP, 2007, p. 93.
59. Iqbal Akhund, *Memoirs of a Bystander: A Life in Diplomacy*, p. 96.
60. Altaf Gauhar, *Ayub Khan: Pakistan's First Military Ruler*, pp. 226–27.
61. K.M. Arif, *Khaki Shadows: Pakistan 1947-1997*, p. 66.
62. Iqbal Akhund, *Memoirs of a Bystander: A Life in Diplomacy*, p. 97.
63. Ibid.; K.M.Arif, *Khaki Shadows: Pakistan 1947-1997*, p. 66.
64. M. Asghar Khan, *The First Round: Indo-Pakistan War 1965*, p. 95.
65. M. Asghar Khan, *We've Learnt Nothing from History, Pakistan: Politics and Military Power*, Karachi: OUP, 2005, pp. 235–36.
66. M. Asghar Khan, *The First Round: Indo-Pakistan War 1965*, p. 45.
67. Altaf Gauhar, *Ayub Khan: Pakistan's First Military Ruler*, p. 237.
68. Ibid., p. 237.
69. Nur Khan reminisces '65 war', *Dawn*, 6 September 2005, https://www.dawn.com/news/155474/nur-khan-reminisces (accessed on 11 December 2017).

70. Ibid.
71. S.G. Mehdi, '1965 war – facts, fibs and fiction', *The Pakistan Times*, 6 September 1977, cited in Ahmed Faruqui, *Rethinking the National Security of Pakistan: The Price of Strategic Myopia*, London: Ashgate Publishing Ltd, 2003, p. 57.
72. Mohammad Musa, *My Version: India-Pakistan War 1965*, Karachi: Wajidalis, cited in Ahmed Faruqui, *Rethinking the National Security of Pakistan*, p. 57.
73. Gul Hasan Khan, *Memoirs of Lt Gen. Gul Hassan Khan*, p. 169.
74. Ishtiaq Ahmed, *The Pakistan Military in Politics: Origins, Evolution, Consequences*, p. 146.
75. Altaf Gauhar, *Ayub Khan: Pakistan's First Military Ruler*, p. 230.
76. Gul Hasan Khan, *Memoirs of Lt Gen. Gul Hassan Khan*, pp. 177–78.
77. Ishtiaq Ahmed, *The Pakistan Military in Politics: Origins, Evolution, Consequences*, p. 145.
78. Dilip Mukerjee, *Zulfiqar Ali Bhutto: Quest for Power*, p. 48.
79. Altaf Gauhar, *Ayub Khan: Pakistan's First Military Ruler*, p. 219.
80. Lawrence Ziring, *Pakistan in the Twentieth Century: A Political History*, p. 304.
81. *Dawn*, 23 March 1969, cited in Herbert Feldman, *From Crisis to Crisis: Pakistan 1962-1969*, p. 158, fn. 28.
82. Herbert Feldman, *From Crisis to Crisis: Pakistan 1962-1969*, p. 143.
83. Iqbal Akhund, *Memoirs of a Bystander: A Life in Diplomacy*, p. 103.
84. Ishtiaq Ahmed, *The Pakistan Military in Politics: Origins, Evolution, Consequences*, p. 148.
85. Ibid., p. 148.
86. Shuja Nawaz, *Crossed Swords: Pakistan, Its Army and the Wars Within*, Karachi: OUP, 2008, p. 240.
87. *The New York Times*, 22 April 1966, cited in Safdar Mahmood, *Pakistan Divided*, New Delhi: Chaman Offset, 1983, p. 44.
88. Ibid.
89. K.M. Arif, *Khaki Shadows: Pakistan 1947-1997*, p. 89.
90. Lawrence Ziring, *Pakistan in the Twentieth Century: A Political History*, p. 298.
91. Salman Taseer, *Bhutto: A Political Biography*, Delhi: Vikas Publishing House, 1980, p. 66.
92. Humayun Mirza, *From Plassey To Pakistan*, Maryland: Timespinner, 1999, pp. 290–91.
93. Stanley Wolpert, *Zulfi Bhutto of Pakistan: His Life and Times*, p. 100.
94. Iqbal Akhund, *Memoirs of a Bystander: A Life in Diplomacy*, p. 110.
95. Ibid., p. 262.
96. Kuldip Nayar, *India: The Critical Years*, Delhi: Vikas Publishing House, 1971, p. 199.

97. Ibid.
98. Ibid., p. 101.
99. Tashkent Declaration, Ministry of External Affairs, India, 10 January 1966, http://mea.gov.in/bilateral-documents.htm?dtl/5993/Tashkent+Declaration (accessed on 9 September 2017).
100. Shuja Nawaz, *Crossed Swords: Pakistan, Its Army and the Wars Within*, p. 239.
101. Arshad Sami Khan, *Three Presidents and an Aide: Life, Power and Politics*, p. 70.
102. Benazir Bhutto, *Daughter of the East*, London: Hamish Hamilton, 1988, p. 35.
103. Stanley Wolpert, *Zulfi Bhutto of Pakistan: His Life and Times*, p. 102.
104. Iqbal Akhund, *Memoirs of A Bystander: A Life in Diplomacy*, pp. 126–27.
105. Herbert Feldman, *From Crisis to Crisis: Pakistan 1962-1969*, p. 150, fn. 19.
106. Sultan M. Khan, *Memories and Reflections of a Pakistani Diplomat*, London: The Centre For Pakistan Studies, 1997, p. 181.
107. Ibid.
108. Ibid.
109. Ibid.
110. Ibid.

4.1 Yahya Khan I: Unsteady Hands

1. K.M. Arif, *Khaki Shadows: Pakistan 1947-1997*, Karachi: OUP, 2001, p. 99; Shuja Nawaz, *Crossed Swords: Pakistan, Its Army and the Wars Within*, Karachi: OUP, 2008, p. 251.
2. Arshad Sami Khan, *Three Presidents and an Aide: Life, Power and Politics*, New Delhi: Pentagon Press, 2008, pp. 120–21.
3. K.M. Arif, *Working With Zia*, Karachi: OUP, 1995, p. 36.
4. A. Basit, *The Breaking of Pakistan*, Lahore: Liberty Publishers, 1990, p. 112, cited in K.M. Arif, *Khaki Shadows*, p. 100.
5. Sir Morrice James, *Pakistan Chronicle*, Karachi: OUP, 1993, cited in Sherbaz Khan Mazari, *A Journey to Disillusionment*, Karachi: OUP, 1999, p. 176.
6. K.M. Arif, *Working with Zia*, p. 29.
7. A.R. Siddiqi, *The Military in Pakistan: Image and Reality*, Lahore: Vanguard Books Ltd, 1996, p. 211.
8. K.M. Arif, *Khaki Shadows: Pakistan 1947-1997*, p. 99; Shuja Nawaz, *Crossed Swords: Pakistan, Its Army and the Wars Within*, p. 251.
9. Lawrence Ziring, *Pakistan in the Twentieth Century: A Political History*, Karachi: OUP, 1997, p. 322.

10. A.R. Siddiqi, *The Military in Pakistan: Image and Reality*, p. 125.
11. Jahan Dad Khan, *Pakistan: Leadership Challenges*, Karachi: OUP, 1999, p. 105.
12. K.M. Arif, *Khaki Shadows: Pakistan 1947-1997*, p. 99.
13. G.W. Choudhury, *The Last Days of United Pakistan*, Bloomington: Indiana University Press, 1974, p. 104.
14. Shuja Nawaz, *Crossed Swords: Pakistan, Its Army and the Wars Within*, Karachi: OUP, 2008, p. 251.
15. Jahan Dad Khan, *Pakistan: Leadership Challenges*, p. 105.
16. Ibid., pp. 106–07.
17. A.R. Siddiqi, *The Military in Pakistan: Image and Reality*, pp. 125–26.
18. Jahan Dad Khan, *Pakistan: Leadership Challenges*, p. 108.
19. Mohammad Musa, *Jawan to General*, Karachi: East and West Publishing Company, 1984, p. 187, cited in K.M. Arif, *Working with Zia*, Karachi: OUP, 1995, p. 28.
20. Jahan Dad Khan, *Pakistan: Leadership Challenges*, p. 95.
21. Hassan Abbas, *Pakistan's Drift into Extremism*, New Delhi: Pentagon Press, 2005, reprinted 2007, p. 55.
22. Jahan Dad Khan, *Pakistan: Leadership Challenges*, p. 126.
23. Arshad Sami Khan, *Three Presidents and an Aide: Life, Power and Politics*, pp. 192, 208.
24. Gohar Ayub Khan, *Glimpses into the Corridors of Power*, Karachi, OUP, 2007, p. 115.
25. Hassan Abbas, *Pakistan's Drift into Extremism*, pp. 53–54; G.W. Choudhury, *The Last Days of United Pakistan*, pp. 28–29.
26. Piloo Mody, *Zulfi My Friend*, Delhi: Thomson Press (India) Limited, 1973, p. 104.
27. Sartaj Aziz, *Between Dreams and Realities: Some Milestones in Pakistan's History*, Karachi: OUP, 2009, p. 42.
28. A. Basit, *The Breaking of Pakistan*, pp. 25–26, cited in K.M. Arif, *Khaki Shadows: Pakistan 1947-1997*, p. 100.
29. G.W. Choudhury, *The Last Days of United Pakistan*, p. 50.
30. Ibid., p. 41.
31. Shuja Nawaz, *Crossed Swords: Pakistan, Its Army and the Wars Within*, p. 249.
32. Sultan M. Khan, *Memories and Reflections of a Pakistani Diplomat*, London: The Centre of Pakistan Studies, 1997, p. 242.
33. Arshad Sami Khan, *Three Presidents and an Aide: Life, Power and Politics*, p. 123–24.
34. Ibid.; A.A.K.Niazi, *The Betrayal of East Pakistan*, Karachi: OUP, 1998, Indian edition, New Delhi: Natraj Publishers, 2014, p. 39; Shuja Nawaz, *Crossed Swords: Pakistan, Its Army and the Wars Within*, p. 260.

35. Henry Kissinger, *The White House Years*, first Indian edition, New Delhi: Vikas Publishing House, 1979, p. 850.
36. Cited in Lawrence Ziring, *Pakistan in the Twentieth Century: A Political History*, p. 333.
37. Jamsheed Marker, *Quiet Diplomacy: Memoirs of an Ambassador of Pakistan*, Oxford: OUP, 2010, p. 116.
38. A phrase used in an article. 'The Enigma of a Political Priest', *Holiday*, Dhaka, 21 February 1971, cited in Dilip Mukerjee, *Zulfiqar Ali Bhutto: Quest for Power*, Delhi: Vikas Publishing House, 1972, p. 104.
39. Ibid., p. 114.
40. Khalid Hasan's long essay 'Zulfikar Ali Bhutto' in his book *Rearview Mirror* cites this as the origin of the story, cited in Shuja Nawaz, *Crossed Swords: Pakistan, Its Army and the Wars Within*, p. 264.
41. K.M. Arif, *Working with Zia*, p. 21.
42. *The Pakistan Observer*, 21 December 1970, cited in Safdar Mahmood, *Pakistan Divided*, New Delhi: Chaman Offset, 1983, p. 95.
43. *The Pakistan Observer*, 22 December 1970, cited in ibid.
44. Ibid.
45. Arshad Sami Khan, *Three Presidents and an Aide: Life, Power and Politics*, pp. 146–49.
46. Ibid.
47. Lawrence Ziring, *Pakistan in the Twentieth Century: A Political History*, p. 352.
48. Brian Cloughley, *A History of the Pakistan Army: Wars and Insurrections*, Karachi: OUP, 1999, p. 171.
49. Shuja Nawaz, *Crossed Swords: Pakistan, Its Army and the Wars Within*, p. 266.
50. Henry Kissinger, *The White House Years*, pp. 852–53.
51. M. Asghar Khan, *We've Learnt Nothing from History–Pakistan: Politics and Military Power*, Karachi: OUP, 2005, p. 42.
52. Henry Kissinger, *The White House Years*, p. 861.
53. G.W. Choudhury, *The Pakistan Times*, 22 September 1988, cited in Gen. K.M. Arif, *Working with Zia*, pp. 39–40.
54. Ibid., p. 39.
55. K.M. Arif, *Khaki Shadows: Pakistan 1947-1997*, p. 344.
56. David Dunbar, 'Pakistan: The Failure of Political Negotiations', *Asian Survey*, 1972, cited in Ahmed Faruqui, *Musharraf's Pakistan, Bush's America & the Middle East*, Lahore: Vanguard Books, 2008, p. 36.
57. Iqbal Akhund, *Memoirs of a Bystander: A Life in Diplomacy*, Karachi: OUP, 1997, p. 211.
58. Arshad Sami Khan, *Three Presidents and an Aide: Life, Power and Politics*, p. 179.

59. Shuja Nawaz, *Crossed Swords: Pakistan, Its Army and the Wars Within*, p. 259.
60. Mushahid Hussain and Akmal Hussain, *Pakistan: Problems of Governance*, Centre For Policy Research, New Delhi: Konark Publishers Ltd, 1993, p. 79.
61. Ibid., p. 75.

4.2 Yahya Khan II: 1971—How Not to Fight a War

1. Arshad Sami Khan, *Three Presidents and an Aide: Life, Power and Politics*, New Delhi: Pentagon Press, 2008, p. 151.
2. A.A.K. Niazi, *The Betrayal of East Pakistan*, Karachi: OUP, 1998, Indian edition, New Delhi: Natraj Publishers, 2014, p. 38.
3. Shuja Nawaz, *Crossed Swords: Pakistan, Its Army and the Wars Within*, Karachi: OUP, 2008, p. 264.
4. Ishtiaq Ahmed, *The Pakistan Military in Politics: Origins, Evolution, Consequences*, New Delhi: Amaryllis, 2013, pp. 172–73.
5. K.M. Arif, *Working with Zia*, Karachi: OUP, 1995, pp. 23–24.
6. Ibid., p. 25.
7. Mohamed Hassanein Haykal, 'The General who was defeated', in weekly 'Frankly Speaking' articles in Arabic, MENA, Cairo, 19 April 1973, cited in G.W. Choudhury, *The Last Days of United Pakistan*, Bloomington: Indiana University Press, 1974, pp. 183–84.
8. Arshad Sami Khan, *Three Presidents and an Aide: Life, Power and Politics*, pp. 151–52.
9. Brian Cloughley, *A History of the Pakistan Army: Wars and Insurrections*, Karachi: OUP, 1999, p. 178.
10. A.A.K.Niazi, *The Betrayal of East Pakistan*, p. 46.
11. Sultan M. Khan, *Memories and Reflections of a Pakistani Diplomat*, London: The Centre For Pakistan Studies, 1997, p. 311.
12. Ibid., pp. 305–06.
13. K.M. Arif, *Khaki Shadows: Pakistan 1947-1997*, OUP, Karachi 2001, p. 406.
14. Sultan M. Khan, *Memories and Reflections of a Pakistani Diplomat*, pp. 311–12.
15. Ibid., p. 312.
16. 'Yahya Khan Speaks', *The New York Times*, 29 September 1971, cited in Safdar Mahmood, *Pakistan Divided*, New Delhi: Chaman Offset, 1983, p. 135.
17. Gul Hassan Khan, *Memoirs of Lt Gen. Gul Hassan Khan*, Karachi: OUP, 1993, p. 274.
18. Jahan Dad Khan, *Pakistan: Leadership Challenges*, Karachi: OUP, 1999, pp. 116–17 and 121–22.

19. K.M. Arif, *Khaki Shadows: Pakistan 1947-1997*, pp. 27–28.
20. Hassan Abbas, *Pakistan's Drift into Extremism*, New Delhi: Pentagon Press, 2005, pp. 66–67.
21. Ibid., p. 67.
22. Khadim Hussain Raja, *A Stranger in My Own Country: East Pakistan, 1969-1971*, Karachi: OUP, 2012, p. 97.
23. Ibid., p. 99.
24. Dilip Mukerjee, *Zulfiqar Ali Bhutto: Quest for Power*, Delhi: Vikas Publishing House, 1972, p. 140.
25. Kuldip Nayyar, *Distant Neighbours*, Delhi: Vikas Publishing House, 1972, p. 180.
26. Safdar Mahmood, *Pakistan Divided*, p. 197.
27. Jahan Dad Khan, *Pakistan: Leadership Challenges*, pp. 119–120.
28. Henry Kissinger, *The White House Years*, first Indian edition, Delhi: Vikas Publishing House, 1979, p. 861.
29. Ibid., p. 883.
30. M. Asghar Khan, *We've Learnt Nothing from History: Pakistan Politics and Military Power*, Karachi: OUP, 2005, p. 49.
31. Shuja Nawaz, *Crossed Swords: Pakistan, Its Army and the Wars Within*, pp. 295–96.
32. Arshad Sami Khan, *Three Presidents and an Aide: Life, Power and Politics*, p. 174.
33. Minutes of the WASAG Meeting, Washington, 3 December 1971, Subject: South Asia. Foreign Relations of the US (FRUS), Vol.XI, 1969-1976, pp. 596–99 cited in Shuja Nawaz, *Crossed Swords: Pakistan, Its Army and the Wars Within*, p. 297.
34. Shuja Nawaz, *Crossed Swords: Pakistan, Its Army and the Wars Within*, p. 297.
35. Radio Pakistan, 8 p.m. news, cited in Shuja Nawaz, *Crossed Swords: Pakistan, Its Army and the Wars Within*, p. 298.
36. Brian Cloughley, *A History of the Pakistan Army: Wars and Insurrections*, p. 223.
37. Owen Bennet Jones, *Pakistan: Eye of the Storm*, Lahore: Vanguard Books, 2002, pp. 183–84.
38. Signal No. G-0001 of 0992300 December 1971, cited in K.M. Arif, *Working with Zia*, Karachi: OUP, 1995, p. 35.
39. Jahan Dad Khan, *Pakistan: Leadership Challenge*, p. 123,
40. Lt Gen. A.A.K. Niazi, *The Betrayal of East Pakistan*, p. xxvi
41. K.M. Arif, *Working with Zia*, p. 34.
42. Ibid., p. 34.
43. Abdul Hafiz Kardar, *Pakistan's Soldiers of Fortune*, Lahore: Ferozesons, 1988, cited in Ahmed Faruqui, *Musharraf's Pakistan, Bush's America & the Middle East*, Lahore: Vanguard Books, 2008, p. 36.

44. Robert Jackson, *South Asian Crisis: India, Pakistan and Bangladesh: A Political and Historical Analysis of the 1971 War*: Santa Barbara, Praeger, 1975, cited in Ahmed Faruqui, *Musharraf's Pakistan, Bush's America & the Middle East*, p. 36.
45. Ahmed Faruqui, *Musharraf's Pakistan, Bush's America &the Middle East*, p. 36.
46. Roedad Khan, *Pakistan: A Dream Gone Sour*, Karachi: OUP, 1997, p. 31.
47. Shuja Nawaz, *Crossed Swords: Pakistan, Its Army and the Wars Within*, p. 240.
48. Roedad Khan, Pakistan: *A Dream Gone Sour*, p. 33.
49. Shuja Nawaz, *Crossed Swords: Pakistan, Its Army and the Wars Within*, p. 312.
50. Ibid., p. 295.
51. Ahmed Faruqui, *Musharraf's Pakistan, Bush's America & the Middle East*, p. 31.
52. Many such instances have been published which confirm lack of coordination between the three defence services. *Weekly Sahafat* (Urdu), Lahore, 26 October–1 November 1977, pp. 21–22, cited in Safdar Mahmood, *Pakistan Divided*, p. 199.
53. Richard Sisson and Leo Rose, *War and Secession: Pakistan, India and the Creation of Bangladesh*, University of California Press, 1990, cited in Ahmed Faruqui, *Rethinking the National Security of Pakistan: The Price of Strategic Myopia*, London: Ashgate Publishing Ltd, 2003 p. 58.
54. Lawrence Ziring, *Pakistan in the Twentieth Century: A Political History*, p. 294.
55. Altaf Gauhar, 'Foreword' in Asghar Khan, *The First Round: Indo-Pakistan War 1965*, London: Islamic Information Services Ltd, 1979, Indian edition, Ghaziabad: Vikas Publishing House, 1979, p. xiv.
56. Roedad Khan, *Pakistan: A Dream Gone Sour*, pp. 29–30; Brian Cloughley, *A History of the Pakistan Army: Wars and Insurrections*, p. 172.
57. K.M. Arif, *Khaki Shadows: Pakistan 1947-1997*, p. 135.
58. Gul Hassan Khan, *Memoirs of Lt Gen. Gul Hassan Khan*, p. 299.
59. Jahan Dad Khan, *Pakistan: Leadership Challenges*, p. 121.
60. Roedad Khan, *Pakistan: A Dream Gone Sour*, pp. 33–34.
61. Imran Khan, *Pakistan: A Personal History*, London: Transworld Publishers, 2011, p. 56.
62. Gohar Ayub Khan, *Glimpses into the Corridors of Power*, p. 161.

5.1: Z.A. Bhutto I: Picking Up the Pieces

1. K.M. Arif, *Working with Zia: Pakistan's Power Politics, 1977-88*, Karachi: OUP, 1995, p. 47.
2. Arshad Sami Khan, *Three Presidents and an Aide: Life, Power and Politics*, New Delhi: Pentagon Press, 2008, p. 181.

3. Richard Sisson and Leo R. Rose, *War and Secession*, Berkeley: University of California Press, 1990, p. 306, fn. 28, cited in Sherbaz Khan Mazari, *A Journey to Disillusionment*, Karachi: OUP, 1999, p. 216.
4. Arshad Sami Khan, *Three Presidents and an Aide: Life, Power and Politics*, p. 184.
5. Safdar Mahmood, *Pakistan Divided*, New Delhi: Chaman Offset, 1983, p. 207.
6. Dilip Mukerjee, *Zulfiqar Ali Bhutto: Quest for Power*, Delhi: Vikas Publishing House, 1972, p. 7.
7. Rafi Raza, *Zulfikar Ali Bhutto and Pakistan 1967-1977*, Karachi: OUP, 1997, p. 136.
8. Lawrence Ziring, *Pakistan in the Twentieth Century: A Political History*, Karachi: OUP, 1997, p. 369.
9. K.M. Arif, *Khaki Shadows: Pakistan 1947-1997*, p. 280; Lawrence Ziring, *Pakistan in the Twentieth Century: A Political History*, p. 369.
10. Iqbal Akhund, *Memoirs of a Bystander: A Life in Diplomacy*, Karachi: OUP, 1997, p. 207.
11. F.B. Ali, 'Conduct Unbecoming', *Newsline*, September 2000, cited in Hassan Abbas, *Pakistan's Drift into Extremism*, New Delhi: Pentagon Press, 2005, reprinted 2007, pp. 67–68.
12. Hassan Abbas, ibid., p. 68.
13. Jahan Dad Khan, *Pakistan: Leadership Challenges*, Karachi: OUP, 1999, p. 144.
14. Gul Hassan Khan, *Memoirs of Lt Gen. Gul Hassan Khan*, Karachi: OUP, 1993, pp. 349–50.
15. Hassan Abbas, *Pakistan's Drift into Extremism*, pp. 71–72.
16. K.M. Arif, *Working with Zia: Pakistan's Power Politics, 1977-88*, p. 42.
17. Arshad Sami Khan, *Three Presidents and an Aide: Life, Power and Politics*, pp. 269–70.
18. Stanley Wolpert, *Zulfi Bhutto of Pakistan: His Life and Times*, New York: OUP, 1993, p. 287.
19. Sherbaz Khan Mazari, *A Journey to Disillusionment*, p. 452.
20. K.M. Arif, *Working with Zia: Pakistan's Power Politics, 1977-88*, p. 46.
21. A.A.K. Niazi, *The Betrayal of East Pakistan*, Karachi: OUP, 1998, Indian edition, New Delhi: Natraj Publishers, 2014, pp. 252–53.
22. Faiz Ali Chishti, *Betrayals of Another Kind*, Delhi: Tricolour Books, 1989, p. 119.
23. Roedad Khan, *Pakistan: A Dream Gone Sour*, Karachi: OUP, 1997, p. 169.
24. A.A.K. Niazi, *The Betrayal of East Pakistan*, pp. 255–64.
25. Ibid., p. 267.
26. Secret 'GHQ Report on Indo-Pakistan war December [19]71', Document number 3769/DA. Pakistan Army GHQ Archives. Though unsigned, inquiries by Shuja Nawaz indicate that it was headed by Gen. Awan. Shuja Nawaz, *Crossed Swords: Pakistan, Its Army and the Wars Within*, Karachi: OUP, 2008, pp. 310–11, 313.

27. Ibid., p. 311.
28. Ibid.
29. Benazir Bhutto, *Daughter of the East*, London: Hamish Hamilton, 1988, p. 53.
30. Biharis were the non-Bengali Muslim immigrants into East Pakistan from India following Partition in 1947.
31. Secret brief for the president's summit meeting from the COAS, forwarded by Gen. Tikka Khan to the DMO on 11 June 1972. Pakistan Army GHQ Archives, cited in Shuja Nawaz, *Crossed Swords: Pakistan, Its Army and the Wars Within*, p. 328.
32. Stanley Wolpert, *Zulfi Bhutto of Pakistan: His Life and Times*, pp. 189–90; Salman Taseer, *Bhutto: A Political Biography*, Delhi: Vikas Publishing House, 1980, p. 137.
33. Oriana Fallaci (trans. John Shepley), *Interview with History*, New York: Houghton Mifflin, 1976, cited in Brian Cloughley, *A History of the Pakistan Army: Wars and Insurrections*, Karachi: OUP, 1999, p. 253.
34. Shuja Nawaz, *Crossed Swords: Pakistan, Its Army and the Wars Within*, pp. 330–31.
35. Benazir Bhutto, *Daughter of the East*, p. 57.
36. Piloo Mody, *Zulfi My Friend*, Delhi: Thomson Press (India) Limited, 1973, p. 148.
37. Benazir Bhutto, *Daughter of the East*, p. 58.
38. Sherbaz Khan Mazari, *A Journey to Disillusionment*, p. 264.
39. V.T. Joshi, *Pakistan: Zia to Benazir*, New Delhi: Konark Publishers Pvt. Ltd, 1995, p. 17.
40. Ibid., pp. 105–06.
41. Ibid., p. 51.
42. Sultan M. Khan, *Memories and Reflections of a Pakistani Diplomat*, London: The Centre for Pakistan Studies, 1997, p. 431.
43. A.A.K. Niazi, *The Betrayal of East Pakistan*, p. 248.
44. Henry Kissinger, *The White House Years*, first Indian edition, Delhi: Vikas Publishing House, 1979, p. 907.

5.2: Z.A. Bhutto II: The Arrogance of Power

1. Salman Taseer, *Bhutto: A Political Biography*, New Delhi: Vikas Publishing House, 1980, p. 21; Stanley Wolpert, *Zulfi Bhutto of Pakistan: His Life and Times*, New York: OUP, 1993, p. 15.
2. Salman Taseer, *Bhutto: A Political Biography*, p. 27. During his stint in the US in 1947, Bhutto dropped the softer 'Zulfiqar' and began spelling his name 'Zulfikar', something like how Jinnah had changed his name. Henceforth the name would be spelt as Zulfikar.
3. Stanley Wolpert, *Zulfi Bhutto of Pakistan: His Life and Times*, p. 19.

4. Interview with Piloo Mody, *Illustrated Weekly of India*, Bombay, 23 January 1972, cited in Dilip Mukerjee, *Zulfiqar Ali Bhutto: Quest for Power*, Vikas Publishing House, Delhi, 1972, pp. 27–28.
5. Salman Taseer, *Bhutto: A Political Biography*, p. 19.
6. Dilip Mukerjee, *Zulfiqar Ali Bhutto: Quest for Power*, p. 28.
7. Sherbaz Khan Mazari, *A Journey to Disillusionment*, Karachi: OUP, 1999, pp. 247–48.
8. Stanley Wolpert, *Zulfi Bhutto of Pakistan: His Life and Times*, p. 22.
9. Oriana Fallaci, 'Interview with History', cited in Salman Taseer, *Bhutto: A Political Biography*, p. 24.
10. Salman Taseer, *Bhutto: A Political Biography*, p. 21; Sherbaz Khan Mazari, *A Journey to Disillusionment*, p. 268.
11. K.M. Arif, *Working with Zia, Pakistan's Power Politics, 1977-88*, Karachi: OUP, 1995, p. 146.
12. Kausar Niazi, *Zulfiqar Ali Bhutto of Pakistan: Last Days*, Delhi: Vikas Publishing House, 1992, p. 106.
13. Cited in Syeda Hameed, *Born to Be Hanged: Political Biography of Zulfikar Ali Bhutto*, New Delhi: Rupa Publications 2017, p. x.
14. Faiz Ali Chishti, *Betrayals of Another Kind*, Delhi: Tricolour Books, 1989, p. 37.
15. Sultan M. Khan, *Memories and Reflections of a Pakistani Diplomat*, London: The Centre for Pakistan Studies, 1997, p. 405.
16. K.M. Arif, *Working with Zia, Pakistan's Power Politics, 1977-88*, pp. 127–28.
17. Ibid., p. 128.
18. Sherbaz Khan Mazari, *A Journey to Disillusionment*, p. 269, fn. 58.
19. Syeda Hameed, *Born to Be Hanged: Political Biography of Zulfikar Ali Bhutto*, p. 144.
20. Sherbaz Khan Mazari, *A Journey to Disillusionment*, pp. 335–36; Stanley Wolpert, *Zulfi Bhutto of Pakistan: His Life and Times*, p. 240.
21. J.A. Rahim's press statement issued on 9 August 1977 published verbatim in White Paper on the Performance of Bhutto Regime, Vol. III, Government of Pakistan, Islamabad, 1979, cited in Sherbaz Khan Mazari, *A Journey to Disillusionment*, p. 385.
22. Syeda Hameed, *Born To Be Hanged: Political Biography Of Zulfikar Ali Bhutto*, p. 2.
23. Stanley Wolpert, *Zulfi Bhutto of Pakistan: His Life and Times*, p. 4.
24. Mary Anne Weaver, *Pakistan: In the Shadow of Jihad and Afghanistan*, USA: Straus and Girous, 2002, Indian edition, New Delhi: Viking, Penguin Books India, 2003, p. 181.
25. James P. Farwell, *The Pakistan Cauldron: Conspiracy, Assassination and Instability*, USA: Potomac Books, 2011, Indian edition, New Delhi: Pentagon Press, 2012, p. 59.

26. Tariq Ali, *The Duel: Pakistan on the Flight Path of American Power*, New York: Scribner, 2008, p. 104.
27. Jamsheed Marker, *Cover Point: Impressions of Leadership in Pakistan*, Karachi: OUP, 2016, p. 94.
28. Tariq Ali, *The Duel: Pakistan on the Flight Path of American Power*, p. 107.
29. Salman Taseer, *Bhutto: A Political Biography*, p. 111.
30. Sherbaz Khan Mazari, *A Journey to Disillusionment*, p. 235, *fn* 31.
31. Kausar Niazi, *Zulfiqar Ali Bhutto of Pakistan: Last Days*, p. 150.
32. Sultan M. Khan, *Memories and Reflections of a Pakistani Diplomat*, London: The Centre for Pakistan Studies, 1997, pp. 412–13.
33. James P. Farwell, *The Pakistan Cauldron: Conspiracy, Assassination and Instability*, p. 64.
34. Jamshed Marker, *Quiet Diplomacy: Memoirs of an Ambassador of Pakistan*, Karachi: OUP, 2010, p. 383.
35. Shyam Bhatia, *Goodbye Shahzadi: A Political Biography of Benazir Bhutto*, New Delhi: Lotus Collection, Rolli Books, 2008, p. x.
36. Benazir Bhutto, *Daughter of the East*, 1988, p. 72.
37. Brian Cloughley, *A History of the Pakistan Army–Wars and Insurrections*, Karachi: OUP, 1999, p. 142; Stanley Wolpert, *Zulfi Bhutto of Pakistan: His Life and Times*, pp. 70–71.
38. Iqbal Akhund, *Trial and Error: The Advent and Eclipse of Benazir Bhutto*, Karachi: OUP, 2000, p. 322.
39. Iqbal Akhund, *Memoirs of a Bystander: A Life in Diplomacy*, Karachi: OUP, p. 137.
40. Dilip Mukerjee, *Zulfiqar Ali Bhutto: Quest for Power*, pp. 28–29.
41. Excerpts from court documents presented to Rajya Sabha, *Official Reports*, 54th session, Appendix LIV, Part I, pp. 110–11, cited in Dilip Mukerjee, *Zulfiqar Ali Bhutto: Quest for Power*, pp. 29–30.
42. *Dawn*, 1 July 1967, cited in Dilip Mukerjee, ibid.
43. Ibid.
44. Interview with Oriana Fallaci, *L'Europeo*, April 1972, cited in Christina Lamb, *Waiting for Allah: Pakistan's Struggle for Democracy*, New Delhi: Viking, Penguin Books, 1991, p. 48.
45. Sherbaz Khan Mazari, *A Journey to Disillusionment*, pp. 72–73.
46. Gohar Ayub Khan, *Glimpses into the Corridors of Power*, Karachi: OUP, 2007, pp. 140–41.
47. White Paper on the Performance of the Bhutto Regime, Vol. I, Government of Pakistan, Islamabad, 1979, cited in Sherbaz Khan Mazari, *A Journey to Disillusionment*, pp. 75, 77.
48. *Dawn*, 29 October 1958, cited in Salman Taseer, *Bhutto: A Political Biography*, p. 40.
49. Emma Duncan, *Breaking the Curfew: A Political Journey Through Pakistan*, London: Arrow Books Ltd, 1990; first published by Michael Joseph in 1989, p. 234.

50. Ibid.
51. Arshad Sami Khan, *Three Presidents and an Aide: Life, Power and Politics*, New Delhi: Pentagon Press, 2008, p. 43.
52. Salman Taseer, *Bhutto: A Political Biography*, p. 47.
53. Jahan Dad Khan, *Pakistan: Leadership Challenges*, Karachi: OUP, 1999, p. 131.
54. Jamsheed Marker, *Cover Point: Impressions of Leadership in Pakistan*, p. 100.
55. Salman Taseer, *Bhutto: A Political Biography*, p. 91.
56. *Dawn*, 25 November 1967, cited in. Dilip Mukerjee, *Zulfiqar Ali Bhutto: Quest for Power*, p. 58.
57. M. Asghar Khan, *We've Learnt Nothing from History–Pakistan: Politics and Military Power*, Karachi: OUP, 2005, p. 60.
58. Ibid., p. 35.
59. Sartaj Aziz, *Between Dreams and Realities: Some Milestones in Pakistan's History*, Karachi: OUP, 2009, p. 48.
60. Gohar Ayub Khan, *Glimpses into the Corridors of Power*, pp. 137, 150–51.
61. Gul Hassan Khan, *Memoirs of Lt Gen. Gul Hassan Khan*, Karachi: OUP, 1993, p. 388.
62. Rafi Raza, *Zulfikar Ali Bhutto and Pakistan, 1967-77*, Karachi: OUP, 1997, p. 294.
63. Ayesha Jalal, *The Struggle for Pakistan*, Cambridge, Massachusetts: Cambridge University Press, 2014, p. 206.
64. Jamsheed Marker, *Cover Point: Impressions of Leadership in Pakistan*, p. 105.
65. Ibid., p. 54.
66. Tariq Ali, *The Duel: Pakistan on the Flight Path of American Power*, New York: Scribner, 2008, p. 63.
67. For details see the previous chapter.
68. Kausar Niazi, *Zulfiqar Ali Bhutto of Pakistan: Last Days*, p. 80.
69. Gohar Ayub Khan, *Glimpses into the Corridors of Power*, p. 158.
70. See the author's *Pakistan: Courting the Abyss*, Noida: HarperCollins India, 2016, p. 98.
71. Sherbaz Khan Mazari, *A Journey to Disillusionment*, p. 164.
72. Tariq Ali, *The Duel: Pakistan on the Flight Path of American Power*, p. 110.
73. *Business Recorder*, 29 January 2008, cited in ibid.
74. Iqbal Akhund, *Trial and Error: The Advent and Eclipse of Benazir Bhutto*, pp. 37–38.
75. Stanley Wolpert, *Zulfi Bhutto of Pakistan: His Life and Times*, p. 273.
76. Ibid.
77. Rafi Raza, *Zulfikar Ali Bhutto and Pakistan 1967-1977*, p. 243, and Hassan Abbas, *Pakistan's Drift into Extremism*, p. 87.
78. Kausar Niazi, *Zulfiqar Ali Bhutto of Pakistan: Last Days*, pp. 228–30.

79. 'General Elections [Top Secret], ISI document for prime minister, 5 October 1976, cited in Husain Haqqani, *Pakistan: Between Mosque and Military*, Lahore: Vanguard Books, 2005, p. 116.
80. Stanley Wolpert, *Zulfi Bhutto of Pakistan: His Life and Times*, pp. 270–72.
81. Lawrence Ziring, *Pakistan in the Twentieth Century: A Political History*, Karachi: OUP, 1997, p. 413.
82. Kausar Niazi, *Zulfiqar Ali Bhutto of Pakistan: Last Days*, p. 68.
83. K.M. Arif, *Working with Zia: Pakistan's Power Politics, 1977-88*, p. 63.
84. Kausar Niazi, *Zulfiqar Ali Bhutto of Pakistan: Last Days*, p. 60.
85. Sherbaz Khan Mazari, *A Journey to Disillusionment*, p. 456.
86. K.M. Arif, *Working with Zia: Pakistan's Power Politics, 1977-88*, pp. 77–78.
87. Kausar Niazi, *Zulfiqar Ali Bhutto of Pakistan: Last Days*, pp. 123–25.
88. Sherbaz Khan Mazari, *A Journey to Disillusionment*, pp. 455–56.
89. Kausar Niazi, *Zulfiqar Ali Bhutto of Pakistan: Last Days*, p. 68.
90. Benazir Bhutto, *Daughter of the East*, p. 73.
91. Kausar Niazi, *Zulfiqar Ali Bhutto of Pakistan: Last Days*, p. 89.
92. According to Syeda Hameed, the irony was that in 1931 Mohammd Ahmed Khan was honorary magistrate of Kasur. The exact spot where he was killed was the same where he had supervised the hanging of Shaheed Bhagat Singh. Shadman Chowk was where the central jail was located. Syeda Hameed, *Born to Be Hanged: Political Biography of Zulfikar Ali Bhutto*, p. 197.
93. Jamsheed Marker, *Cover Point: Impressions of Leadership in Pakistan*, p. 109.
94. Syeda Abida Hussain, *Power Failure: The Political Odyssey of a Pakistani Woman*, Karachi: OUP, 2015, p. 157.
95. Benazir Bhutto, *Daughter of the East*, pp. 120–21.
96. K.M. Arif, *Working with Zia: Pakistan's Power Politics, 1977-88*, p. 206.
97. Shyam Bhatia, *Goodbye Shahzadi: A Political Biography of Benazir Bhutto*, p. 24. Since Murtaza was not in the country at the time, he would have to be referring to someone else who had seen the body.
98. Ibid., p. 83–84.
99. Iqbal Akhund, *Trial and Error: The Advent and Eclipse of Benazir Bhutto*, p. 318.

6: Zia-ul-Haq: A Chess Player in a Nation of Cricketers

1. For the sake of full disclosure, the author too was born in Jalandhar and studied at St Stephen's.
2. Gohar Ayub Khan, *Glimpses into the Corridors of Power*, Karachi: OUP, 2007, p. 180.

3. Mazhar Ali Khan, *Pakistan: The Barren Years: The Viewpoint, Editorials and Columns of Mazhar Ali Khan 1875-1992*, Karachi: OUP, 1998, pp. 394–95.
4. Christina Lamb, *Waiting for Allah: Pakistan's Struggle for Democracy*, New Delhi: Viking, Penguin Books India, 1991, p. 84.
5. Jamsheed Marker, *Cover Point: Impressions of Leadership in Pakistan*, Karachi: OUP, 2016, p. 123.
6. Roedad Khan, *Pakistan: A Dream Gone Sour*, Karachi: OUP, 1997, pp. 82–83.
7. Ibid., pp. 83–84.
8. Ibid., pp. 86–87.
9. Faiz Ali Chishti, *Betrayals of Another Kind*, Delhi: Tricolour Books, 1989, pp. 97, 121.
10. Jamsheed Marker, *Cover Point: Impressions of Leadership in Pakistan*, p.131.
11. Brian Cloughley, *A History of the Pakistan Army: Wars and Insurrections*, Karachi: OUP, 1999, p. 265.
12. K.M. Arif, *Khaki Shadows: Pakistan 1947-1997*, Karachi: OUP, 2001, p.144.
13. Faiz Ali Chishti, *Betrayals of Another Kind*, p. 23.
14. K.M. Arif, *Khaki Shadows: Pakistan 1947-1997*, p. 147.
15. Ibid., p. 199.
16. Ibid., p. 142.
17. Jamsheed Marker, *Cover Point: Impressions of Leadership in Pakistan*, p. 128.
18. K.M. Arif, *Khaki Shadows: Pakistan 1947-1997*, p. 149.
19. Faiz Ali Chishti, *Betrayals of Another Kind*, pp. 108–09.
20. Syeda Abida Hussain, *Power Failure: The Political Odyssey of a Pakistani Woman*, Karachi: OUP, 2015, pp. 195–96.
21. K.M. Arif, *Khaki Shadows: Pakistan 1947-1997*, p. 145.
22. Lawrence Ziring, *Pakistan in the Twentieth Century: A Political History*, Karachi: OUP, 1997, p. 455.
23. K.M. Arif, *Khaki Shadows: Pakistan 1947-1997*, p. 144.
24. Gul Hassan Khan, *Memoirs of Lt Gen. Gul Hassan Khan*, Karachi: OUP, 1993, p. 403.
25. Ibid., p. 401.
26. K.M. Arif, *Khaki Shadows: Pakistan 1947-1997*, p. 154.
27. Quoted in F.B. Ali, 'Conduct Unbecoming', *Newsline*, September 2000, p. 37, cited in Hassan Abbas, *Pakistan's Drift into Extremism*, New Delhi: Pentagon Press, 2005, reprinted in 2007, pp. 75–76.
28. Faiz Ali Chishti, *Betrayals of Another Kind*, pp. 28, 101–02.
29. Hassan Abbas, *Pakistan's Drift into Extremism*, p. 98.
30. Faiz Ali Chishti, *Betrayals of Another Kind*, p. 92.

31. Iqbal Akhund, *Trial and Error: The Advent and Eclipse of Benazir Bhutto*, Karachi: OUP, 2000, pp. 100–01.
32. Iqbal Akhund, *Memoirs of a Bystander: A Life in Diplomacy*, Karachi: OUP, 1997, p. 351.
33. K.M. Arif, *Khaki Shadows: Pakistan 1947-1997*, p. 154.
34. Hassan Abbas, *Pakistan's Drift into Extremism*, p. 91.
35. M. Asghar Khan, *We've Learnt Nothing from History: Pakistan Politics and Military Power*, Karachi: OUP, 2005, p. 188; Gul Hassan Khan, *Memoirs of Lt. Gen. Gul Hassan Khan*, pp. 400–01.
36. Gul Hassan Khan, *Memoirs of Lt Gen. Gul Hassan Khan*, p. 400–401.
37. Kausar Niazi, *Zulfiqar Ali Bhutto of Pakistan: Last Days*, Delhi: Vikas Publishing House, 1992, pp. 95–96.
38. Stanley Wolpert, *Zulfi Bhutto of Pakistan: His Life and Times*, New York: OUP, 1993, p. 262.
39. K.M. Arif, *Working with Zia*, Karachi: OUP, 1995, p. ix.
40. Faiz Ali Chishti, *Betrayals of Another Kind*, p, 97.
41. Benazir Bhutto, *Daughter of the East*, London: Hamish Hamilton, 1988, p. 68.
42. Shyam Bhatia, *Goodbye Shahzadi: A Political Biography of Benazir Bhutto*, New Delhi: Lotus Collection, Rolli Books, 2008, p. 4.
43. Stanley Wolpert, *Zulfi Bhutto of Pakistan: His Life and Times*, p. 263.
44. Ibid.
45. Ibid., pp. 263–64.
46. Salman Taseer, *Bhutto: A Political Biography*, Delhi: Vikas Publishing House, 1980, p. 194.
47. Faiz Ali Chishti, *Betrayals of Another Kind*, p. 56.
48. Jamsheed Marker, *Cover Point: Impressions of Leadership in Pakistan*, p. 124.
49. Hassan Abbas, *Pakistan's Drift into Extremism*, p. 86.
50. Faiz Ali Chishti, *Betrayals of Another Kind*, p. 49.
51. Mushahid Hussain, *Pakistan Politics: The Zia Years*, New Delhi: Konark Publishers Ltd, 1991, p. 265, cited in Mushahid Hussain and Akmal Hussain, *Pakistan: Problems of Governance*, Centre For Policy Research, New Delhi: Konark Publishers Ltd, 1993, p. 133.
52. Iqbal Akhund, *Memoirs of a Bystander: A Life in Diplomacy*, Karachi: OUP, 997, pp. 356–57.
53. Roedad Khan, *Pakistan: A Dream Gone Sour*, p. 69.
54. K.M. Arif, *Khaki Shadows: Pakistan 1947-1997*, p. 174.
55. Jamsheed Marker, *Cover Point: Impressions of Leadership in Pakistan*, p. 122.
56. Roedad Khan, *Pakistan: A Dream Gone Sour*, p. 70.
57. K.M. Arif, *Working with Zia*, pp. 166–67.
58. Mushahid Hussain and Akmal Hussain, *Pakistan: Problems of Governance*, pp. 134–35.

59. K.M. Arif, *Working with Zia*, p. xi.
60. Kausar Niazi, *Zulfiqar Ali Bhutto of Pakistan: Last Days*, pp. 210–11.
61. Jahan Dad Khan, *Pakistan: Leadership Challenges*, Karachi: OUP, 1999, p. 173.
62. Shuja Nawaz, *Crossed Swords: Pakistan, Its Army and the Wars Within*, p. 353.
63. K.M. Arif, *Working with Zia*, pp. 96–97.
64. *The Los Angeles Times*, 7 July 1977, cited in K.M. Arif, *Working with Zia*, p. 108.
65. K.M. Arif, *Khaki Shadows: Pakistan 1947-1997*, p. 153.
66. K.M. Arif, *Working with Zia*, p. x.
67. Ayesha Jalal, *The Struggle for Pakistan*, Cambridge, Massachusotts: Cambridge University Press, 2014, p. 240.
68. Imran Khan, *Pakistan: A Personal History*, London: Transworld Publishers, 2011, pp. 75–76.
69. Syeda Abida Hussain, *Power Failure: The Political Odyssey of a Pakistani Woman*, p. 226.
70. Iqbal Akhund, *Trial and Error: The Advent and Eclipse of Benazir Bhutto*, pp. 14–15.
71. K.M. Arif, *Working with Zia*, p. 235.
72. V.T. Joshi, *Pakistan: Zia to Benazir*, New Delhi: Konark Publishers Pvt Ltd, 1995, p. 32.
73. James P. Farwell, *The Pakistan Cauldron: Conspiracy, Assassination and Instability*, Lincoln, Nebraska: Potomac Books, 2011, Indian edition, New Delhi: Pentagon Press, 2012, p. 74.
74. Hassan Abbas, *Pakistan's Drift into Extremism*, p. 99.
75. Nilima Lambah, *A Life across Three Continents: Recollections of a Diplomat's Wife*, Delhi: Lotus Collection, Roli Books, 2008, p. 75.
76. I.A. Rehman, '40 Years of Zia: How Zia redefined Pakistan' *Dawn*, 2 July 2017, https://www.dawn.com/news/1342697/40-years-of-zia-how-zia-redefined-pakistan, (accessed on 2 December 2017).
77. Farzana Sheikh, *Making Sense of Pakistan*, London: C. Hurst & Co., 2009, pp. 58, 64 and 76.
78. Jamsheed Marker, *Quiet Diplomacy: Memoirs of an Ambassador of Pakistan*, Karachi: OUP, 2010, second impression 2010, p. 357.
79. Rodney Jones in *The Washington Quarterly*, Summer 1989, cited in Iqbal Akhund, *Trial and Error: The Advent and Eclipse of Benazir Bhutto*, p. 247.
80. Dennis Kux, *The United States and Pakistan, 1947-2000: Disenchanted Allies*, London: OUP, 2001, p. 361.
81. Faiz Ali Chishti, *Betrayals of Another Kind*, p. 102.
82. Ibid., pp. 102–03.
83. Ibid., p. 106.
84. Jamsheed Marker, *Quiet Diplomacy: Memoirs of an Ambassador of Pakistan*, p. 347.

85. Mushahid Hussain and Akmal Hussain, *Pakistan: Problems of Governance*, p. 137.
86. Ibid., pp. 149–50.
87. James P. Farwell, *The Pakistan Cauldron: Conspiracy, Assassination and Instability*, p. 73.
88. Mary Anne Weaver, *Pakistan: In the Shadow of Jihad and Afghanistan*, New York: Straus and Girous, 2002, Indian edition, New Delhi: Viking, Penguin Books India, 2003, p. 65.

7: Benazir Bhutto: Paradise Lost

1. Imran Khan, *Pakistan: A Personal History*, London: Transworld Publishers, 2011, p. 59.
2. Shyam Bhatia, *Goodbye Shahzadi: A Political Biography of Benazir Bhutto*, New Delhi: Lotus Collection, Rolli Books, 2008, p. 34.
3. 'My Dearest Daughter: A letter from the death cell', Bhutto's letter to Benazir from his death cell, dated 21 June 1978, reproduced by Sani H. Panhwar, member Sindh Council, PPP, www.bhutto.org, pp. 66–67, (accessed on 9 September 2017).
4. Iqbal Akhund, *Trial and Error: The Advent and Eclipse of Benazir Bhutto*, Karachi: OUP, 2000, p. 318.
5. William Dalrymple, 'Pakistan's flawed and feudal princess', *The Guardian*, 30 December 2007, https://www.theguardian.com/commentisfree/2007/dec/30/pakistan.world (accessed on 9 June 2017).
6. Ibid.
7. Christina Lamb, *Waiting for Allah: Pakistan's Struggle for Democracy*, New Delhi: Viking, Penguin Books India, 1991, p. 54.
8. William Dalrymple, 'Pakistan's flawed and feudal princess'.
9. Christina Lamb, *Waiting for Allah: Pakistan's Struggle for Democracy*, p. 278.
10. Ron Suskind, *The Way of the World: A Story of Truth and Hope in an Age of Extremism*, New York: HarperCollins, 2008, p. 261.
11. Iqbal Akhund, *Trial and Error: The Advent and Eclipse of Benazir Bhutto*, p. 26.
12. Rafia Zakaria, *The Upstairs Wife: An Intimate History of Pakistan*, Boston: Beacon Press, 2015, p. 143.
13. V.T. Joshi, *Pakistan: Zia to Benazir*, New Delhi: Konark Publishers Pvt. Ltd, 1995, p. 13.
14. Shyam Bhatia, *Goodbye Shahzadi: A Political Biography of Benazir Bhutto*, p. xii.
15. Dilip Mukerjee, *Zulfiqar Ali Bhutto: Quest for Power*, Delhi: Vikas Publishing House, 1972, p. 30.

16. Mary Anne Weaver, *Pakistan: In the Shadow of Jihad and Afghanistan*, New York: Straus and Girous, 2002, Indian edition, New Delhi: Viking, Penguin Books India, 2003, p. 175.
17. Benazir Bhutto, *Daughter of the East*, London: Hamish Hamilton, 1988, p. 33; Mary Anne Weaver, *Pakistan: In the Shadow of Jihad and Afghanistan*, p. 181.
18. Mary Anne Weaver, ibid., pp. 181–82.
19. Benazir Bhutto, *Daughter of the East*, p. 16.
20. Ibid., p. 51.
21. Ibid., p. 56.
22. Ibid., p. 66.
23. Ron Suskind, *The Way of the World: A Story of Truth and Hope in an Age of Extremism*, p. 357.
24. Benazir Bhutto, *Daughter of the East*, pp. 71–72.
25. Christina Lamb, *Waiting for Allah: Pakistan's Struggle for Democracy*, p. 46.
26. Benazir Bhutto, *Daughter of the East*, p. 75.
27. Iqbal Akhund, *Trial and Error: The Advent and Eclipse of Benazir Bhutto*, p. 96; Nafisa Hoodbhoy, *Aboard the Democracy Train: A Journey Through Pakistan's Last Decade of Democracy*, London: Anthem Press, 2011, pp. 11–12.
28. Mary Anne Weaver, *Pakistan: In the Shadow of Jihad and Afghanistan*, p. 188.
29. Ibid, pp. 185–87.
30. Iqbal Akhund, *Trial and Error: The Advent and Eclipse of Benazir Bhutto*, p. 1.
31. Christina Lamb, *Waiting for Allah: Pakistan's Struggle for Democracy*, p. 36.
32. Ibid., p. 39; Mary Anne Weaver, *Pakistan: In the Shadow of Jihad and Afghanistan*, p. 191.
33. Husain Haqqani, *Magnificent Delusions: Pakistan, United States and an Epic History of Misunderstanding*, New York: Public Affairs, 2013, p. 277.
34. Shyam Bhatia, *Goodbye Shahzadi: A Political Biography of Benazir Bhutto*, p. 55.
35. Shuja Nawaz, *Crossed Swords: Pakistan, Its Army and the Wars Within*, Karachi: OUP, 2008, p. 414.
36. Mushahid Hussain and Akmal Hussain, *Pakistan: Problems of Governance*, Centre For Policy Research, New Delhi: Konark Publishers Ltd, 1993, p. 39.
37. Ibid, pp. 39–40.
38. Reference is to a failed Hamid Gul–inspired mujahideen operation to capture Jalalabad, Afghanistan.

39. Mushahid Hussain, 'Civil-Military Relations', *Frontier Post*, Lahore, 5 May 1991, cited in Hassan Abbas, *Pakistan's Drift into Extremism*, New Delhi: Pentagon Press, 2005, reprinted in 2007, p. 137.
40. Christina Lamb, *Waiting for Allah: Pakistan's Struggle for Democracy*, p. 278.
41. Nafisa Hoodbhoy, *Aboard the Democracy Train: A Journey Through Pakistan's Last Decade of Democracy*, pp. 21–22.
42. V.T. Joshi, *Pakistan: Zia to Benazir*, New Delhi: Konark Publishers Pvt. Ltd, 1995, pp. 13–14.
43. Mary Anne Weaver, *Pakistan: In the Shadow of Jihad and Afghanistan*, p. 191.
44. Ibid., p. 205.
45. Iqbal Akhund, *Trial and Error: The Advent and Eclipse of Benazir Bhutto*, p. 57.
46. Ibid., p. 53.
47. Ibid., p. 280.
48. Mary Anne Weaver, *Pakistan: In the Shadow of Jihad and Afghanistan*, pp. 206–07.
49. Gohar Ayub Khan, *Glimpses into the Corridors of Power*, Karachi: OUP, 2007, p. 251.
50. Arshad Sami Khan, *Three Presidents and an Aide: Life, Power and Politics*, New Delhi: Pentagon Press, 2008, p. 274.
51. Christina Lamb, *Waiting for Allah: Pakistan's Struggle for Democracy*, p. 277.
52. Iqbal Akhund, *Trial and Error: The Advent and Eclipse of Benazir Bhutto*, p. 148, fn. 28.
53. Christina Lamb, *Waiting for Allah: Pakistan's Struggle for Democracy*, pp. 276–77.
54. Hassan Abbas, *Pakistan's Drift into Extremism*, p. 142.
55. Arshad Sami Khan, *Three Presidents and an Aide: Life, Power and Politics*, pp. 277–78.
56. Mary Anne Weaver, *Pakistan: In the Shadow of Jihad and Afghanistan*, pp. 184–85 .
57. V.T. Joshi, *Pakistan: Zia to Benazir*, p. 19.
58. Mary Anne Weaver, *Pakistan: In the Shadow of Jihad and Afghanistan*, p. 211.
59. V.T. Joshi, *Pakistan: Zia to Benazir*, pp. 12–13.
60. Roedad Khan, *Pakistan: A Dream Gone Sour*, Karachi: OUP, 1997, p. 160.
61. Syeda Abida Hussain, *Power Failure: The Political Odyssey of a Pakistani Woman*, Karachi: OUP, 2015, p. 572.
62. Helms Introduces Bhutto, and Gets It Wrong, Associated Press, 7 April 1995, https://www.sfgate.com/news/article/Helms-Introduces-Bhutto-and-Gets-It-Wrong-3037837.php (accessed on 8 March 2018).

63. Mary Anne Weaver, *Pakistan: In the Shadow of Jihad and Afghanistan*, pp. 195–96.
64. John E. Burns, 'Bhutto Clan Leaves Trail of Corruption in Pakistan', *The New York Times*, 9 January 1998, cited in James P. Farwell, *The Pakistan Cauldron: Conspiracy, Assassination and Instability*, Lincoln, Nebraska: Potomac Books, 2011, Indian edition, New Delhi: Pentagon Press, 2012, p. 71.
65. Benazir Bhutto, *Daughter of the East*, p. 303.
66. Iqbal Akhund, *Trial and Error: The Advent and Eclipse of Benazir Bhutto*, p. 17.
67. Nafisa Hoodbhoy, *Aboard the Democracy Train: A Journey Through Pakistan's Last Decade of Democracy*, p. 69.
68. Ibid.
69. Syeda Abida Hussain, *Power Failure: The Political Odyssey of a Pakistani Woman*, p. 620.
70. Mary Anne Weaver, *Pakistan: In the Shadow of Jihad and Afghanistan*, p. 208.
71. Shyam Bhatia, *Goodbye Shahzadi: A Political Biography of Benazir Bhutto*, p. xiii.
72. 'My Dearest Daughter: A Letter from the death cell', Bhutto's letter to Benazir from his death cell, dated 21 June 1978, reproduced in PDF form by Sani H. Panhwar, member, Sindh Council of PPP, www.bhutto.org, p. 67 (accessed on 9 September 2017).
73. Shyam Bhatia, *Goodbye Shahzadi: A Political Biography of Benazir Bhutto*, p. 102.
74. Gohar Ayub Khan, *Glimpses into the Corridors of Power*, p. 236.
75. Iqbal Akhund, *Trial and Error: The Advent and Eclipse of Benazir Bhutto*, p. 129.
76. Ibid.
77. Ibid., pp. 133–34.
78. Shyam Bhatia, *Goodbye Shahzadi: A Political Biography of Benazir Bhutto*, p. 39.
79. Ibid., pp. 41–42.
80. Ibid., p. 61.
81. Ibid., p. 68.
82. Iqbal Akhund, *Trial and Error: The Advent and Eclipse of Benazir Bhutto*, pp. 208–09.
83. Condoleezza Rice, *No Higher Honour: A Memoir of My Years in Washington*, London: Simon & Schuster, 2011, p. 608; Ron Suskind, *The Way of the World: A Story of Truth and Hope in an Age of Extremism*, p. 205.
84. Ibid.
85. Condoleezza Rice, *No Higher Honour: A Memoir of My Years in Washington*, p. 608.

86. Ibid.
87. Ibid., p. 609.
88. Ibid., 606–07.
89. Nafisa Hoodbhoy, *Aboard the Democracy Train: A Journey Through Pakistan's Last Decade of Democracy*, p. 191; Ron Suskind, *The Way of the World: A Story of Truth and Hope in an Age of Extremism*, p. 292.
90. Condoleezza Rice, *No Higher Honour: A Memoir of My Years in Washington*, p. 610.
91. Ron Suskind, *The Way of the World: A Story of Truth and Hope in an Age of Extremism*, p. 282.
92. Condoleezza Rice, *No Higher Honour: A Memoir of My Years in Washington*, pp. 610–11.
93. Ibid., p. 611; Ron Suskind, *The Way of the World: A Story of Truth and Hope in an Age of Extremism*, p. 334.
94. Heraldo Munoz, *Getting Away with Murder: Benazir Bhutto's Assassination and the Politics of Pakistan*, Indian edition, New Delhi: Viva Books Private Ltd, 2014, p. 26.
95. Ibid., p. 127.
96. Ron Suskind, *The Way of the World: A Story of Truth and Hope in an Age of Extremism*, p. 267.
97. Heraldo Munoz, *Getting Away with Murder: Benazir Bhutto's Assassination and the Politics of Pakistan*, p. 27.
98. Ron Suskind, *The Way of The World: A Story of Truth and Hope in an Age of Extremism*, pp. 335–36.
99. Nafisa Hoodbhoy, *Aboard the Democracy Train: A Journey Through Pakistan's Last Decade of Democracy*, p.196.
100. Ron Suskind, *The Way of the World: A Story of Truth and Hope in an Age of Extremism*, p. 291.
101. Heraldo Munoz, *Getting Away with Murder: Benazir Bhutto's Assassination and the Politics of Pakistan*, pp. 133–34.
102. James P. Farwell, *The Pakistan Cauldron: Conspiracy, Assassination and Instability*, p. 203.
103. Heraldo Munoz, *Getting Away with Murder: Benazir Bhutto's Assassination and the Politics of Pakistan*, p. 185.

8: Nawaz Sharif – The Comeback Kid

1. Usman Dar, https://www.facebook.com/UDarOfficial/posts/ 680734888683273, 20 August 2014 (accessed on 2 December 2017).
2. Ibid.
3. Jilani Khan claimed to have studied dance and music at Santiniketan. See Syeda Abida Hussain, *Power Failure: The Political Odyssey of a Pakistani Woman*, Karachi: OUP, 2015, p. 188.

4. Sohail Warraich, *Gaddar Kaun: Nawaz Sharif Ke Kahani Unke Zaban*, (Urdu) Lahore: Sagar Publishers, 2012, pp. 65–67.
5. Hassan Abbas, *Pakistan's Drift into Extremism*, New Delhi: Pentagon Press, 2005, reprinted in 2007, p. 135.
6. Ibid.
7. Syeda Abida Hussain, *Power Failure: The Political Odyssey of a Pakistani Woman*, p. 298.
8. Usman Dar, https://www.facebook.com/UDarOfficial/posts/680734888683273, 20 August 2014 (accessed on 2 December 2017).
9. Sohail Warraich, *Gaddar Kaun: Nawaz Sharif Ke Kahani Unke Zaban*, pp. 51–52.
10. Shuja Nawaz, *Crossed Swords: Pakistan, Its Army and the Wars Within*, Karachi: OUP, 2008, p. 412.
11. Hassan Abbas, *Pakistan's Drift into Extremism*, pp. 135–36.
12. Sartaj Aziz, *Between Dreams and Realities: Some Milestones in Pakistan's History*, Karachi: OUP, 2009, p. 90.
13. Ibid., p. 111.
14. Pervez Musharraf, *In the Line of Fire: A Memoir*, New York: Free Press, 2006, p. 138.
15. Declan Walsh, 'Pakistan's Ex-leader in Exile: Pervez Musharraf's Quiet New Life in London', *The Guardian*, 9 September 2009, https://www.theguardian.com/world/2009/sep/09/pakistan-pervez-musharraf-exile-london (accessed on 7 December 2017).
16. Christina Lamb, *Waiting for Allah: Pakistan's Struggle for Democracy*, New Delhi: Viking, Penguin Books India, 1991, p. 68.
17. Ibid.
18. Imran Khan, *Pakistan: A Personal History*, London: Transworld Publishers, 2011, pp. 131–33.
19. Ibid., pp.132–33.
20. Kim Barker, *The Taliban Shuffle: Strange Days in Afghanistan and Pakistan*, New York: Anchor Books, 2012, p. 181.
21. Ayaz Amir, 'Dullness, stagnation and corrupt mediocrity', *The News*, 16 December 2016, https://www.thenews.com.pk/print/172146-Dullness-stagnation-and-corrupt-mediocrity (accessed on 2 December 2017).
22. Emma Duncan, *Breaking the Curfew: A Political Journey Through Pakistan*, London: Arrow Books Ltd, first published by Michael Joseph, 1989, p. 96.
23. Shahid-ur-Rahman, 'Who Owns Pakistan', http://arz-e-pak.com/documents/ebooks/WhoOwnPakistan.pdf p. 150, (accessed on 2 December 2017).
24. Usman Dar, https://www.facebook.com/UDarOfficial/posts/680734888683273, 20 August 2014, (accessed on 2 December 2017).

25. Figures are given in dollar terms here and elsewhere as the exchange rate was different then.
26. Shahid-ur-Rahman, 'Who Owns Pakistan', pp. 150–51.
27. Ibid., p. 103.
28. Ibid., p. 44.
29. Ayaz Amir, 'Dullness, stagnation and corrupt mediocrity', cited by Dr Aamir Khan, 'Removing Nawaz Sharif', *Daily Times*, 23 June 2017, http://dailytimes.com.pk/opinion/24-Jun-17/removing-nawaz-sharif (accessed on 2 December 2017).
30. Kim Barker, *The Taliban Shuffle: Strange Days in Afghanistan and Pakistan*, p.182.
31. Imran Khan, *Pakistan: A Personal History*, p. 133.
32. Iqbal Akhund, *Trial and Error: The Advent and Eclipse of Benazir Bhutto*, Karachi: OUP, 2000, p. 45.
33. Ibid., pp. 328–29.
34. Hassan Abbas, *Pakistan's Drift into Extremism*, pp. 164–65.
35. Christina Lamb, *Waiting for Allah: Pakistan's Struggle for Democracy*, p. 57.
36. Khaled Ahmed, *Pakistan: Behind the Ideological Mask*, Lahore: Vanguard Books, 2004, pp. 262–63.
37. Gohar Ayub Khan, *Glimpses into the Corridors of Power*, Karachi: OUP, 2007, p. 280.
38. Christina Lamb, *Waiting for Allah: Pakistan's Struggle for Democracy*, p. 67.
39. Maleeha Lodhi, *Pakistan's Encounter with Democracy*, Lahore: Vanguard, 1994, pp. 243–45, cited in Ilhan Niaz, *The Culture of Power and Governance of Pakistan 1947-2008*, Karachi: OUP, 2010, p. 123.
40. Nasim Hassan Shah, *Memoirs and Reflections*, Islamabad: Alhamra Publishing, 2002, p. 124, cited in Ilhan Niaz, *The Culture of Power and Governance of Pakistan 1947-2008*, p. 191.
41. Mushahid Hussain and Akmal Hussain, *Pakistan: Problems of Governance*, Centre For Policy Research, New Delhi: Konark Publishers Ltd, 1993, p. 105.
42. Syeda Abida Hussain, *Power Failure: The Political Odyssey of a Pakistani Woman*, p. 344.
43. Pakistan Institute of Legislative Development And Transparency (PILDAT), 'Assessment of the quality of Democracy in Pakistan 2016', http://www.pakistantoday.com.pk/2017/02/01/pakistan-less-democratic-in-2016-than-a-year-before-pildat/ p. 10, (accessed on 2 December 2017).
44. Gohar Ayub Khan, *Glimpses into the Corridors of Power*, pp. 257–59.
45. Aasim Zafar Khan 'No-go areas of parliament', *The News on Sunday*, 22 January 2017, http://tns.thenews.com.pk/go-areas-parliament/#.WIQjhvl9600 (accessed on 2 December 2017).

46. Kalbe Ali, 'PM attended Senate once this parliamentary year', *Dawn*, 12 March 2016, http://www.dawn.com/news/1245199/pm-attended-senate-once-this-parliamentary-year (accessed on 2 December 2017).
47. 'PM's attendance record', editorial in *The Express Tribune*, 20 January 2016 https://tribune.com.pk/story/1030512/pms-attendance-record/ (accessed on 3 December 2017).
48. Muhammad Mehboob,'PM compares political rivals to terrorists', *The Nation*, 7 May 2016, http://nation.com.pk/national/07-May-2016/pm-compares-political-rivals-to-terrorists (accessed on 2 December 2017); 'A peculiar comparison', *The Express Tribune*, 8 May 2016, www.tribune.com.pk (accessed on 2 December 2017.)
49. Syeda Abida Hussain, *Power Failure: The Political Odyssey of a Pakistani Woman*, p. 410.
50. Ibid., p. 559.
51. Gohar Ayub Khan, *Glimpses into the Corridors of Power*, pp. 297–98.
52. Hassan Abbas, *Pakistan's Drift into Extremism*, pp. 162–63.
53. Gohar Ayub Khan, *Glimpses into the Corridors of Power*, p. 302.
54. Ibid., p. 303.
55. Ibid.
56. Azhar Sohail, *Agencion ki Hakumat*, (Urdu) Lahore: Vanguard, 1993, p. 10, cited in Hassan Abbas, *Pakistan's Drift into Extremism*, p. 137.
57. Imran Khan, *Pakistan: A Personal History*, p. 75.
58. Christina Lamb, *Waiting for Allah: Pakistan's Struggle for Democracy*, p. 90.
59. Abdul Sattar, 'No Power on Earth', *The News*, 2 May 2017, https://www.thenews.com.pk/print/201906-No-power-on-earth (accessed on 2 December 2017).
60. Mushahid Hussain and Akmal Hussain, *Pakistan: Problems of Governance*, p. 104.
61. The reference was to the way the then army chief Lt Gen. Gul Hassan was removed by Z.A. Bhutto. See chapter on 'Bhutto: Picking up the pieces'.
62. Gohar Ayub Khan, *Glimpses into the Corridors of Power*, p. 224.
63. Shuja Nawaz, *Crossed Swords: Pakistan, Its Army and the Wars Within*, p. 449.
64. Aftab Alam (ed.), *Pakistan's Fourth Military Coup*, Delhi: Raj Publications, 2001, p. 32.
65. Shuja Nawaz, *Crossed Swords: Pakistan, Its Army and the Wars Within*, p. 450.
66. Ibid.
67. Sohail Warraich, *Gaddar Kaun: Nawaz Sharif Ke Kahani Unke Zaban*, p. 175.
68. Bruce Riedel, 'American Diplomacy and the 1999 Kargil Summit at Blair House', *Center for the Advanced Study of India*, University of

Pennsylvania, 2002.http://citeseerx.ist.psu.edu/viewdoc/download?doi=10.1.1.473.251&rep=rep1&type=pdf (accessed on 2 December 2017). Riedel was taking notes in the Clinton–Sharif meeting. The account in the succeeding paragraphs is based on his article.

69. Riazul Haq,'Panama leaks scandal: Opposition asks PM seven blunt questions', *The Express Tribune*, 12 May 2016, http://tribune.com.pk/story/1101932/panama-leaks-scandal-opposition-asks-pm-seven-blunt-questions/, (accessed on 2 December 2017).
70. Zahid Hussain, 'Probing 'Panamagate', 13 April 2017, *Dawn*, https://www.dawn.com/news/1251731, (accessedon 2 December 2017).
71. Nasir Iqbal, 'JIT report carries seeds of upheaval', *Dawn*, 11 July 2017, https://www.dawn.com/news/1344488/jit-report-carries-seeds-of-upheaval (accessed on 2 December 2017); Danish Hussain, 'Qatari prince's letters dismissed as a myth', *Express Tribune*, 11 July 2017, https://tribune.com.pk/story/1455067/qatari-princes-letters-dismissed-myth/ (accessed on 2 December 2017).
72. Nasir Iqbal,'JIT report carries seeds of upheaval': *Dawn*,11 July 2017, https://www.dawn.com/news/1344488/jit-report-carries-seeds-of-upheaval (accessed on 2 December 2017).
73. 'PM worked for offshore firm, confirms Dubai law company', *Dawn*, 20 July 2017, https://www.dawn.com/news/1346473/pm-worked-for-offshore-firm-confirms-dubai-law-company (accessed on 2 December 2017).
74. Rizwas Shahzad, 'NAB files four corruption references against Sharif family, Ishaq Dar in accountability courts', *Express Tribune*, 8 September 2017, https://tribune.com.pk/story/1501064/nab-files-four-corruption-references-sharif-family-ishaq-dar-accountability-courts/ (accessed on 2 December 2017).
75. Umair Jamal, 'What is next for the Sharif family?' *Pakistan Today online*, 16 July 2017, https://www.pakistantoday.com.pk/2017/07/16/what-is-next-for-the-sharif-family/ (accessed on 2 December 2017).
76. Tariq Butt, 'Sharif's two-pronged policy on JIT', *The News*, 25 June 2017, https://www.thenews.com.pk/print/213027-Sharifs-two-pronged-policy-on-JIT (accessed on 2 December 2017); '"Panama case is a test of two-nation theory"' says PM's son-in-law', *Pakistan Today*, 25 June 2017, him.www.pakistantoday.com.pk/2017/06/24/panama-case-is-accountability-of-two-nation-theory-not-pm-nawaz-pms-son-in-law (accessed on 2 December 2017).
77. 'No review', *The News*, 17 September 2017, www.thenews.com.pk/print/230509-No-review (accessed on 2 December 2017).
78. Shahzad Chaudhry, 'A state without a leader', *The News*,14 July 2017, https://www.thenews.com.pk/print/216345-A-state-without-a-leader (accessed on 2 December 2017).

9: Pervez Musharraf: Shoot and Scoot

1. Mary Ann Weaver, *Pakistan: In the Shadows of Jihad and Afghanistan*, New York: Straus & Giroux, 2002, Indian edition, New Delhi: Viking, Penguin Books India, 2003, pp. 20–21.
2. Hassan Abbas, *Pakistan's Drift into Extremism*, New Delhi: Pentagon Press, 2005, Reprint, 2007, p. 179.
3. Pervez Musharraf, *In the Line of Fire: A Memoir*, New York: Free Press, 2006, p. 41.
4. Ibid., pp. 49, 72–73.
5. Mary Anne Weaver, *Pakistan: In the Shadow of Jihad and Afghanistan*, p. 7.
6. Shuja Nawaz, *Crossed Swords: Pakistan, Its Army and the Wars Within*, Karachi, OUP, 2008, p. 506.
7. Mary Anne Weaver, *Pakistan: In the Shadow of Jihad and Afghanistan*, p. 22.
8. Syeda Abida Hussain, *Power Failure: The Political Odyssey of a Pakistani Woman*, Karachi: OUP, 2015, p. 564.
9. Shyam Bhatia, *Goodbye Shahzadi: A Political Biography of Benazir Bhutto*, New Delhi: Lotus Collection, Rolli Books, 2008, p. 85.
10. *The Herald*, April 1990, cited in N.C. Behera, *State, Identity and Violence: Jammu, Kashmir and Ladakh*. Centre for Policy Research, New Delhi: Manohar Publishers, 2000, p. 196.
11. Pervez Musharraf, *In the Line of Fire: A Memoir*, pp. 79–80.
12. Shuja Nawaz, *Crossed Swords: Pakistan, Its Army and the Wars Within*, p. 500.
13. Sohail Warraich, *Gaddar Kaun: Nawaz Sharif Ke Kahani Unke Zaban*, Lahore: Sagar Publishers, 2012, p. 136.
14. Pervez Musharraf, *In the Line of Fire: A Memoir*, p. 77.
15. Hassan Abbas, *Pakistan's Drift into Extremism*, p. 170.
16. Shuja Nawaz, *Crossed Swords: Pakistan, Its Army and the Wars Within*, 2008, pp. 510–11.
17. Ibid., pp. 511.
18. For details see the author's *Pakistan: Courting the Abyss*, Noida: HarperCollins India, 2016, p. 295.
19. Shuja Nawaz, *Crossed Swords: Pakistan, Its Army and the Wars Within*, p. 514.
20. Ibid., p. 514–15.
21. Pervez Musharraf, *In the Line of Fire: A Memoir*, p. 96.
22. Sohail Warraich, *Gaddar Kaun: Nawaz Sharif Ke Kahani Unke Zaban*, p. 219.
23. Sartaj Aziz, *Between Dreams and Realities: Some Milestones in Pakistan's History*, Karachi: OUP, 2009, p. 259.

24. Ibid., p. 253.
25. Ibid., p. 254.
26. Hassan Abbas, *Pakistan's Drift into Extremism*, pp. 171–72.
27. Sohail Warraich, *Gaddar Kaun: Nawaz Sharif Ke Kahani Unke Zaban*, pp. 221–22.
28. Sartaj Aziz, *Between Dreams and Realities: Some Milestones in Pakistan's History*, p. 254.
29. Shuja Nawaz, *Crossed Swords: Pakistan, Its Army and the Wars Within*, p. 517.
30. Sartaj Aziz, *Between Dreams and Realities: Some Milestones in Pakistan's History*, p. 258.
31. Ibid., p. 273.
32. Shuja Nawaz, *Crossed Swords: Pakistan, Its Army and the Wars Within*, p. 520.
33. Mary Anne Weaver, *Pakistan: In the Shadow of Jihad and Afghanistan*, p. 30.
34. Pervez Musharraf, *In the Line of Fire: A Memoir*, pp. 97–98.
35. Tom Clancy with Gen. Tony Zinni (Retd) and Tony Koltz, *Battle Ready*, New York: Putnam, 2004, p. 347.
36. Shuja Nawaz, *Crossed Swords: Pakistan, Its Army and the Wars Within*, p. 522.
37. Sohail Warraich, *Gaddar Kaun: Nawaz Sharif Ke Kahani Unke Zaban*, p. 280.
38. Gohar Ayub Khan, *Glimpses into the Corridors of Power*, Karachi:OUP, 2007, pp. 323–25, 330.
39. Sohail Warraich, *Gaddar Kaun: Nawaz Sharif Ke Kahani Unke Zaban*, pp.144–45, 154–55.
40. Shuja Nawaz, *Crossed Swords: Pakistan, Its Army and the Wars Within*, p. 521.
41. Pervez Musharraf, *In the Line of Fire: A Memoir*, p. 98.
42. Shahzad Chaudhry, 'The anatomy of a coup', *The News*, 22 July 2016, https://www.thenews.com.pk/print/136675-The-anatomy-of-a-coup (accessed on 11 June 2017).
43. Ahmed Faruqui, *Rethinking the National Security of Pakistan: The Price of Strategic Myopia*, Farnham, UK: Ashgate Publishing Ltd, 2003, p. 7.
44. Bruce Riedel, 'American Diplomacy and the 1999 Kargil Summit at Blair House', *Center for the Advanced Study of India*, University of Pennsylvania, 2002, http://citeseerx.ist.psu.edu/viewdoc/download?doi=10.1.1.473.251&rep=rep1&type=pdf (accessed on 2 December 2017).
45. Owen Bennet Jones, *Pakistan: Eye of the Storm*, Lahore: Vanguard Books, 2002, p. 38.
46. Sartaj Aziz, *Between Dreams and Realities: Some Milestones in Pakistan's History*, p. 287.

47. Ibid., pp. 287–88.
48. Pervez Musharraf, *In the Line of Fire: A Memoir*, pp. 109–10.
49. Sartaj Aziz, *Between Dreams and Realities: Some Milestones in Pakistan's History*, p. 289.
50. Pervez Musharraf, *In the Line of Fire: A Memoir*, p. 110.
51. Ibid., p. 109.
52. Ibid., p. 121.
53. Shahzad Chaudhry, 'The anatomy of a coup'.
54. Pervez Musharraf, *In the Line of Fire: A Memoir*, p. 149.
55. Bruce Riedel, 'American Diplomacy and the 1999 Kargil Summit at Blair House'.
56. Hassan Abbas, *Pakistan's Drift into Extremism*, pp. 191–92.
57. Mary Anne Weaver, *Pakistan: In the Shadow of Jihad and Afghanistan*, p. 47.
58. Imran Khan, *Pakistan: A Personal History*, London: Transworld Publishers, 2011, p. 260.
59. Ibid., p. 222–23.
60. Ibid., pp. 260–61.
61. Nafisa Hoodbhoy, *Aboard the Democracy Train: A Journey Through Pakistan's Last Decade of Democracy*, London: Anthem Press 2011, p. 89.
62. Imran Khan, *Pakistan: A Personal History*, p. 222.
63. Ibid., pp. 257–58.
64. Heraldo Munoz, *Getting Away with Murder: Benazir Bhutto's Assassination and the Politics of Pakistan*, Indian edition, New Delhi: Viva Books Private Ltd, 2014, p. 183.
65. Christophe Jaffrelot, *The Pakistan Paradox: Instability and Resilience*, New Delhi: Random House, 2015, pp. 283–84.